KU-163-711

Kelly Grovier

Kelly Grovier was educated at the University of California, LA, and at Oxford, where he wrote his doctorate on the eighteenth-century philosopher and adventurer 'Walking' Stewart. He is the author of *A Lens in the Palm* (Carcanet) and a regular contributor to the *Times Literary Supplement* and the *Observer*. He is the co-founder of the scholarly journal *European Romantic Review* and a lecturer at the University of Wales, Aberystwyth. *The Gaol* was a BBC Book of the Week.

Praise for *The Gaol*

'Gripping . . . Grovier's treatment of the material organisation of the place is excellent . . . Newgate's role in the evolution of London, in the creation of crime in the public imagination, in the development of the concept of the prison, is unmatched, and Grovier relates it compellingly' *Daily Telegraph*

'Grovier introduces a gallery of rogues and tells their fates with relish' *Daily Mail*

'Scintillating . . . Teeming with sharply observed portraits of Newgate's unfortunate inmates, Grovier's study is a sparkling tribute to a grim cultural phenomenon' Christopher Silvester, *Daily Express*

'The author has a keen eye for the grisly detail . . . In many ways *The Gaol* is an upmarket extension of *The Newgate Calender*, the blood-and-guts, five-volume blockbuster full of all the gory details, that was on every eighteenth-century bookshelf' *Mail on Sunday*

'A murky, devilish, romp of a book' *Diplomat*

'Beguiling lyricism . . . He is interested in Newgate's place in the collective psyche, a "more intimate story" than historians have managed . . . vividly evoked' *Sunday Telegraph*

'Grovier's colourful history traces how this incubator of horror and cruelty became such an iconic presence within popular history, combining a wealth of gruesome detail with portraits of the many characters associated with it' *Metro*

LIVERPOOL JMU LIBRARY

3 1111 01365 6440

Also by Kelly Grovier

A Lens in the Palm

WITHDRAWN

The Gaol

The Story of Newgate –
London's Most Notorious Prison

KELLY GROVIER

JOHN MURRAY

First published in Great Britain in 2008 by John Murray (Publishers)
An Hachette UK Company

First published in paperback in 2009

4

© Kelly Grovier 2008

The right of Kelly Grovier to be identified as the Author of the Work has been
asserted by him in accordance with the Copyright, Designs and Patents Act 1988.

All rights reserved. Apart from any use permitted under UK copyright law no part
of this publication may be reproduced, stored in a retrieval system, or transmitted, in
any form or by any means without the prior written permission of the publisher,
nor be otherwise circulated in any form of binding or cover other than that in
which it is published and without a similar condition being imposed on the
subsequent purchaser.

A CIP catalogue record for this title is available from the British Library

ISBN 978-0-7195-6133-7

Typeset in Bembo by Servis Filmsetting Ltd, Stockport, Cheshire

Printed and bound by Clays Ltd, St Ives plc

John Murray policy is to use papers that are natural, renewable and recyclable
products and made from wood grown in sustainable forests. The logging and
manufacturing processes are expected to conform to the environmental regulations
of the country of origin.

John Murray (Publishers)
338 Euston Road
London NW1 3BH

www.johnmurray.co.uk

for my mother and father

Contents

CONTENTS

Illustrations

'. . . if you would peruse in unbroken – ay, overlapping – continuity the history of a community, look not in the church registers and the courthouse records, but beneath the successive layers of calcimine and creosote and white-wash on the walls of the jail . . .'

William Faulkner, 'The Jail'
(Nor Even Yet Quite Relinquish –)

Preface

If you walk east from Trafalgar Square towards the City of London, as the theatre restaurants of Covent Garden give way to the Law Courts of the Strand and barrister chambers of Fleet Street and Ludgate Hill, there is a turning on the left, one hundred yards from the western façade of St Paul's Cathedral, that you might overlook amid the flurry of briefcases and cabs and pinstripe suits. This is Ave Maria Lane, so-called, it is said, for the prayer that was recited on the corner by medieval monks processing along a time-erased route through the precincts of the walled city. One hundred and twenty yards on the left of the ancient byway, a private cul-de-sac loops back west and is cordoned off by an iron gate, beyond which hangs the kind of custom-painted sign that one ought to take notice of: 'No Admittance'. This is Amen Court – a short horseshoe of a street serving a terrace of immaculate redbrick houses, tucked away behind the bustling chambers and inns of court that shoulder all around. 'Amen', one might assume, as it once marked the end of the line.

At the back of this quiet tree-lined court, a small playground has been built in the ivy-latticed shadow of a massive stone wall, the sombre countenance of which rises incongruously against the swings and seesaws that echo with afternoon laughter. None of the residents here seem to know – I've asked – that beneath the tanbark and sand where the children in this isolated corner of central London play on slides and swings, lie fragments of the long-forgotten remains of countless murderers and madmen, poisoners and pickpockets, highwaymen and thieves. For centuries, this strip of land lay alongside a narrow passage known as 'Deadman's Walk'. It stretched behind the back wall of the most menacing structure in all the British Empire: Newgate Prison.

Newgate was neither the oldest nor the largest gaol in England. When it was finally torn down, brick by brick, at the beginning of the twentieth century, after nearly a millennium of existence, its destruction sparked no riots or revolution, as the Fall of the Bastille had triggered in Paris in July 1789. No kings are known ever to have been cast inside it, nor was it ever fought over as a crucial stronghold in a time of war. Yet somehow Newgate Prison loomed in the British imagination like no other structure before or since.

First constructed on the fringe of a Roman river fort at an unremembered moment in Iron Age Britain, over the ensuing centuries Newgate would slowly drift to the very centre of cultural consciousness. Along the way, The Gaol, as it was iconically called by inhabitants of the emerging city, became the unofficial stage on which many of the nation's most thrilling dramas unfolded. From the Peasants' Revolt in the fourteenth century to the mass martyrdoms of Catholics and Protestants in the sixteenth, from the Great Fire in the seventeenth century to the Gordon Riots in the second half of the eighteenth, Newgate perennially stood at the epicentre of social convulsion.

This is where the real-life Robin Hood and the larger-than-life Captain Kidd ended their days, where flamboyant footpads (or highwaymen) such as Claude Duval and James Maclaine left legions of women visitors to the prison swooning. The Scottish outlaw Robert MacGregor (a.k.a. Rob Roy) was held in Newgate and so was the infamous philanderer Giacomo Casanova, who described its ambiance as 'a hell such as Dante might have conceived'. Nor was Newgate merely incidental to the lives of the already famous. A crucible of celebrity, the forbidding institution was responsible for forging the reputations of countless conspirators and conmen, poisoners and escapologists, from the Flowerpot plotters of the Popish Plot to the irrepressible Jack Sheppard who broke free of its stony grip on two miraculous occasions. By the late eighteenth century, according to the prison reformer John Howard, half of all crimes committed in and around London were being planned inside Newgate. For centuries The Gaol was the grimy axle around which London slowly twisted.

That Newgate should have etched itself so deeply into the memory of England is perhaps not so surprising given the prison's enduring links with literary figures. This is where the scoundrel Thomas Malory is thought to have written *Le Morte D'Arthur*; where rapier-wielding playwrights Ben Jonson and Christopher Marlowe were made to cool their slippered heels. Daniel Defoe squeezed what he had suffered inside the prison through his quill and out spilled *Moll Flanders*. What remains to this day one of the most successful theatrical productions on the English stage, John Gay's rumbustious *Beggar's Opera*, was nearly called 'The Newgate Opera' after the structure that inspired it. From Dr Johnson and George Crabbe to Ainsworth and Dickens, the fascination with Newgate thickened like a London pea souper from the eighteenth to the nineteenth centuries. Nor were poets and prose writers alone in their obsession with the prison. Artists too were drawn to its cloistered chaos. William Hogarth, George Cruikshank, Gustave Doré and Vincent van Gogh can each trace major works in their respective oeuvres back to the mystique of The Gaol.

By the beginning of the seventeenth century, every aspect of Newgate – from its indelible stench to the diseases it fermented, from the corruption of its officials to the heroism of some of its inmates – had imprinted itself on to the soul of the capital. Visitors paid handsomely for a sniff inside, their queues clogging the streets. Broadsheets sensationalising the alleged crimes and confessions of those awaiting execution in the prison's Condemned Hold – or worse, in the subterranean 'Limbo' – sold in unprecedented numbers, creating a readership whose influence can still be felt to this day.

Indeed Newgate survives in the very fabric of our language. The vivid lingo of felons, or what became known as Newgate cant, presented a distinct lexical code, which was continually being cracked and collected into dubious dictionaries, long before even the appearance of Dr Johnson's masterwork. Excerpts from this secret language serve as the titles and epigraphs of each of the chapters that follow. Many phrases linked to Newgate cant linger on and still surface in common currency. If you think I'm 'pulling your leg', look again at the expression itself. Keen spectators at the frequent hanging fairs, where condemned convicts were trundled the two and a half miles from the prison to Tyburn – the principal site of execution near present-day Marble Arch – would purchase expensive seats from one of the pew operators, such as Mammy Douglas, whose living relied on the carnival atmosphere created by hangings. The paying audience expected a spectacle: the more writhing the better. In the ensuing mêlée, family members competed with Resurrection Men for control of the bladderless body. Occasionally, a merciful hangman would be the first to grab hold of the flailing limbs. But whoever it was who managed to yank the ankles and break the felon's neck, thereby curtailing the macabre performance, would be accused, in a bizarre transference of the gruesome truth, of having pulled the audience's leg.

Still, having one's leg pulled was preferable to being 'left in the lurch'. While most dictionaries of phrase and fable trace that expression back to genteel parlour games of cribbage or the seventeenth-century French game 'Lourche', an irresistible if untraceable urban legend has it that the saying is an allusion to the horse-drawn sledge, or 'lurch', on which convicts were bundled, their legs and wrists bound with rope, for the journey

A NEW
Canting DICTIONARY:

Comprehending All the

TERMS, Antient and Modern,

Used in the Several

TRIBES

O F

Gypsies, Beggars, Shoplifters, High-waymen, Foot-Pads, and all other *Clans* of *Cheats* and *Villains*.

INTERSPERSED

With Proverbs, Phrases, Figurative Speeches, &c.

Being a Complete Collection of all that has been publish'd of that Kind. With very large Additions of Words never before made Publick.

Detecting, under each Head or Order, the several Tricks or Pranks made use of by Varlets of all Denominations ; and therefore Useful for all Sorts of People (especially *Travellers* and *Foreigners*) to enable them to secure their Money and preserve their Lives.

With a Preface, giving an Account of the Original, Progress, &c. of the *Canting Crew* ; and recommending Methods for *diminishing* these Varlets, by *better Employment of the Poor*.

To which is Added,
A complete Collection of SONGS *in the* Canting Dialect.

LONDON, Printed ; And Sold by the Booksellers of *London* and *Westminster.* 1725.

1. *Title-page of one of the many dictionaries that codified the Newgate slang, or 'cant' spoken throughout the London underworld*

from Newgate to the gallows. Though it was customary for drivers of the cart to stop at one of the designated alehouses in St Giles or along the 'Tyburn Way' (now Oxford Street) in order for the condemned to have a final drink, especially cruel chauffeurs were known to hop off for a swift one themselves while leaving the parched and terrified felon *in the lurch* to contemplate his imminent fate in soul-wrenching sobriety.

Where earlier, excellent studies of the prison have documented the criminal and architectural history of the structure, my aim is to tell a more intimate story and to explore the meaning of Newgate as an unparalleled icon, an incubator of inspiration. In doing so, I have attempted to resuscitate forgotten stories and to place them alongside better-known ones in order to capture a sense of the prison's shifting essence from era to era. Organised around three of the most devastating catastrophes to define its existence – the inferno from which Newgate was born in 1086, the Great Fire of 1666, and the blaze that engulfed The Gaol during the Gordon Riots in 1780 – this is the story of a resilient relic, which resisted history's every effort to raze it. Given Newgate's astonishing longevity, no book could hope exhaustively to enshrine all of its most famous alumni. Doubtless any lover of London's rich heritage will spot omissions of anecdotes that could compellingly have contributed to the mosaic I have endeavoured to piece together in the following pages. My challenge, though, has been to choose which stories best illustrate the evolving identity of a place that at once helped shape, and was shaped by, the dynamic unfolding of British history. The lives assembled here, whether dignified or damnable, admirable or abominable, have each helped grind one of the most astonishing social lenses in Western culture – an aperture, though occluded by time, through which the ghosts of the English past can still be brought into extraordinary focus.

I
KINDLE

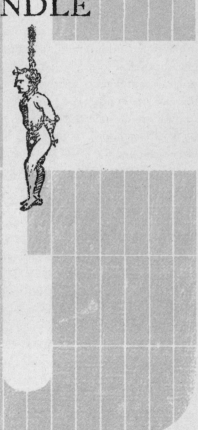

1

Whit

'**WHIT**, *Newgate. As,* Five Rum–padders are rub'd in the Darkmans out of the Whit, and are pik'd into the Deuseavile; *Five Highway-men in the Night broke Newgate, and are gone into the Country.'*

A New Canting Dictionary: Comprehending All the Terms, Antient and Modern, Used in the Several Tribes of Gypsies, Beggars, Shoplifters, Highwaymen, Foot-Pads, and all other Clans of Cheats and Villains (London, 1725)

On 7 October 1903, Philip Norman stood in a gaping hole punched in the centre of London's urban crust. Setting his shovel aside, he bent down to wipe away a layer of soft yellow sand and coarse gravel revealing a solid swathe of pink mortar clinging to something anchored underneath. His hand paused briefly, then began brushing frantically – his knuckles knocking aside great chunks of rubble to expose the rough plane of a long, straight fossil below the surface. When Philip stopped and straightened himself to take in the full extent of the ancient pedestal he had just uncovered, he was in no doubt that, in a small way and without having jotted a single word, his aching hands had just rewritten the history of London.

Elected Treasurer of the distinguished Society of Antiquaries of London in 1898, 61-year-old Philip Norman was a much-respected urban archaeologist who had spent decades unpicking the compressed strata in which the city's secrets lay trapped.

His was the golden age of archaeological pioneers, of Augustus Pitt-Rivers and William Flinders Petrie, who had founded the great societies and museums devoted to the discipline. An accomplished water-colourist who left a handsome collection of his paintings to the London Museum, Philip had a keen eye for appreciating how the overlapping layers of opaque media bleed and blur. Before arriving at the excavation site on the corner of Old Bailey and Newgate Street, where a fresh foundation was being laid for an extensive new Criminal Court two hundred yards north-west of St Paul's Cathedral, the seasoned digger had done his homework.

The new Criminal Court would be built over the jagged chasm where the notorious Newgate Prison was gradually being eradicated, brick by brick, from the material memory of the landscape. Designed by the celebrated eighteenth-century architect and founding member of the Royal Academy, George Dance the Younger, this incarnation of the prison was regarded as London's most impressive building after St Paul's when it was constructed in 1770. Dance's prison was a replacement for an even earlier structure that had been disfigured (or 'damnified', as one contemporary account put it) in the Great Fire of 1666. This earlier building had been erected in 1423 with money left by the dying philanthropist and many-times Lord Mayor of London, Richard Whittington, who, near the end of his life, was mortified by the horrifying conditions that had been allowed to fester unchecked for centuries. Whittington's gaol, or 'The Whit' as it was popularly christened (85 feet by 50 feet, and five storeys in height) superseded what is thought to have been the original gaol built on the site at the end of the twelfth century – possibly called 'Chamberlain's Gate' or 'West Gate', to which there are only the vaguest references in medieval writing. Remnants of all four eras of The Gaol – Dance's prison (1770–1902), the post-Great Fire prison (1666–1770), Whittington's gaol (1423–1666), and the original structure (?–1423) – would have been visible to the trained eye of Philip Norman.

*2. Portrait of Richard Whittington, the many-times Lord
Mayor of London, who left in his will a large sum for the
refurbishment of the prison. A statue of his beloved cat was
said to have adorned the façade of the new gaol in
commemoration of Whittington's generosity*

For the origins of that initial structure, the senior archaeologist had little more to go on than the hand-me-down
accounts compiled by Renaissance chroniclers such as John
Stow. In his *A suruay of London contayning the originall, antiquity,
increase, moderne estate, and description of that citie, written in the
yeare 1598*, Stow does his best to collate the fragmented and
half-remembered histories of each of the old gates to the city:
Aldgate to the east; Bishopsgate, Moorgate and Cripplegate
to the north; and Aldersgate and Ludgate to the west. In
between these last two:

> . . . on the west, and by North, is termed *Newgate,* as latelier
> builded then the rest. This gate was first erected about the
> raigne of *Henry* the second, or *Richard* the first, vpon this occa-
> sion. The Cathedrall Church of Saint *Paule,* being burnt about
> the yeare 1086, in the raigne of *Willam* the Conqueror,

Mauritius then Bishoppe of London, rapayred not the old
church, as some haue supposed, but began the foundation of a
new worke, such as men then iudged would neuer haue béene
performed, it was to them so wonderfull for height, length, and
breadth, as also in respect it was raysed vppon arches or vaults,
&c.

Following Stow, most historians in the intervening centuries
accepted the notion that Newgate was deserving of its name
and that it was in fact 'latelier builded then the rest'. Indeed, a
whole logic sprang from Stow's narrative to support this theory.
In the wake of the devastating fire that had destroyed St Paul's
in 1086, Mauritius commanded that a more impressive church
be built over the embers. Construction of the vast churchyard
and cemetery that were designed to complement the new
cathedral church, according to the story, disrupted the flow of
traffic between Ludgate in the west and Aldgate in the east. As
a result, travellers had to choose between two long detours
'which passage, by reason of so often turning', Stow surmised,
'was very combersome, and daungerous both for horse and
man'.

For remedie whereof, a new gate was made, and so called, by
which men and cattell with all manner of carriages, might passe
more directly (as afore) from *Aldegate,* through West Cheape by
Paules on the North side, through Saint *Nicholas Shambles,* and
Newgate market to *Newgate,* and from thence to any part
Westwarde ouer *Oldborne* bridge, or turning without the gate
into Smithfielde, and through *Iseldon* to any part North and by
West. This gate hath of long time béene a Gayle, or prison, for
fellons and trespassors, as appeareth by records in the raigne of
King *Iohn,* of which amongst other I find one testifying [to]
that in the yeare 1218.

According to conventional belief, in other words, the need for
a 'new gate' arose when a new threat began weighing on medieval English society, that of the highwayman, who preyed on

the carriages and cattle forced to circumnavigate the congested city.

But as Philip Norman scrabbled in the rich mixture of soil, sand and chalky rubble that had not been exposed to the light of day for the better part of a millennium, he found himself suddenly distrustful of the conventional chronology. Something didn't add up. From the back of his mind, the forgotten conjecture of an eighteenth-century historian, William Maitland, came rushing to the surface. In his two-volume *History and survey of London from its foundation to the present time* (1775), Maitland insisted on having seen with his own eyes the testimony of a primitive archaeologist who had allegedly unearthed 'the Vestigia of the Roman Military Road called Watling-Street . . . pointing directly to this Gate'. Though the report is now untraceable, it was enough to persuade Maitland that Newgate had been 'one of the four original Gates built over the said Roman Highway in this Place', and therefore one of the very oldest co-ordinates in London's history.

Philip was standing a few feet to the right of where 'ghostly demarcations' of the military road referred to by Maitland would have led, if that theory were correct, from the Fleet River in the west to a double-arched gateway in the north-west wall of the hill fort, Londinium. Between the second and fourth centuries, a formidable two-mile wall had hooped, horseshoe-like, around the Roman settlement, from the Tower in the east up to what is now Finsbury Circus in the north and curving back down to near Blackfriars Bridge on the Embankment, with no wall (at least until the fourth century) extending along the river bank.

On arriving at the excavation site, Philip had been able to inspect a freshly unearthed stretch of the old wall, which had run the short distance southwards towards Ludgate. 'The beautiful yellow sand and gravel beneath were exposed to sight and there was a fine opportunity of studying the structure, which, being more or less isolated and standing up to a considerable height, formed a picturesque object.' At its base, the section of wall was 8½ feet thick, and was a petrified soup of Kentish ragstone, Roman tile, ferruginous sandstone and ironstone blocks. Brought largely from the Maidstone district of Kent, the materials would have taken some '1,300 barge journeys' to transport. The wall was held together by a rough mortar, striated with levels of livid red brick. The effect was fearsome to behold, so much so that it provoked a twelfth-century monk, William Fitz Stephen of Canterbury, to describe it as having 'been tempered with the blood of beasts' (*'Caemento cum sanguine animalium temperato'*).

'According to the usual method of building the London wall,' Philip later recorded, 'a trench about 12 feet wide had been dug in the natural soil, the lower part of which, for a depth of 1 foot 8 inches to 2 feet, was filled with puddled clay mixed with fragments of Kentish ragstone.' At some unremembered point in the evolution of medieval English, the word 'bayle' (from the verb *baillier*, 'to enclose') blurred itself into the word 'bailie' (a variant of *baillif*, or 'chief magistrate') to become the term by which both this stretch of London wall, from Newgate to Ludgate, as well as the courthouse that was constructed alongside it, would forever be known: 'bali', 'le Baille', 'the grete bayli', and of course, 'Old Balee'.

The opportunity to behold such a rare relic of London's buried past was itself exhilarating, but what was truly extraordinary was the wholly unexpected discovery of the ancient plinth, one hundred feet to the north of the remnant wall, under what would have been the left side of the last incarnation of the prison – the one that was still being demolished. In relation to the layout of George Dance the Younger's sprawling prison, in other words, Philip was positioned near the back left corner (or rather, in the yawning hole that had been opened eleven feet beneath where the building had stood), just below the infamous 'Press Yard'.

The yard took its name from the hideous medieval practice that had long since been outlawed: 'pressing' or *peine forte et dure*

– 'the long and forceful punishment'. Until 1870, Stephen Halliday says, felons in Britain were required to forfeit their property after sentencing, leaving families ruined. Legally, the only way around this penalty was for the accused to refuse to enter a plea. According to statute, a prisoner could only be tried if he or she consented to having his or her case heard by a jury, and this was expressed in the form of entering a plea. Until the middle of the fifteenth century, refusal to offer such consent was punished by long stints in prison or by starvation. When this failed to persuade defendants to co-operate, crushing or pressing by heavy stones was introduced as a means of persuasion. Stretched and stapled to the floor, a prisoner was fitted with a plank across his or her chest and at prescribed intervals, metal weights were added to it. Eventually, the accused was either compelled to plead, or his chest collapsed. 'He shall be sent back to prison whence he came,' according to the sixteenth-century judge and legal writer Sir William Saundford,

> and laid in some low dark house, where he shall lie naked on the earth, without any litter, rushes or other clothing. And he shall lie upon his back, with his head covered and his feet, and one arm shall be drawn to one quarter of the house with a cord, and the other arm to another quarter, and in the same manner let it be done with his legs; and let there be laid upon his body iron and stone, as much as he can bear, or more; and the next day following he shall have three morsels of barley bread without drink, and the second day he shall have drink three times, as much at each time as he can drink, of the water next unto the prison, except it be running water, without any bread: And this shall be his diet till he die.

Such was the appalling fate of Major George Strangeways in 1658. Strangeways had been accused of murdering his brother-in-law, John Fussell, with a pistol. Refusing to countenance the prosecution against him unless he was assured that, if convicted, he would be executed in precisely the same manner as Fussell, the defendant was subjected to pressing. In his case, the ordeal

3. Peine forte et dure, *or 'the long and forceful punishment', was reserved for inmates who refused to enter a plea. Such was the fate of Major George Strangeways in 1658*

lasted only ten minutes. Unable to bear the agony of Strangeways' suffering, the guards added their own weight to the stones stacked upon his chest 'that they might sooner release his soul'. The mere sight of the medieval 'apparatus', *The Chronicles* goes on to say, was enough to make the highwayman Thomas Phillips change his mind, after being led into the yard in 1723. His accomplice, William Spiggot, however, required more convincing. After withstanding the awesome pressure of nearly 400 lb., Spiggot's will gave in before his chest did.

But by the time Dance's building was constructed – his design shifting the prison slightly south along the Old Bailey, thus converting it from an actual 'gate' arching over a street to a large penal warehouse standing alongside it – crushing had ceased and the Press Yard was ironically one of the more coveted areas in which a prisoner could be held. In order to be lodged in a ward adjacent to it, a prisoner would have to pay a substantial fee. At the turn of the nineteenth century, the Press Yard was one of the most expensive residences in the city. This is where the Scottish folk hero Rob Roy was held in 1727 before being sentenced to transportation. Roy had used the Jacobite rebellion of 1715 as a cover for pillaging raids on his former ally, the Duke of Montrose, and very quickly attracted admirers who likened him to Robin Hood. On his way from his ward in the Press Yard to Black Friars dock and a penal ship bound for Barbados, the rebel received a royal pardon and was allowed to return to his native Balquhidder where he lived out the rest of his life.

Such good fortune was not the fate of most of those associated with the Jacobite cause who were lodged in the Press Yard. In February 1696, John Bernardi, a former captain and loyalist to James II, was arrested in a tavern on Tower Hill along with a former associate, Captain Ambrose Rookwood, for their alleged roles in a Jacobite conspiracy to murder the King and return a Stuart to the throne. The plot was Rookwood's idea and he was expeditiously convicted and executed, but evidence against Bernardi was harder to scrape together. With Habeas Corpus suspended, Bernardi was made to languish in Newgate for the next forty years, as reign after reign came and went, without ever being charged with any offence. During the first few years, Bernardi was able to maintain reasonably comfortable accommodation in rooms overlooking the Press Yard, but eventually his savings and the charity offered by others dwindled. In 1712 he married while inside Newgate and raised ten children there who were occasionally allowed to play within the narrow confines of the barren yard.

*4. Gustave Doré's vision of prisoners exercising in
The Gaol in 1872. Vincent van Gogh, in 1890,
would convert this scene into one of his most famous
paintings*

One has difficulty squaring that image with the one for
which the Press Yard is, to this day, ingrained in the popular
imagination. It was here that the celebrated Victorian illustrator of literary and biblical subjects, Gustave Doré, on a visit to
Newgate in 1872 etched the view of prisoners walking in a
cramped circle that Vincent van Gogh, a few months before
committing suicide in 1890, would turn into one of the most
iconic images of the age – converting the inmate in the centre
foreground of the revolving parade into a powerful and pathetic

self-portrait. Tramping in an endless circle of despair, the thirty-three inmates of Doré's and of van Gogh's works – one drawn on top of the other like Dance's prison on top of Whittington's, Whittington's on top of Mauritius's – wear away at the stone slabs that had, until recently, paved the wretched square of earth directly above where Philip Norman was now standing.

As Philip knelt down on the fragmented fabric of soil to examine the ancient pedestal that he had just uncovered, he could see that it comprised four separate blocks 'fastened together with iron clamps fixed in with lead'. The ten-foot plinth was supported by layers of mortar, ragstone and puddled clay, and had clearly formed part of the foundation of a long-since-demolished Roman building. Pre-dating by hundreds of years the supposed construction in the twelfth century of the first 'new gate' on the site – built in response, it was said, to the danger and disruption caused by the new cathedral church being constructed to replace the decimated St Paul's – the existence of such a remnant would require a reassessment of the blueprint of the Roman settlement. In every way resembling the foundations of known Roman gatehouses, notably in nearby Silchester, the plinth suddenly became the oldest-known relic in London.

Far from being the last of the seven portals into and out of the fort to be constructed, 'Newgate' was clearly one of the first, and very likely built some time in the third century. The gate itself would have consisted of 'two parallel passages, each 12 feet long and 13 feet wide', flanked on either side by towers at the base of which would have been guardrooms. In all likelihood, Philip was standing by the south-west corner of one of the two guardrooms where those in charge of the gate, and therefore responsible for deciding who came and went from the Roman fort, would have resided. A feature writer for *The Times* was in little doubt about the significance of the foundation, which he described as 'unlike any recorded elsewhere in

London . . . an object lesson for all those who take an interest in the history of the greatest city the world has seen'.

While the unexpected discovery of fragments from an original gatehouse on the site recalibrated the early geometry of the capital, it also threw up a great many questions. There are no surviving records from the nearly four centuries of Roman occupation of the fort that might help illuminate how the structure was used or adapted, whether it underwent substantial changes or reconstruction, whether it ever suffered attack or damage, or when it was eventually demolished or replaced. The most that can be said with any certainty is that in 1188 the King suddenly decreed that a derelict strip of land adjacent to the gatehouse should be purchased for the purpose of constructing a gaol. The sum of £36 0s.11d. was set aside as payment to a smith and two carpenters whose names may have faded into the fog of time, but whose handiwork laid the foundations for one of the most intriguing and, literally, incendiary social platforms in British cultural history.

In legal terms, the birth of Newgate coincides with the birth of memory. A statute passed in 1276 designated 1189, the beginning of Richard I's reign, as the official end of 'time immemorial', or 'before memory', and the start of English common law.

Precisely when the original structure of Newgate came to serve the same purpose as the 1188 extension is not known. For at least the next two centuries, accommodation within the initial building would have been fiercely sought after by royal courtiers and administrators who saw Newgate as situated conveniently neither inside nor outside of town. The transition from gatehouse to prison must therefore have been a gradual one. While we know that by 1218 at least one of the turrets had been converted into a cell at a cost to the Royal Exchequer of £100, in 1253, Peter de Rivallis, Treasurer of the King's Wardrobe, was still being rewarded for his services to Henry III with residency inside Newgate. That blurred ambivalence, of providing covetable accommodation on the one hand and cramped incarceration on the other, of being at once a gateway and a terminus, a place which both fascinated and repelled society, would characterise The Gaol's existence for the next six hundred and fifty years.

While Newgate's conversion into a place of detention is difficult to pin down to a particular year, the moment when the structure acquired an adjacent Sessions House into which defendants held on the prison side could be transferred for prosecution – or 'delivered' as the very unspiritual process was called – is easier to locate on the timeline of London's history. Before the sixteenth century, courts in London and Middlesex – the civic jurisdiction into which Newgate officially fell – would be convened in almost any ad hoc space that the sheriffs could secure in the city. A makeshift Sessions House in nearby Smithfield, amid the stench of faeces from the cattle market that operated there, eventually crumbled into obsolescence in the fourteenth century and thereafter there are stories of trials being conducted in the attics of victims' homes or in the reception rooms of defendants. Alehouses were frequently converted into venues for legal proceedings and there is mention in the fifteenth century of a brothel being commandeered for a quick delivery. To expedite a more efficient judicial process, the Court of Aldermen in 1539 sanctioned the construction of a dedicated Sessions House just south of Newgate along the city wall in Old Bailey from which, to this day, the court would unofficially derive its name. Acknowledging that, until that time, there was 'no coinveynent place wtyn this cytye for that purpose where the sayd delyverie shal be made' and that the 'Shryeffes of London for the time beying be greatly burdened for a conyenent place to be hyred yerely . . . It is nowe agreed for the comfort of all thys Cytye that a conveyent place be made for that purpose holsomly to be orderyd and prepared upon the common grownde of thys Cytye yn the olde bayly of London wt all spede at the charge of the Chmbre of London.'

5. Newgate in the sixteenth century

The design and appearance of the original Old Bailey are now forgotten. Like its more fearsome neighbour, though, the courthouse would undergo extensive refurbishment over the centuries, especially following its destruction in the Great Fire. Proposed improvements to its layout were generally linked to the lethal issue of gaol fever – that virulent strain of typhus which, wafting over from The Gaol, could wipe out scores of inmates and judges in what became known grimly as a 'Black Assize'. When a new Sessions House was erected in the 1670s, the courtroom was left uncovered, irrespective of the British weather, thus inviting comparisons with the unofficial theatre of Newgate–Old Bailey and the open-air playhouses that continued to operate in the city even after the destruction of the second Globe Theatre in 1642.

Though initially created to serve the demands of Newgate, the Old Bailey would outlast the prison structure, eventually claiming for itself the very ground on which The Gaol once stood. As the sands of centuries of adventure and vice, of courage and suffering, shifted under Philip Norman's feet, he was aware that the ghosts of Newgate could never be eradicated from the cold consciousness of the earth, nor indeed should they be.

LIVERPOOL JOHN MOORES UNIVERSITY
LEARNING SERVICES

2

Bone

'**BONE**, to apprehend, seize, take or arrest. *I'll Bone ye*; I'll cause you to be Arrested. *We shall be Bon'd*, we shall be apprehended for the Robbery. *The Cove is Bon'd, and gone to the Whit*; The Rogue is taken up, and carried to Newgate, or any other Gaol . . . *I have Bon'd her Dudds, Fagg'd, and Brush'd*; I have taken away my Mistress's Cloaths, beat her, and am troop'd off.'

In 1570, the slow and grotesque death of a fat man called Andrew Alexander was reported with unmitigated joy across London. This 'cruel enimie', so one account ran, 'died verye miserably, being so swolne that he was more lyke a monster than a man, and was so rotten within, that no man coulde abide the smell of him'. One might well expect such bitter glee to be reserved for the demise of an unrepentant murderer or a cowardly traitor. But Andrew Alexander belonged to an even rarer and more reviled class of social villains: the Keepers of Newgate.

Officially, so the story goes, the management of Newgate had, since its hazy transformation from purpose-built gatehouse to makeshift prison, been the responsibility of two annually elected sheriffs – one 'a reputable man, free of the city' chosen by the Mayor, the other selected by the Court of Common Council. Refusal to accept the appointment carried severe consequences: a one-hundred-pound fine for the first to decline, and should the other likewise 'absent himself', 'all his goods, lands, and tentements shall be arrested'. The inauguration ritual, according to the medieval dictates inscribed by Whittington's executor, John Carpenter, in the austere statute compendium *Liber Albus* (or 'White Book of the City of London'), was held on 28 February, the eve of St Michael, following a lavish banquet in the cathedral-like grandeur of the ancient Guildhall. This magnificent secular nave occupied the site of the Roman amphitheatre, where legend has it that the two defeated giants, Gog and Magog, had been chained by Brutus when he founded Britain. From that mythical place, the two sheriffs were made to 'go together to the prison of Newgate, and there . . . receive all the prisoners by indenture made between them and the old Sheriffs'. The ceremony was a solemn one, presided over by the Mayor, who presented one of the newly inaugurated sheriffs with the official seal of Newgate, the cocket, and the other with the heavy ring of prison keys. Symbolically, the bestowal of the keys would prove to be among the most momentous and fearsome occasions in English custom. With every twist of these notched batons – which measured roughly a foot in length, an inch thick at the narrowest point along their necks, and weighed approximately two pounds each – the keys gathered into themselves a terrible power. Visitors to the prison would refuse to come into contact with them. At the end of the eighteenth century, a witness to the theft of the keys would testify to the evil that they were thought to possess. 'You would not touch them,' the prosecuting attorney asked the witness, 'for fear they would contaminate you?' To which the visibly unsettled gentleman replied, 'No, sir. I would not come near them.'

Once entrusted with the cocket and keys, the sheriffs were soberly enjoined by the Mayor to 'place into safeguard there at their own peril, without letting the gaol go to fenn or farm' the enemies of the kingdom. 'At their own peril': the well-paid and prestigious position of sheriff came with real risks. If a prisoner managed to escape from the gaol, the sheriffs were held personally liable – individually facing fines of 100 shillings for each escapee. If the disappearing prisoner was a convicted debtor, the sheriffs were expected to reimburse the creditor the sum in question. For repeated misconduct, or failure to appear when summoned by the Mayor, a sheriff risked being 'ousted from his office and adjudged incapable of holding any other office in the said city, thenceforth for ever, without restitution thereof'.

Nor were these hollow threats. In 1255, John de Frome, who had murdered the Queen's cousin, succeeded in liberating himself from the prison. Enraged, Henry III fined the city 3,000 marks and had the sheriffs thrown in gaol for a month. The early memoranda rolls of the city of London are filled with entries itemising the amounts for which the sheriffs were made to compensate the creditors of escaped debtors. On 27 October 1363, Thomas Umfrey, citizen and mercer, was able to recover the then debilitating sum of £56 from James Andrew and John de St Albans, the former sheriffs of the prison, for allowing Gilbert Alkberwe, who was in Umfey's debt, to escape from Newgate. In the light of such potential peril, it is not surprising that the sheriffs began concocting ways of protecting themselves. The most effective of these was what amounted to the sale of the office of Keeper. Anyone willing to take control of the day-to-day management of the prison could bid for the privilege. Those able to raise the largest bonds, which the sheriffs would in turn use as insurance against future fines, were hired. Once appointed, the Keeper was left alone to recoup his expenses in whatever manner he saw fit.

The practice of selling the keepership of the prison to the highest bidder was in insolent violation of the very city ordinances to which the sheriffs had sworn allegiance before the Mayor. The Keeper was to be, according to statute, 'a man, sufficient and of good nature, to keep the said gaol in due manner' and was to be selected by the sheriffs 'without taking anything of him for such keeping thereof, by covenant made in private or openly'. 'Gaylors buying their offices', it was ominously predicted, 'will deale hardly with pitifull prisoners'.

That so many individuals were willing not only to raise enormous sums in order to secure the keepership, but to take on the additional burden of financing repairs of the prison, which came with the appointment, indicates just how potentially profitable the public regarded the position. In order to earn back their high overheads, the Keepers sought reimbursement from the only body that they had direct control over: the prisoner's. Everything that the inmates did, voluntarily or involuntarily, from the moment that they entered Newgate, came at a cost. To sleep in a room that was merely cramped, cold and dank, rather than lice- or excrement-strewn, would cost you. If you had been sentenced to shackling, each chain carried a price. When the irons came off, that cost more. Most had no bedding and slept on freezing slabs of stone. Those who could afford it, purchased a narrow plank and a filthy blanket.

The innovative lengths to which generations of gaolers went in order to devise increasingly cruel methods of wringing cash out of prisoners are mind-boggling, if not stomach-turning. Among the more hideous implements experimented with was a device disturbingly christened the 'scull cap' or 'cap of maintenance' – an ironic play on the name given to the velvet and ermine cap worn ceremonially by the Mayor. At first glance, with its hemispherical metal rims and pendula of pointed spokes, the contraption resembled a mariner's astrolabe. One contemporary visitor to the prison, the so-called 'Popish midwife', Elizabeth Cellier, saw the device in operation on one of her 'charitable visits' and described it as among the gaoler's 'Engines of Tyranny'. It 'was fixed to the head', Cellier remembered in a chapter devoted to 'Tyrannical Barbarisme . . . in His Majesties Goal [sic] of Newgate', 'with a thing like the Rowel of a Spur, being put in her Mouth, cleaves to the Roof with such extream Torture, that it is not

*6. Leg irons, as worn here by the Elizabethan
playwright Thomas Nashe, were among the many
'Engines of Tyranny' said to have been employed by
Newgate's Keepers*

to be exprest; this the Woman endured several times, till at last, by making her Address to some good people, and telling the manner of her usage, they did contribute to the Gaolers demands, and so she with great difficulty obtained her Liberty.'

Aware of the inevitable abuses that such a system encouraged, contemporary statutes struggled to establish humane parameters for the extraction of fees. The Keeper, so the *Liber Albus* sets out, 'shall make oath before the Mayor and Aldermen, that neither he, nor any other for him, shall take fine or extortionate charge from any prisoner for putting on or taking off his irons, or shall receive monies extorted from any prisoner.' That is not to say that fees were discouraged: 'it shall be fully lawful,' the ordinance goes on to clarify, 'for the said gaoler to take from each person, when set at liberty, four pence for his fee, as from ancient times has been the usage.' What was expressly prohibited, however, though widely practised, was the levying of fees for merely being admitted to the prison in the first place: 'he shall take from no person at his entrance there, nor shall he issue [execution] suddenly, by command of the Mayor and Aldermen, without other process. And if he shall be found to commit extortion upon anyone, he shall be ousted from his office, and be punished at the discretion of the Mayor and Aldermen and Common Council of the City.'

The regulations were intended to curb the cruelty of such early Keepers as Edmund le Lorimer, a callous crony of Edward II, whose sadistic sport was squeezing money from already impecunious inmates by overburdening their bodies with shackles. The removal of each gratuitous iron could be purchased at the price of 1s. 4d. – more than three times what was considered just. Among Edmund's other crimes was the practice of refusing bail to eligible inmates in order to keep as many paying customers inside as possible. Edmund was eventually convicted by a jury of a number of abuses including accepting a bribe of 20 marks from a desperate friend, the sergeant John le Parker, supposedly in exchange for helping him to avoid the gallows. Edmund took the money but John still hanged. For his long reign of systematic unkindness, Edmund was stripped of his office and briefly imprisoned in the Fleet before being granted, to no one's surprise, a royal pardon.

Cruelty was passed down from Keeper to Keeper like a congenital disease. In 1333, one of Edmund's successors, Hugh de Croydon, was at the centre of another lengthy investigation. Hugh was accused of the preposterous, though profitable, practice of accepting 'bail' from condemned murderers awaiting execution. At the same time he threatened to shackle anyone suspected of even the most minor offence in the roughest dungeon of the prison unless they paid him to be spared. The inquiry into Hugh's abuses dragged on for eight years until he was finally removed by a congregation consisting of the Mayor, sheriffs and aldermen of the city on 20 March 1341. Three years later, Hugh was hauled up before the city officials again, this time for allegedly dismantling part of a neighbour's house along Old Bailey in order to make room for an extension to his own. But conscience, we're told, finally cornered Croydon. Late in retirement, racked with guilt, the disgraced Keeper was suddenly moved to leave a hefty endowment in his will to be divided annually among the prisoners.

Potential for profit was wrung from every aspect of the prisoners' wretched lives. By the middle of the fourteenth century, the Keepers had begun embargoing food and drink brought in by friends and family members of the inmates in order to force them to purchase the paltry, over-priced rations prepared by the Keepers themselves. So appalling were the provisions offered by the gaolers that a proclamation was passed in 1370 prohibiting any prison official from baking bread, brewing beer or profiting from the sale of any other foodstuff in The Gaol. The ban remained in force only until the 1390s.

In the 1440s, a series of riots inside Newgate resulted in several escapes, drawing attention not only to the deteriorating conditions within the prison but to the widespread corruption among the Keepers and staff whom many held responsible for The Gaol's moral and physical dilapidation. In the summer of 1450 a mutiny left the prison defenceless and the Keeper, Alexander Manning, facing the kind of scrutiny that the prison sheriffs had largely managed to evade. Though defended by Queen Margaret, Manning was thrown into gaol for having 'greatly misconducted himself in his office' through the 'negligent custody of the prisoners' in his charge, 'to the great disturbance of the city' and barred from ever again working in Newgate. It was probably not the first time he had been punished. Around this same time we read of a gaoler by the name of 'Mannyng' who, three years earlier, 'wickedly and negligently permitted the bier of a dead prisoner to stand in the King's Highway, causing a nuisance and great danger to the King who was passing there'. Refusing to move the body 'after many admonitions made to him', he was given 'nine days in the compter'. In the aftermath of the escapes of 1450, the

Common Council met and decided that closer supervision of the prison was necessary.

Among the changes introduced in Newgate during the second half of the fifteenth century were limits on what could be levied for such basics as room and board. It was determined that a gentleman of the city should not be charged more than three shillings a week for his bed, and a yeoman not more than two. Keepers were told that they could ask no more than 1d. for a loaf of bread or for a bushel of coals, and no more than 2d. for a gallon of ale. In order to keep tabs on the Keepers' conduct, regular inspections would be carried out by a committee of visitors comprising two curates and two commoners. Any gaoler caught overcharging prisoners or prohibiting them from enjoying food brought in from outside would be fined 20s. in the first instance, 40s. in the second, and would be dismissed if caught a third time.

The new measures were conscientious, humane, long overdue, and almost entirely without impact. They certainly did little to control the sadistic instincts of that sixteenth-century gaoler who became a living caricature of the cruel Keeper – Andrew Alexander. According to the contemporary London chronicler John Foxe, Alexander, 'exceeded all others' in his abject brutality. Foxe lingers over the treatment by Alexander of an old friend of his, Master Philpot, who had been imprisoned to await burning at the stake for his religious beliefs. Foxe describes the heartless frisking of Philpot, the confiscation of his ring, the refusal to loosen his heavy shackles, and the dragging of Philpot to the most oppressive section of the medieval prison, that corner menacingly alluded to as 'Limbo'.

When Alexander fell ill after decades of sinister service – swelling to an obscene size, plump with putrefaction – he was seen as a fitting symbol for Newgate's own demise. He had become his prison. The 'Keeper of Newgate' soon became a stock villain in contemporary ballads – an archetype against whom almost any outlaw could be seen as heroic. In a forgotten lyric by the late-seventeenth-century poet Alexander Radcliffe, a generic 'Keeper' insidiously solicits the co-operation of the wives and lovers of wanted highwaymen in apprehending them. The verse is narrated by a wife – Hypermnestra, after the Greek myth of the one daughter in fifty who did not kill her husband – who refuses to co-operate, and gladly swaps her freedom (and her clothes) with those of her roguish husband in a ruse that outwits the Keeper.

> At last you sleep securely without warning
> Of the strange Alterations in the Morning:
> I knew betimes the Keepers wou'd be there,
> And all the Night I sweat, 'tween Sport and Fear;
> At last I rose, and 'bout the Room I walk'd,
> And thus at Randum to my self I talk'd;
> Have I not sworn a Thousand Oaths at lest,
> That I'd betray my Husband with the rest?
> What must I do? 'Tis true, I am his Wife,
> What! must I damn my Soul to save his Life?
> Hang all the Oaths in Christendom, said I;
> He is my Husband, and he must not die.
> With that I drew your Breeches on in hast,
> The Codpiece was so big, I was amaz'd;
> I walk'd into your Coat, hanging on Peg.
> I lost my head within your Perewig . . .

Having woken and warned her husband, who manages to escape, Hypermnestra is herself seized, the Keeper having mistaken her for one of the wanted highwaymen. The poem ends farcically with Hypermnestra addressing the husband she will never see again, dictating her own preposterously melodramatic epitaph:

> Here lies a Wife, who rather than she'd fail
> To save her Husband's Life, dy'd in a Jayl:
> My Irons load me so, I'm fit to cry,
> I would write more, but cannot; so God b'ye.

Radcliffe's poem anticipates by only a few years an altogether unamusing real-life dilemma faced by a wife called upon by a Keeper to betray her husband. In 1715 George Flint, a printer and political writer, began publishing a newspaper in support of Jacobite causes. Flint's writings were instantly regarded as treacherous by the government and in 1716 he was arrested for high treason along with two of his printers, Isaac Dalton and James Alexander. The three were fined and thrown into Newgate to await trial. Convinced that a conviction would result in execution, Flint resolved to escape. With his wife's help, he managed to disguise himself as a footman, walk out of the front doors of the prison without any difficulty, and hide at home before taking to the seas. When the Keeper visited his wife and interrogated her as to Flint's whereabouts, she insisted that he 'was dangerously sick in bed and not fit to be disturbed' – a display of insolence that earned her a stint in the prison's Condemned Hold where she was 'used after a most barbarous manner to extort a confession'.

Occasionally one finds a fleeting mention of a Keeper of uncharacteristic tolerance and charity. In the decades after the relentless unkindnesses of Alexander, who was known to shout maniacally through the crowded corridors, 'Rid my prison! Rid my prison!', the more compassionate Simon Houghton was reputed to have extended unprecedented freedom to inmates whose only apparent crime was their allegiance to the Pope. Houghton, whose wife was 'an obstinate recusant' and was thought to have converted to Catholicism, was said to look the other way when several Catholic convicts would huddle together in quiet liturgy. If a letter from Sir Thomas Lake to Lord Salisbury, dated 22 February 1611, is to be believed, Houghton was disciplined severely by the King for his derelictions of duty.

Throughout the seventeenth century, the policy of torturing prisoners as a legitimate means of generating revenue met with fewer and fewer official challenges. The toothless task forces of

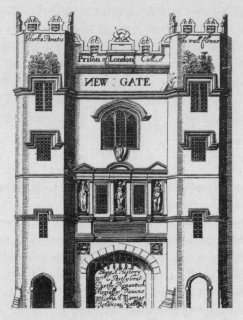

7. *Newgate in 1679*

the fourteenth and fifteenth centuries had finally given way to bureaucratic ennui and a moral complacency that accepted the Keepers' argument that they had a right to earn a living by any means necessary. Outside the prison, those who objected to the behaviour of the prison staff risked prosecution for seditious libel if they dared to make their opinions known in print. At the close of the century, James Whiston courageously published an assault on the culture of cruelty that raged inside the prison, entitled *England's calamities discover'd with the proper remedy to restore her ancient grandeur and policy* (1696), which took aim at the callous conduct of the Keepers. Newgate, Whitson railed,

> is an example that corrupts us all; for how commonly do the
> under officers, gaoler, &c., excuse their barbarity and unrea-

sonable exactions, in alleging that they have no other way to make up the interest of their purchase money? So that they are hereby forced to lay the whole design of their advantage upon the calamities of the miserable; which inhumanity is too frequently connived at by the magistrate, suffering justice to be over-ruled by the persuasion of many golden temptations.

The bloated patron maintains his family in pride, and an imperious wife, or, perhaps, impudent mistress, in excess and luxury, with what he has unconscionably drained from the ruin of the unfortunate.

Luckily for Whiston, as Rumbelow notes, his pamphlet was ignored.

Then there were those whose personal unpleasantness did not prevent them from performing their duties with some aplomb. In 1701, an efficient thief-taker called Bodenham Rewse poured a life's savings, accumulated by collaring debtors and highwaymen, into purchasing the more secure position of head turnkey. The going price for deputy Keeper – as the role amounted to – was well over £300. But the steep price proved a fortuitous investment for Rewse when, years later, after a string of suspicious escapes, the inept Keeper, William Pitt, was himself incarcerated on charges of high treason, leaving Rewse holding the keys. Despite allegations of on-the-job drunkenness and trouble with a wife who objected to having had venereal disease passed on to her from the prostitutes in prison with whom Rewse regularly consorted, he was described by one observer, the author of *An accurate description of Newgate* (1724), as having ensured that 'the Decorum maintain'd in Newgate, is not inferior to that of a well-regulated Family, which I recommend to the Consideration of every honest Person, whose Troubles are such, as not to be determined in a few Days after [being] Arrested.'

More than once, the right of the sheriffs to appoint the Keeper was contested by the Mayor and Corporation of the City. In 1638, Henry Wollaston found himself suddenly waylaid and roughly frisked on a visit to the municipal offices in the Guildhall. Wollaston had been quickly and quietly promoted to Keeper by the sheriffs six weeks earlier, following the sudden death of James Francklin, a favourite of the Lord Mayor. Unhappy with the choice and resentful at not having been consulted, the Lord Mayor unleashed on the unsuspecting Wollaston a pair of heavies who confiscated the Keeper's keys. Outraged by Wollaston's mistreatment, the sheriffs insisted that since they were 'liable to punishments for any escapes, and amerciaments [fines] for non-appearance of prisoners in Her Majesty's courts of justice' and faced 'other such damages and fears', it was only fair that they should be allowed to decide who managed the prison. It is not recorded whether Henry Wollaston ever got his keys or his dignity back.

The eighteenth century was witness to more than one Keeper whose reputation cut against the insidious stereotype. Among the most beloved, Abel Dagge – to whom the poet and friend of Dr Johnson, Richard Savage, was committed in September 1742 for a debt of £8 owed to a Mrs Read, or 'Madam Wolf Bitch', as she was affectionately known by the debtor – served not in London's Newgate, but in a prison with the same name in Bristol. Dagge looked after Savage and made every effort to obtain a speedy release for him. On more than one occasion John Wesley had the opportunity of observing Dagge, who came to represent for the Methodist preacher the very model on whom all gaolers should pattern themselves. 'The first case,' Wesley once wrote, 'must be to find a good man for a gaoler; one that is honest, active and humane. Such was Abel Dagge . . . I regretted his death and revere his memory.'

In a bid to curb the Keepers' appetite for corruption a fixed salary of £200 a year was introduced in 1734, to which was added a handsome liquor allowance. By the middle of the nineteenth century, the salary would more than double and the perks would be increased to include a spacious residence and an exemption from taxes. But despite these incentives, there was little that outside authorities could in practice do to dissuade gaolers from capitalising on their captive audience. The legacy of lucrative squeezing, practised with astonishing success by the Keeper William Pitt who, during the Jacobite Rebellion, managed to extort nearly £4,000 from inmates in a matter of months, was enough to keep the greed alive.

3

Glimmer

'**GLIMMER**, *Fire.*'

Since the Middle Ages, Smithfield – the large 'smooth field' that stretched three hundred yards to the north of Newgate – respired with the stench of huddled horses and cramped cattle waiting to be traded. On London's muddy margins, the ten acres of open ground just beyond the city walls were seized upon as a suitable space for events that belonged on the fringes of social consciousness – jamborees of jousting, a tournament honouring the King's mistress, or the slow roasting to death of hundreds of heretics. The short stride that the condemned would take from Newgate, on the periphery, to the desolate expanse of Smithfield could be viewed as a cultural axis against which some of the most horrific human endings of the sixteenth century slowly turned.

Like the Tower on the opposite corner of the city, Newgate became a crucible of conscience in the Tudor period, within whose dungeons reverberated the silence of both Catholic and Protestant prisoners who refused to recant their beliefs. In 1531, an evangelical theologian called John Frith found himself on the wrong side of Henry VIII's conception of the structure of the spiritual universe after publishing a volume entitled *Disputacion of Purgatorye*. The tract denied the existence of purgatory as a supernatural plane on which the imperfect were purified. Frith was no stranger to the discomforts of controversy. As a student at Cambridge, his heterodox beliefs had earned him a stretch in a college prison cell, among 'the impure exhalations of unsound salt fish' and the decomposing bodies of more than one dead classmate. On the run since his release, he spent time in the stocks at Reading, dodging the unsavoury projectiles of passers-by, after being dubbed a vagabond by the city officials.

But it was Frith's eloquent dismantling of the orthodox belief in purgatory, historians tell us, that made him a marked man. By calling attention to the lack of any scriptural authority for such a concept, Frith was well aware that he was pitting himself against such powerful exegetical heavyweights as John Fisher, the Bishop of Rochester, and, more menacingly still, Henry VIII's Chancellor, Sir Thomas More. The publication of the heretical *Disputacion* provoked More to issue a warrant for Frith's arrest. Although able effortlessly to slide in conversation from Latin to Greek, the lithe young theologian was caught before he could slip from Essex to Antwerp, having donned a disguise to facilitate his escape. He was arrested in October 1532 at Milton Shore and immediately transported to the Tower. But rather than reaching any kind of intellectual or religious compromise with his persecutors, Frith insolently set about composing a controversial commentary on the nature of the sacraments that he knew would exacerbate the situation. His fingers, according to subsequent accounts of his martyr-dom, strained to scrape out each syllable from under the weight of the chains that bound his arms and shoulders.

Eventually transferred from the Tower to Newgate, in what would become part of the appalling pilgrimage that scores of heretics were forced to undertake, Frith's spirits were sustained by correspondence with his one-time mentor, William Tyndale. 'If the pain be above your strength,' Tyndale grimly advised him, 'pray to your Father to shorten it.' In Newgate, Frith continued to scribble in defiance of More's intimidation. Refusing the King's calls to recant, or else be condemned to a pole and a pyre, Frith was interrogated at St Paul's on 20 June and soon afterwards found 'gyltie of the most detestable here-sies'. Two weeks later, 'for the salvation of [his] soul', he was marched symbolically under the arch of Newgate and out of the city's ancient limits. He was then led to a windy and dung-strewn Smithfield, where extra hands had been busy since dawn corralling cattle to make way for spectators and stacking fuel for a bonfire. By all accounts, the 30-year-old Frith accepted his fate with unflinching fortitude. To balance the beam on which he was strung, another alleged heretic, called Andrew Hewitt, was tied up behind Frith. As a strong breeze flattened the flames, dragging the execution out for hours, Frith could be heard above the hiss and crackle attempting to reassure Hewitt, whose unconcealed agony was said to have unsettled some members of the crowd.

Burning to death in Smithfield during the Tudor period was a punishment reserved almost exclusively for Protestants con-victed of heresy. Catholics who refuted the Act of Supremacy, asserting Henry VIII was the head of the Church of England, could expect to be hauled off to Tyburn where they would suffer the gruesome fate of hanging, drawing and quartering. In 1534, royal commissioners began making their rounds to religious communities, demanding demonstrations of alle-giance to the recently passed Act of Succession, which made Elizabeth, daughter of Anne Boleyn, heir to the Crown while declaring Mary, daughter of Katherine of Aragon, a bastard. When in May, the Charterhouse prior, John Houghton, refused to utter that oath, or a subsequent one recognising Henry's supremacy, his obstinacy triggered a merciless inter-rogation by Thomas Cromwell, the King's chief enforcer, which ended in a conviction for 'high treason'.

On 4 May 1535, thousands of people poured into the fields around Tyburn, jostling for a vantage point from which to watch the group of condemned Carthusians being dragged on hurdles from Newgate up the Tyburn Way. In all, five nooses were measured that day. Cut down while still conscious,

Houghton would have been made to watch while his testicles were sliced from his groin and roasted on a small spit before him. After his head was hacked from the neck, his torso scored with a skiver and quartered with difficulty, his right arm was taken back to the Charterhouse where it was hammered to the door as a grim reminder to those thus far spared the severe price of disobedience. Before the agony commenced, above the clatter of cleavers and rustle of ropes, Houghton managed to deliver a dignified declaration from the platform: 'Our holy mother the church hath decreed and appointed otherwise than the king and parliament hath ordained, and therefore, rather than disobey the church, I am ready to suffer. Pray for me, and have mercy on my brethren, of whom I have been the unworthy prior.'

A rare exception to the rule distinguishing the punishment of heretical Protestants as opposed to treasonous Catholics was the ordeal endured by the Franciscan friar and alleged confessor to Katherine of Aragon, John Forest. A frequent preacher at Paul's Cross (which once stood near where St Paul's Cathedral lies today), Forest was a 'favourite of the King', according to Peter Marshall, until the sturdy friar refused to accept the royal divorce. For a time Forest relocated to Newcastle, hoping the dust might settle. But by the late 1530s he was back in London preaching a conservatively Catholic line, which he well knew would antagonise Cromwell. Forest was condemned to Newgate until he was ready to accept the King's offer to rescind the punishment in exchange for a simple recantation before the congregation at Paul's Cross.

'The heresies that Forest would have to abjure', as Bishop Latimer spelled out, hit at the very heart of his faith:

> First that the Holie Catholike Church was the Church of Rome, and that wee ought to beeleve out the same. Second, that wee should beleeve on the Pope's pardon for remission of our sinnes. Thirdlie, that wee ought to beleeve and doe as our fathers have donne aforetyme fowertene yeares past. Fourthlie, that a priest maie turne and change the paines of hell of a sinner, truly

penitent, contrite of his sins, by certaine penance enjoyned him
in the paines of purgatorie; which said articles be most abhomi-
nable heresies, blasphemie against God . . .

But the clutch of Carmelite and Carthusian inmates with
whom Forest consorted in Newgate resolved not to sacrifice
their principles for the tawdry reward of life. Like Frith before
him, Forest was chained to a pyre before an expectant audience
in Smithfield on 22 May 1538. Cromwell attended the conflagration that he had helped to ignite, as did Thomas Cranmer
and an entourage of city officials.

It is difficult to predict what will finally be the cause of death
in execution by burning. If the condemned were fortunate, he
or she would succumb to carbon monoxide poisoning, or suffo-
cate, before the flames could take hold of the flesh. If the pyre
were relatively small, or if the executioner forbade the convict's
family or friends from adding faggots to the fire to accelerate the
incineration, the heretic could suffer the interminable torture of
having the flames advance from the soles of his feet to the calves
and thighs, up the abdomen and chest, spreading to the arms and
neck before engulfing the slowly slipping face.

For Forest's execution, a huge 'wooden statue from the
Welsh pilgrimage site of Llandderfel' was brought in as extra
kindling. The sculpture was of the sixth-century Welsh saint,
Derfyl Gadarn, whose fabled bravery in battle was such that it
was said he could fetch 'outlaws out of hell'. Soon after the
friar's death, rumours began to swirl throughout England and
Wales concerning the fulfilment of a curious prophesy: that
one day the holy image of Gadarn would set a 'forest on fire'.
The tale gave birth to a popular ballad that would forever link
the two figures in the lethal smoke that choked Smithfield:

> David Darvell Gatheren,
> As saith the Welshmen,
> Fetched outlaws out of hell;
> Now is he come with spere and shilde

In harness to burn at Smithfield,
For in Wales he may not dwell.
And Forest the Friar,
That obstinate liar,
That wilfullie shall be dead,

In his contumacie,
The gospell doth denie,
The king to be supreme head.

Between his accession in 1509 and his death in 1547, Henry's convoluted and self-serving political and religious whims are thought to have been responsible for over seventy thousand executions. Among the last to make the fatal journey from Newgate to Smithfield was the Protestant writer Anne Askew. By the time the dignified Askew – who had resolutely refused to accept as legitimate an arranged marriage between herself and Thomas Kyme, a Catholic farmer – was arrested for distributing Protestant literature, the needle in the compass of Henry's brain was once again pointing towards Rome. Facing a series of terrifying interrogations from a queue of bishops, including Henry's favourite thumbscrewer, Edmund Bonner, Askew refused to recant her convictions, eventually becoming the first woman to be put to the rack in the Tower.

Anne Askew's unflinching fortitude as she was tortured in the Tower and subsequently in Newgate, where she was transferred to await execution, became the stuff of legend. The reformist scholar and publisher of her writings John Bale captured the courage with which she endured her torments:

For Anguysh and payne of her broken ioyntes and broused armes and eyes, she curseth not the tyme that euer she was borne, as the maner of the vnfaythfull is. But she hyghlye magnyfyeth and prayseth God for it. Neyther was she peruerted with flatterynge promyses, nor yet ouercommen with terryble threttenynges of deathe. Neyther doubted she the stynke of Newgate, nor yet the burnynge fyer in Smythfelde.

8. Smithfield: the execution of Anne Askew in July 1546

On a stormy morning in July 1546, the Lord Chancellor and the Lord Mayor joined other dignitaries on a high wooden pew to watch the broken body of the 25-year-old Askew, which had been borne on the shoulders of the city's sergeants from her cell in Newgate to the freshly kindled pyre in Smithfield. 'At the first puttyng-to of the fyar,' according to an eyewitness, 'theyre felle a lytle dewe, or a few pleasante droppes apon us that strode by, and a pleasant cracking from heaven.'

The pageant of martyrdom that stretched between Newgate and Smithfield in the sixteenth century established a link between the two sites that had been plotted at least two hundred years earlier. In the summer of 1381, two groups of rebels from the counties of Essex and Kent converged on London to protest against the imposition of a crippling poll tax. In the wake of the Black Death, the patience of the English people was at breaking point and there was little tolerance for the aggressive tactics of the abusive tax collectors. For their leader, the Kentish rebels had turned to a local roofer called Wat Tyler about whom almost nothing is now known except that his daughter had allegedly been assaulted by one of the obnoxious officials. By 12 June, Tyler and his forces were lying in wait on the wind-swept plains of Blackheath to the south-east of the city while the Essex band assembled to the east at Mile End.

Reports of the impending invasion of the capital reached the 14-year-old king, Richard II, who anxiously despatched negotiators to agree a settlement. But once they realised the size of the insurgency the emissaries lost their nerve and beat a hasty retreat. Tyler's rebels misinterpreted the gesture as an affront to their concerns and resolved to wreak havoc on the city. Arriving in Southwark, the peasant rebels broke open the Marshalsea Prison and laid claim to London Bridge. Within hours, Fleet Prison too had fallen. Among the individual targets of the revolt was John of Gaunt, the steward of England and architect of the offending tax, whose lavish Savoy Palace was burned to the ground. All across London, noblemen and lawyers were dragged from their smouldering homes and beheaded in the streets. Emboldened, the rebels made their way to the newly christened 'Chancery Lane' and the 'New Temple' there (founded two centuries earlier by the Knights Templar) which held the city's law rolls. The rioters tore the documents to pieces and prepared themselves for the big prize: Newgate.

Petrified by the accelerating pace of destruction, Richard met the Essex rebels at Mile End where he agreed to an aston-ishing string of demands that he hoped might bring the unprecedented onslaught to an end. Despite the King's conces-sion on conditions governing the sale and rent of land, as well as the abolition of feudal services and an end to serfdom, the violence raged on. From the Tower, the rebels seized the trem-bling figures of the Archbishop of Canterbury and Sir Robert Hale, the King's Treasurer, whom they butchered unmercifully. As Newgate erupted into an unquenchable furnace, its inmates engulfed in a billowing screen of flames, Richard offered to meet Tyler himself on 15 June in Smithfield.

Accounts differ as to what transpired next. Some suggest it was a threatening gesture by Tyler while others speculate that it was merely his insolent air that provoked the Lord Mayor, William Walworth, to draw a dagger and send Tyler tumbling from his horse, there to be finished off by Richard's minions. Disorientated and leaderless, the rebellion soon dispersed. The Peasants' Revolt, now remembered as the birth of violent dissent in Britain, helped fix the consequential co-ordinates of Newgate and Smithfield, between which the nation's imagination would continue to agitate for centuries.

For some six years, from the end of Henry VIII's reign in 1547 to the accession of his religiously adversarial daughter, Mary, in July 1553 – a period that comprised the brief and mercifully effete tenures of Edward VI and Queen Jane – the embers of the first wave of Smithfield martyrs were trampled into the ground by the hoofs of market cattle. The pageant of traitors between Newgate and Smithfield ceased, and the air around St Bartholomew's, for a moment, cleared itself of the acrid stench of burning flesh. But before the new Queen, hell-bent on turning back the clock to the pre-Dissolution days of union with Rome, had officially proclaimed a prohibition against Protestant preaching, the human spits in Smithfield were already being reassembled.

Among the first to suffer the consequences of the lethal pendulum of pious preference was the Bible translator John Rogers. Detained in Newgate without trial for over a year, Rogers was confident that his imprisonment would not withstand legal scrutiny and, in November 1554, joined fellow inmates in composing a letter to the Queen demanding either immediate release or immediate trial. In the meantime, Mary persuaded Parliament to pass, only days after Rogers's appeal, legislation reasserting heresy as a capital offence. Appearing before a council convened in January 1555, Rogers defended

9. *The burning of John Rogers in February 1555*

himself eloquently against allegations of heresy, but to no avail. A final request, that he might be able to speak with his wife and their eleven children, one of whom he had yet to meet, was declined. On 4 February, 'being Monday in the morning, he was suddenly warned by the Keeper of Newgate's wife to prepare himself for the fire.' 'If it be so,' he is said to have said, 'I need not tie my points.'

Crowds blocked the narrow throat of present-day Giltspur Street, which ran between Newgate and Smithfield. When asked by the sheriff, a Mr Woodroofe, whether he was prepared to repudiate his 'abominable doctrine and the evil opinion of the sacrament of the altar', Rogers, as his weeping family looked on, replied, 'That which I have preached, I will seal with my blood.' The scene of Rogers's ensuing immolation was at once transfixing and unbearable to watch. 'The fire was put unto him,' John Foxe recorded, 'and when it had taken hold both upon his legs and shoulders, he, as one feeling no smart, washed his hands in the flame, as though it had been in cold water.'

And so it went. By the time that Mary's childless reign had come to an abortive end in November 1558, some three hundred Protestants, refusing to abjure their faiths, had been fed, one by one, into the Smithfield pyre. To the secret congregations from which the martyrs had been snatched, driven underground, Newgate became a point of final dispatch, out of which clandestine epistles from their doomed leaders had been smuggled. When the reformist chaplain John Rough was lodged there in December 1557, accused of importing contraband Bibles into London from Leiden, his final days were spent filling page after page of courageous exhortation. 'My course, brethren, have I run,' he wrote, 'salute one another in my name. Be not ashamed of the gospel of the cross, by me preached, nor yet of my suffering; for with my blood I affirm the same. I go before; I suffer first the baiting of the butchers' dogs . . .'

Although the era of burning heretics at the stake eventually came to a close, the barbaric immolation of women condemned for other 'treasonable' offences, including the murder of one's spouse, would continue long after the principal site of execution shifted to Newgate in 1783. In 1777, a proposal to expand the list of crimes punishable by fire to include coining (the illegal minting of currency) met with a rollicking rebuke from Sir William Meredith. He expressed his astonishment at the heartlessness of his parliamentary peers who could countenance such cruelty. 'I indeed have always understood treason,' Meredith railed, 'to be nothing less than some act or conspiracy against the life or honour of the King, and the safety of the state; but what the King or state can suffer by my taking now and then a bad sixpence or a bad shilling, I cannot imagine . . . By this nick-name of treason, however,' he continued, there lies at this moment in Newgate, under sentence to be burnt alive, a girl just turned fourteen; at her master's bidding she hid some white-washed farthings behind her stays, on which the jury found her guilty as an accomplice with her master in treason. The master was hanged last Wednesday; and the faggots all lay ready, no reprieve came till just as the cart was setting out, and the girl would have been burnt alive on the same day, had it not been for the humane but casual interference of Lord Weymouth. Good God! Sir, are we taught to execrate the fires of Smithfield, and are we lighting them now to burn a poor harmless child for hiding a white-washed farthing! And yet, this barbarous sentence, which ought to make men shudder at the thought of shedding blood for such trivial causes, is brought as a reason for more hanging and burning.

The ghosts of the martyrs who were marched to their deaths from Newgate would never cease to haunt the hoof-mulched soil of Smithfield. Over a century after the embers of the last pyre had flickered out, Dickens could summon in his novel *Oliver Twist* the spirit of despair that would forever hover over this tattered swatch of the city's imagination:

It was market morning. The ground was covered, nearly ankle deep, with filth and mire; a thick stream, perpetually rising from the reeking bodies of the cattle and mingling with the fog . . . the crowding, pushing, driving, beating, whooping and yelling; the hideous and discordant din that resounded from every corner of the market; and the unwashed, unshaven, squalid and dirty figures constantly running to and fro, and bursting in and out of the throng; rendered it a stunning and bewildering scene, which quite confounded the senses.

4

Crank

'Counterfeit-CRANK, *a genteel Cheat, a Sham or Impostor,*
appearing in divers Shapes; one who sometimes counterfeits Mens
hands, or forges Writings; at other Times personates other Men:
Who is sometimes a Clipper or Coiner; at other Times deals in
Counterfeit Jewels, and pretends to pledge or sell them for less
than Worth, and is never heard of again. Sometimes he sets up
for a strolling Mountebank or Player, and pretends to Cures and
parts he knows nothing of: To Day he is a Clergyman in Distress;
to Morrow a reduced Gentleman: In short, a Counterfeit-Crank
is a perfect Proteus, who can transform himself into all Shapes to
serve his villainous Purposes.'

London is a city of imposture and disguise. It is a place where
the compulsion to masquerade runs deeper than the passing
observance of festival traditions or the fleeting temptation to
defraud for a few pence. While the costumed players and
painted clowns, fire-eaters and magicians of the great fairs, such
as St Bartholomew's in Smithfield, satisfied the urge to pretend
in public, Londoners were forever surprising themselves with
the need to dupe and be duped. It only enhanced Newgate's
mystique that in the context of the great impostors who would
take the spotlight from time to time, the prison should also
serve as an anti-theatre, an authenticator of identities, a backstage to which performers would briefly retire (if involuntarily)
from their self-directed scenes on the streets, before the bow of

the public pillory or the curtain call at Tyburn and that last, lethal curtsy.

One such player was 18-year-old Elizabeth Crofts of Aldersgate Street (a brisk five-minute hustle from Newgate, north-east of the prison in the direction of present-day Barbican) who managed to capture London's attention on 14 March 1554 and hold it for nearly a week. These were the heydays of Queen Mary's persecution of Protestants and religious tension was running at fever pitch. No one now knows what the precise relationship between Elizabeth, a servant maid, and a band of Protestant mischief-makers led by someone called 'Drakes' had been, or even whether Elizabeth shared their fervent religious views. All that history records is that somehow or other the group convinced Elizabeth to secrete herself behind a makeshift wall along Aldersgate Street, and to issue anti-Papist pronouncements through a specially devised whistle or tube. The eerie whispers, which wafted through the neighbourhood, were like prophecies from another world.

Passers-by stopped to listen to the 'half-articulate effusions', dubbing them the voice of an angel, 'the Spirit in the Wall'. 'Her words proceeded,' it was said, 'in such a tone, as seemed to have nothing mortal in it.' Many were convinced it was the Holy Spirit manifesting itself in a time of turmoil. Crowds quickly gathered and began debating what exactly was being said. 'Shhh! . . . now, that murmur there . . . was that a denouncement of King Philip?' By the second days eighteen thousand people had crammed themselves along the Aldersgate Street wall. Drakes and a pair of co-conspirators, Miles and Hill, circulated among the listeners stirring up speculation as to what the 'spirit' had just said. 'Was that not a condemnation of the Queen?' To test the apparition's allegiances someone shouted out 'God save the Queen!' But the wall fell silent. Another howled, 'God save the Catholic Church!' Not a sound from the wall. Then a nervous gentleman at the back of the throng, hiding his face in the collar of his coat, yelled, 'God save Elizabeth!' alluding to Mary's Protestant sister, and a trembling voice from behind the wall decreed: 'So be it.' London gasped. Suspicions began to swirl that divine intervention would soon depose Mary. But the rumpus came to a sudden end when a sceptic with a crowbar attacked the wall's flimsy structure. As plank after plank was ripped off, the angelic 'spirit in the wall' was exposed to be nothing more than a crouching child clutching a kazoo.

Elizabeth was dragged to Newgate and taken before the Archdeacon of Middlesex to explain her involvement in a ruse to unsettle the city's loyalty to the Queen. Apologising for having insulted 'God and the Queen's majesty', she 'wept bitterly' and revealed the identities of those who had put her up to the scheme. While the fate of her accomplices is unrecorded, Elizabeth's punishment was to 'stand upon a scaffold neer St Paul's Cross, on the 15th of July . . . and that being done, to make a publick declaration of that lewd imposture', after which she bows out of the historical record.

Other impostors, however, found it more difficult to quit the public stage and managed to appear again and again, as if daring society to unmask them. Such was the case with the remarkable modalities of Mary Moders. 'Of all that this Age have produced,' one of her first biographers, Francis Kirkman wrote, 'none does so clearly demonstrate the Truth of our Frailness and Imbecility, when governed by our own wild desires, then [sic] this enduring Narrative.' Born in 1642, the charming daughter of a Canterbury fiddler, Mary starts out respectably enough as the young wife of a local shoemaker. When both of their children died in infancy, Mary determined to take leave not only of her commitments, but also of her identity. While an elopement to the West Indies was aborted when her husband discovered the plot, she soon succeeded in absconding to Dover where a surgeon called Thomas Day proposed marriage. It was not long after the wedding that Mary's marital status was exposed and she was tried in a local court for bigamy. In the first of several near-misses for the serial missus, Mary avoided conviction by convincing the jury that she was confused and under the impression that her first husband was dead.

Intent on reinventing herself yet again, Mary moved to the Continent after her acquittal and settled briefly in Cologne. She immersed herself in German culture and resolved to master the language. So successful was she in her new role that she was mistaken for a Westphalian noblewoman. The mix-up implanted in her mind the seeds of a sensational scheme. She invested the little money she had in a few accoutrements of social elevation – an expensive necklace and posh frock, lace and silk shoes – and made her way quickly back to England. En route to London, bypassing Dover and her former home in Canterbury, she forged a portfolio of documents on which she could rely for proof of her substantial wealth as the 'ill-used child' and heiress of 'Count Henry Van Wolway, sovereign prince of the Empire'. The self-styled 'German Princess' found lodgings with an innkeeper by the name, appropriately enough, of King, who, as it happened, had the perfect prince in mind for her. King's brother-in-law, John Carleton, an 18-year-old law clerk, was happy to oblige. Attired in a silk suit, the fragrant Carleton presented himself to the audacious impostor who agreed to accept his hand (and money) in marriage.

But the gambit was short-lived. When news of the royal affair reached Canterbury, an anonymous letter alerted Carleton to his wife's duplicitous past. Charged with bigamy, Mary was seized and escorted to Newgate, where she refused to relinquish her fabricated character. In that, needless to say, she was not alone; 'no man goes into Newgate twice,' according to a later commentator on the question of identity in The Gaol, 'with the same name, trade, or place of nativity.' Mary's sustained performance attracted huge and adoring crowds as a steady stream of admirers, including Samuel Pepys, circulated through the corridors of the prison to catch a glimpse of the unflappable actress. When Mary was offered the platform of a witness box in the Old Bailey, her powers of imposture were, by all accounts, a marvel to behold, as the prosecution's fumbled case collapsed before the jury. Mary's first husband, John Stedman, never materialised. Without anyone from her past to contradict her outrageous story, Mary's identity became anything that the charismatic defendant wanted it to be. Insisting that she was indeed Maria de Wolway, but that a rumoured fortune was merely a wishful fabrication, according to her biographer Janet Todd, Mary was acquitted to uproarious applause in the court and adulation throughout the city.

In what must be one of the oddest cultural tangos in British social history, Mary's notoriety put in motion an implausible three-step of art-imitating-life-imitating-art-again as her story inspired a wave of theatrical productions in which she herself was cast in the leading role. An inept farce by Thomas Porter featuring one of the most celebrated actors of the day, Cave Underhill, was followed by a play entitled *The German Princesse*, which opened at the Duke's Theatre, in which Mary impersonated herself impersonating a princess who insists that she is not impersonating anyone at all. As ever, Pepys was in attendance. Though he once had admired Mary's 'wit and spirit', Pepys confided in his diary his disappointment with the performance. 'To the Duke's house, and there saw "The German Princesse" acted by the woman herself; but never was anything so well done in earnest,' Pepys wrote, 'worse performed in jest upon the stage. And indeed the whole play, abating the drollery of him that acts her husband, is very simple, unless, here and there, a witty sprinkle or two.' Not since the infamous fence, Mary Frith – better known in her day and after as 'Moll Cutpurse' – had taken to the stage in man's clothing at the start of the seventeenth century had such audacity held London in thrall.

Given the public's enthusiastic endorsement of her invented personas, it is not surprising that Mary should continue to pursue a life of shape-shifting – adopting and disposing of

*10. The infamous cross-dressing seventeenth-century fence,
Mary Frith, better-known as 'Moll Cutpurse'.*

identities left and right as she manipulated lover after gullible
lover, amassing a modest wealth along the way. In the end,
however, she lost her touch if not her nerve. Six years after
taking the stage, she was spotted stealing a pewter tankard. By
then few jurymen could countenance her surreal excuses and
she was convicted of theft. A brief stretch in Jamaica, where
she had been transported, ended when Mary violated the
terms of her sentencing and returned to London to resume her
old habits. When the Keeper of Newgate recognised her at the
home of a suspected thief, Mary must have known she stood
as little chance of survival as a cat at the end of its ninth life.
Though the German Princess took her final bow at Tyburn on
22 January 1673, clutching a picture of John Carleton with
which she asked to be buried, her identity changes continued
to intrigue readers for many decades.

Pamphlet after pamphlet appeared, some purporting to have
been written by Mary herself, attempting to disentangle fact

from fiction. In one of the most popular of these publications, *The counterfeit lady unveiled, being a full account of the birth, life, most remarkable actions, and untimely death of Mary Carleton, known by the name of the German princess*, its author, Francis Kirkman, famously pinpointed the conundrum faced by any subsequent biographer: 'If I should promise to give you a true account of her whole life,' he explained, 'I should deceive you, for how can Truth be discovered of her who was wholly composed of Falsehood?' Another pamphlet, the anonymously published *memoires of Mary Carleton, commonly stiled the German princess* (1673), concludes with an epitaph, expressing doubt that her deceitful ways could be stifled by the mere disguise of death:

> Here lies one much against her will,
> Who did lye living; and dead, lies still . . .
> And tho' now coffin'd up in Chest,
> Ne'er think that she'l there tamely rest.
> Assure your self alive, or dead,
> She can't keep constant to her bed.
> Therefore look to't, lest out she steal,
> And cheat the worms of a set meal.

Twenty-five years before the demise of the German Princess, a no less astonishing crook crossed Newgate's stage in the guise of a prince. If one thinks Mary Moders bold for undertaking to impersonate a royal figure on whom no one in England was likely ever to have laid eyes, how much more audacious were the efforts of Cornellis Ivans. What exactly possessed Ivans to pass himself off as the Prince of Wales (the future Charles II) remains a mystery. According to a contemporary writer, he was hardly a dead ringer, being 'a little man [with] flaxen haire, shorter than the Prince by a head, a little bowed in his Shoulders, with hands like to a Butchers boyes hands, with a narrow blue ribband about his neck, without a George.' Nevertheless, the unemployed French émigré of Welsh extraction, having failed to find himself employment on a boat,

determined to capitalise on what he considered to be a market-
able, if unremarkable, resemblance to the prince.

Setting out on foot in May 1648, Ivans scoured the south
coast of England for a community unlikely to ask questions or
even to know which questions to ask. Having sized up Dover
and then Deal, he settled on Sandwich, 'comming in so strange
a manner as on foot, and in an old black ragged sute, without
any Companions but Lice'. After a few carefully placed remarks
in a tavern about his narrow escape from Queen Henrietta
Maria, who, he claimed, had 'endeavoured to poyson him' back
in France, Sandwich was abuzz with talk of the refugee prince.
Before nightfall he was offered lodgings by a wealthy captain
and warmly welcomed by the Lord Mayor, William Mandey.
Though Ivans stumbled over his story more than once, contra-
dicting details and confusing his political allegiances, the trust-
ing people of Sandwich were 'much inclined to him'. 'Before
he went from *The Bell* Tavern,' according to the *House of Lords
Journal* for May 1648, 'and not above Two Hours after he first
came thither, he was presented by a Gentlewoman (whose
Name he knoweth not) with One Hundred Pieces of Gold,
and Three Bunches of Asparagus.' And so he went, with
'Trumpets sounding his Meat' from tavern to tavern.

Having arrived in tatters, the emperor needed new clothes
and the townspeople were all too willing to invest Ivans with
whatever he required to maintain his princely image. Decked
in a crimson suit laced in gold and silver, Ivans processed
through the town twiddling his fingers monarchically and
accepting all manner of gifts. 'One Thomas Richards,' according to the *Kingdomes Weekly Intelligencer*, 'a man of an extraordinary stature, was chosen to carry the sword . . . walking
before him in a slow and stately posture,' as shouts of 'Room
for the Prince!' rang through the streets. Mutterings of a dis-
crepancy between the profile of the real prince, dusky and tall,
and the diminutive charlatan who was shamelessly impersonating him, came to the ear of a 'Scottish man' Sir Thomas

Dishington, an attendant to Queen Henrietta, who happened to be passing through Sandwich. When Dishington took it upon himself to inform the Lord Mayor that he was entertaining a hoaxer, Mandey was outraged, but not at Ivans. 'I told the Mayor,' Dishington later recalled, 'that he [Ivans] was an impostor, and a villaine: And required the Mayor (as he would be answerable to King and Parliament,) that they would make him sure and forth comming, for which the Mayor (being accompanyed with 30 or 40 Mariners) came to me, the Mayor himself seized on my sword, with their assistant took it from me, and presently committed me to the common Gaole.'

By now, news of the supposed Prince's residency was spreading through the Civil War-torn country, piquing the interest of Roundheads and Cavaliers alike. Kentish forces, eager to seize on the supposed presence in England of the King's son as a catalyst for bringing him back to London, resolved to go to Sandwich and rescue the waylaid prince. Meanwhile, Parliament, suspicious of any such arrival on their shores, despatched a delegation to detain him. With little time to spare, Ivans's admirers, proof against all evidence of his imposture, smuggled him on to a getaway ship bound for the Isle of Thanet. That evening, 'at Master Crispes house at Supper', Ivans was betrayed to the authorities and hauled off to Newgate. And there the 'Hubbub' ends, as mysteriously as it began. After making a full confession before the House of Lords, the fabulous figure of Cornellis Ivans disappears from the fabric of the prison's history, escaping silently into the night. But in whose clothes?

The impostures of Crofts, Moders and Ivans, while welcome diversions in their day, seem droll in comparison to the bizarre events that unfolded in a dank, dog-legged corner of Dr Johnson's London a century after Ivans vanished into the haze of history. It all started in 1759, when Miss Frances Lynes (known to friends and family as 'Fanny') and William Kent moved from Norfolk to London and rented a room from Richard Parsons, clerk of nearby St Sepulchre's, in the guest-house he owned at No. 33 Cock Lane. The address, which would soon be on the lips of every Londoner, is off Giltspur Street and a two-minute stroll from Newgate in the direction of Smithfield Market. Kent was the widower of Fanny's sister, Elizabeth, who had died in childbirth a few months earlier.

On an evening in early summer, when Kent was called away on business, Fanny consented to allow the landlord's daughter, ten-year-old Elizabeth, to sleep beside her. That evening, the house was unsettled by an eerie and persistent scratching, which kept the residents of No. 33 up most of the night. The nocturnal knocking and scraping continued for several weeks after Kent's return and began to attract the curiosity of neighbours. Before long, Fanny, still shaken by the recent death of her sister, began attaching to the unexplained sounds a premonition of her own untimely demise. The tension created by the disturbance was exacerbated by a growing animosity between Kent and the landlord, Parsons, who felt short-changed on rent. When Fanny discovered that she was expecting Kent's child, they resolved to leave Cock Lane and move to cheaper digs in Holborn. There, Fanny Lynes died on 2 February 1760, in a suite of grubby rooms in the dead of winter, battling 'an eruptive fever'. She was six months pregnant and riddled, it was said, with smallpox.

Unnerved by Fanny's sudden death, the neighbourhood around Cock Lane strove to put behind it the uncanny connection between the strange sounds, which had since ceased, and the macabre omen that Fanny had read into them. And it did, until, that is, the knocking and scratching returned. The resumption of the sounds, which seemed to originate from the room where Parsons's two children, including the now 12-year-old Elizabeth, slept, caused a stir throughout the city. A medium, Mary Frazer, was summoned to Cock Lane and in due course determined that the noises were the desperate efforts of the ghost of Fanny Lynes to engage with the living. 'Scratching Fanny', as the ghost became known, allegedly

11. *The mystery of the Cock Lane ghost captivated London in*
1762

responded to questions with a single sharp rap for 'yes' and a thudding double-thunk for 'no'.

At first, listeners were content with answers to the most trivial of questions – 'whether a watch, when held up, be white, blue, yellow, or black; how many clergymen are in the room'. It wasn't long, however, before the lines of inquiry took a more sinister turn. Why was Fanny so shiftless? Was there something she wanted to say? After a series of leading questions, followed by ambiguous rattles and indeterminate thuds, those in attendance were convinced that Fanny Lynes had returned to Cock Lane to reveal that she had not died of smallpox after all, but had been murdered by William Kent.

London was beside itself. Crowds flocked to the crooked street, jostling for the chance to stand around the bed of Elizabeth Parsons and witness the sensational séances for themselves. 'To have a proper idea of the scene, as it is now carried on,' wrote Oliver Goldsmith, who became obsessed with the sensation though he didn't believe that there was any supernatural component to it, 'the reader is to conceive a very small room with a bed in the middle; the girl, at the usual hour of going to bed, is undressed, and put in with proper solemnity; the spectators are next introduced . . . and wait in silent expectation for the opening of the scene.' Once she has announced her invisible presence by way of a salutary rustle or scrape, 'Scratching Fanny' proceeds to establish her reliability as a medium by answering a few innocuous questions. 'Though sometimes right, and sometimes wrong, she pretty invariably persists in one story,' Goldsmith noted, 'namely, that she was poisoned, in a cup of purl, by red arsenic, by Mr Kent, and that she heartily wishes him hanged.'

Before long, a lynch-mob mentality began to swell and the safety of William Kent was suddenly far from certain. Panic grew when Elizabeth and her father were heard asserting that the ghost had shown herself to them, 'without hands, in a shroud . . . all luminous and shining', a claim corroborated by a neighbour. It was at this juncture that Samuel Johnson, whose reputation as a man of unflappable sensibility had been established seven years earlier with the publication of his celebrated *Dictionary*, determined to get to the bottom of the sensational saga unfolding a short stroll from his home in Gough Square, off Fleet Street. Suspicious that Elizabeth was behind the hoax, Dr Johnson, together with his friends Horace Walpole and Oliver Goldsmith, devised a series of 'tests' to which the triumvirate were allowed to subject the young girl.

The first of these involved a close, under-the-duvet, chaperoning of Elizabeth by a female maid, who was made to hold the child as she slept. The test proved inconclusive as those in attendance could not agree whether supernatural sounds were audible. From there the tests became increasingly constrictive, involving fetters and chain-mail in which the girl was all but mummified. But apart from the uncomfortable clankings of iron every time Elizabeth rustled, no sounds were heard that night. When Elizabeth was at last informed that she could sleep unmolested, but, should the ghost fail to present itself, her father would be dragged to Newgate, the 12-year-old was seen, through a peephole punched in her door, to produce from under her nightdress a small board against which she thrummed her knuckles and scraped her nails like a street musician playing a homespun instrument.

As Walpole, Johnson and Goldsmith nodded in smug satisfaction at the wisdom and conclusiveness of their methodology, Elizabeth's parents, together with the 'sham' medium Frazer, were carted off to prison and charged with conspiracy. It is some indication of the city's tolerance that on each of the three occasions on which Richard Parsons was sentenced to stand in the pillory at the end of Cock Lane, having been convicted at the Guildhall on 10 July of coercing his daughter to perpetrate a hoax, the crowds refused to hurl either expletives or excrement. Indeed, it was perhaps Johnson who suffered the most from exposing the culprit. His pomposity was not appreciated by a city that preferred to operate on the premise that a former brothel in Cock Lane might well be the portal between the living and the dead, and that 'Scratching Fanny' was proof enough to justify their faith. The satirical poet Charles Churchill, delighted, according to Johnson's biographer Thomas Babington Macaulay, that 'a naughty girl of eleven had been amusing herself by making fools of so many philosophers', lampooned the lexicographer in a popular poem entitled *The Ghost*, in which Johnson is unflatteringly rechristened 'Pomposo' and derided as 'insolent and loud / Vain idol of a scribbling crowd'.

And there the mystery rested for nearly a century until an artist clambered into the crypt of the church where William Kent had quietly buried Fanny Lynes, looking for gothic subjects to sketch. 'While drawing in the crypt of St John's, Clerkenwell, in a narrow cloister on the north side, (there being at that time coffins, fragments of shrouds, and human remains lying about in disorder),' wrote the Scottish painter James Archer, 'the sexton's boy pointed to one of the coffins, and said that it was "Scratching Fanny". This reminding me of the Cock Lane Ghost, I removed the lid of the coffin, which was loose, and saw the body of a woman . . . The face was perfect, handsome, oval, with an aquiline nose,' Archer observed. Such eerie preservation, as Archer and countless crime writers since have noted, is a classic sign of arsenic poisoning.

5

Pink'd

'**PINK'D**, *prick'd with a Sword in a Re-encounter or Duel.* He pink'd his Dubblet, *He run him through.*'

To the development of medieval and Renaissance poetry and drama, Newgate Gaol is a vanishing point − a site of erasure and disappearance. So early and insistent is its link with English literature and literary figures that one is tempted to read the prison itself as a fading text on which has been inscribed a whole history of human anguish and endurance.

One of the alluring qualities of Newgate as an undeciphered fragment is its very resistance to decoding. Attempt to retrieve what appears to be etched in the margins of the prison's murky past, and the clues dissolve before your very eyes. As a register of poets and of the subjects that inspired them from the twelfth to the seventeenth centuries, Newgate is at once crowded and blank. From the genesis of Robin Hood to the writing of Sir Thomas Malory's *Le Morte D'Arthur* and the lethal escapades of Christopher Marlowe, Thomas Nashe and Ben Jonson, the prison shuffles through the early volumes of English literature a ream of unreadable pages and lost leads.

In the second half of the thirteenth century, Roger Godberd, the elusive leader of a highway gang operating around Nottinghamshire, was apprehended in Hereford by Reginald de Grey and brought to Newgate where he was held 'as a felon of the Lord King'. The allegations against Godberd, that he and his band had pillaged an abbey in Wiltshire – stealing its horses and treasures and murdering one of its monks – matches the supposed crimes committed by the legendary bandit, Robin Hood. Ballads celebrating the adventures of the charismatic rapscallion began circulating in the fourteenth century and one of the mainstays of the familiar story is that the colourful thief is given sanctuary from the Sheriff of Nottingham by Sir Richard at the Lee, the Lord of Verysdale. Similarly, before his own capture, Godberd had attracted the patronage of a prominent knight called Richard Foliot, whose protection of Godberd's gang cost him a castle that lay on the outskirts of – where else? – Sherwood Forest.

As a possible historical model for Robin Hood, Godberd is among the most compelling candidates, though one neglected by some scholars, perhaps because so little is known about him after he disappeared into the shadows of Newgate some time around 1272. While the almost complete absence of prison records from that period makes tracing him well-nigh impossible, one can begin to see how Newgate, as a cultural black hole, incubated imagination.

Among the many literary figures left to stew inside The Gaol was the great fifteenth-century Arthurian author, Sir Thomas Malory. Though much mystery surrounds the early life and times of Malory, recent scholarship has established beyond doubt that he was an incorrigible rogue for much of his adult life. By the age of 40 he was adding incidents of rape, rustling and vandalism to a list of felonies that already included burglary and extortion so that the gaolers of London's prisons – from the Marshalsea to the King's Bench, from Newgate to the Fleet – were well acquainted with him. But a string of bails, pardons and narrow escapes from each of these institutions engendered in Malory an infuriating air of invulnerability.

Malory's luck, however, finally broke in 1468 when, suspected of being involved in an elaborate plot to depose the new King, Edward IV, he was lodged in the Tower and very likely bandied back and forth for the next three years between the King's Bench and Newgate. In an age of fickle allegiances, when Yorkists and Lancastrians were forever wresting and relinquishing the upper hand, Malory managed to keep his neck off the chopping block by exploiting the gaps in political continuity. It was during this time that he completed his masterpiece, *Le Morte D'Arthur* – an ingenious assemblage of original Arthurian tales and adaptations from French and English sources. Given the richness of its allusions to other writers, access to an extensive library would have been crucial for Malory. In addition to the holdings near to hand in the Tower, scholars have pointed out the proximity of Newgate to the impressive library that had been endowed by Richard Whittington, the famous benefactor of Newgate in the fifteenth century, in the Franciscan monastery of Greyfriars immediately north of The Gaol. It is doubtless an indication of Malory's charisma and canniness that he was permitted to have precious volumes delivered to him, whether in the Tower or in Newgate.

Substantiating the possible links between Malory and Greyfriars of Newgate Street is the fact that when he died on 14 March 1471, six months after completing the monumental *Morte D'Arthur*, the silver-tongued scoundrel was laid to rest in a chapel of the monastery dedicated to St Francis, a stone's throw from the prison. The interment was a surprising mark of social esteem for someone with as chequered a past as Malory's. This is where Queen Isabella, the so-called She-Wolf of France, was buried in 1358, followed four years later by Joan, Queen of Scotland. But if discord was Malory's lot in life, it wasn't too long before upheaval tracked him down in death. When the monasteries were violently dissolved in the middle of the sixteenth century, the alabaster tombs of Greyfriars were dutifully smashed and raided, the marble tombstones stolen and sold, and the brass ornamentation stripped off. Like much of the tale of The Gaol both before and since, the material legacy of Malory and *Le Morte D'Arthur* was erased for ever.

By the end of the sixteenth century, more assiduous records were being kept by the prison and filed in the Sessions House next door. An entry in the autumn 1589 Rolls has cast a teasing flicker across the pages of one of the scantiest biographies in English literature. In September of that year, two thespians with allegedly thuggish leanings were tossed into Newgate, accused of killing the son of an innkeeper by the name of William Bradley. One of the suspects was Thomas Watson, a suave 34-year-old sonneteer and Latin translator, and the other was a prodigious dramatist and recent composer of a highly successful play, *Tamburlaine the Great* – 25-year-old Christopher Marlowe.

From what can be pieced together from surviving testimony, the incident in question occurred on an early afternoon in mid-September in Hog Lane, near Norton Fulgate, Shoreditch, on the east side of the city. The area had been a haunt for actors and playwrights since James Burbage's 'Theatre' opened a decade earlier. Bradley and Watson had been locked in a feud for several weeks over a debt of some £14 that Bradley owed to a contact of Watson, John Alleyn. A known bruiser and sponger, Bradley had attempted to bully his way out of repayment by threatening to kill Alleyn's solicitor, Hugo Swift, should he continue to pursue the matter. Bradley's tactics were repaid in kind, however, when Alleyn, Swift and Watson demonstrated to Bradley with their fists and sturdy Renaissance slippers that they meant business and had no intention of writing off the debt. Shortly after a boozy lunch in a nearby tavern on 18 September, an enraged Bradley swaggered his gin-soaked way up Hog Lane, where he knew Watson lived, his sword swinging at his side.

Spoiling for a fight, Bradley was unfussed when, after Watson failed to appear, Kit Marlowe entered the scene. Marlowe and Watson were famous friends and as the feud had already spread well beyond the principal parties, Bradley apparently saw no reason to split hairs. Bradley drew his sword and poked the playwright provokingly on the shoulder. But no sooner had Marlowe responded to the outrageous challenge, matching Bradley's wild lunges with a few adept jabs of his own, than Watson himself walked on. Happy to take over for his friend, Watson leapt into the skirmish and traded jousts with the aggressive scoundrel. But when Watson found himself inched backwards by Bradley's surprising determination, now teetering on the edge of a ditch and slowly losing ground as he fended off thrust after inebriated thrust, he saw a small window of opportunity and shoved his rapier through it.

Bradley lay dead and the two-against-one odds to which the various members of the crowd who had gathered could attest did not look good for either Watson or Marlowe. The two men were dragged to Newgate by the attending constable, where they were held on suspicion of murder. Luckily, there was enough corroborating evidence that could be assembled in time for the inquest, which was held the following day, to establish Bradley as the instigator. Watson's and Marlowe's actions were excused on grounds of self-defence. Release from the gaol would therefore merely require a perfunctory pardon from the Queen, which Marlowe received less than a fortnight later. Watson, however, would have to wait nearly five months to receive his.

This was, of course, far from the last lethal scrape in which Marlowe would find himself. Four years later, while under investigation by the Privy Council for atheism and libel, he was fatally stabbed above his right eye in a house in Deptford. To this day controversy swirls as to the precise circumstances surrounding Marlowe's murder, the conjecture leading down alleyways as diverse as a mere drunken brawl and political assassination. Though Marlowe's writings in the intervening years, between his release from Newgate and his violent death at the age of 29, do not seem to have been overly influenced by his short stay in prison, one does not have to flip ahead very far in the catalogue of English drama to find a writer whose work was forever scarred by first-hand experience inside The Gaol.

The particularities of the incident that resulted in the 26-year-old playwright, and future author of *Volpone* and *The Alchemist*, Ben Jonson, ramming a short sword through the chest of his former friend, the actor Gabriel Spencer, in September 1598 remain misty. The two had survived something of an ordeal two years earlier, when they were imprisoned in the Marshalsea after the performance of *The Isle of Dogs*, a play Jonson had co-written with Thomas Nashe. For reasons that seem unfathomable today, the work had caused a considerable stir on grounds of alleged 'lewdness'. The furore resulted in all of the theatres in London being shut down and Nashe astutely slipping off to Great Yarmouth. Jonson and Spencer, who had acted in the play, were dragged off to prison at the insistence of Richard Topcliffe, Queen Elizabeth's infamous pursuivant. Though initially charged with 'mutynous behaviour', according to Ian Donaldson, the matter was quickly dropped and Jonson and Spenser were free to return to their dramatic lives.

But as Jonson's fame exploded in the ensuing months and years, Spencer's spleen grew in direct proportion. Envious at his one-time cellmate's accelerating success, and bleary-eyed after long drinking sessions in the pubs of Shoreditch, Spencer lay in wait for Jonson off Hog Lane, near the entrance to the Curtain Theatre, a few yards from where Marlowe and Bradley had crossed swords almost a decade earlier. Accepting Spencer's challenge, Jonson proposed that they move the duel to the yellowing grasses of the adjoining Hogsden Field, where Jonson repelled a few desperate thrusts before driving his point home. The writer would later explain that his success in slaying Spencer was something of a feat, given the superior weapon wielded by the aggressor, being ten inches longer than Jonson's and nearly twice as expensive. But the authorities were as unimpressed by the scale of Jonson's victory as they were by his insistence that Spenser had started it. To the gaolers of Newgate, murder was murder and Jonson had better prepare himself for the trip to Tyburn.

Luckily for Jonson, life for the literate in Renaissance London was often one of loopholes, and a curious statute in English law that dated back to the twelfth century proved his unexpected salvation. Before his murder in 1170, the Archbishop of Canterbury, Thomas Becket, had insisted that members of the clergy should not be held liable to secular law or tried in non-ecclesiastical courts. Henry II took little notice of Becket's demands until public outrage at the archbishop's assassination forced the King to reconsider. A concession to the Church stitched into the Compromise of Avranches of 1172 excused the clergy from ever having to answer secular charges, except in cases of arson, highway robbery and high treason. It was soon recognised, however, that this provision was wide open to abuse by anyone with access to a colourful robe and willing to assert clerical immunity. As members of the clergy were among the few in society who were taught to read Latin, a literacy test was therefore devised for anyone wishing to claim the protection of the so-called 'Benefit of Clergy'. In practice, this amounted to being asked to read the solemn '*Miserere mei*', Psalm 51, with its pathetic plea, 'Have mercy upon me, O God.'

Given its ability to save a defendant from hanging, the passage soon became known as the 'Neck Verse'. Not surprisingly, canny criminals would commit the psalm to memory in the event that they should be caught and prosecuted. For Ben Jonson, reading the Latin text was no challenge at all. Rather than being punished with execution, a livid letter 'T' was branded on his left thumb as a memento of the place that he had been spared from visiting. The experience inside The Gaol left a deep impression on the texture of Jonson's imagination and subsequent work. His former prison cell, supervised by an archetypal Keeper by the name of Shackles, is among the stark settings to feature in the comedy *The Devil is an Ass*, which he came to write nearly two decades later.

12. Ben Jonson, whose life was spared in 1598 when he invoked the 'Neck Verse'

Though Jonson may have been the most illustrious inmate during the autumn of 1598 who was made to march 'two by two, Newgate fashion' (as Shakespeare would describe the prison's routine in *Henry IV, Part I*), he shared its dank and lice-strewn slabs with an intriguing, if now-forgotten, figure who did as much to inscribe The Gaol's mystique on to the pages of history as any of his better-known contemporaries. Arrested for a highway robbery, the writer Luke Hutton was prohibited from invoking the exemption that would soon save Jonson's neck. The felony, which had been perpetrated on the prisoner's birthday, 18 October (St Luke's Day, as it happened), was not the first offence to have earned Hutton a stay in Newgate. Three years earlier he had been convicted of a hanging offence, but had managed to secure a reprieve when Chief Justice Sir John Popham interceded on his behalf. The hellishness of

The Blacke Dogge of Newgate :
both pithie and profitable
for all Readers.

Vide, Lege, Caue.

Time shall trie the trueth.

13. A ballad by the highwayman, Luke Hutton, published in 1596 helped inscribe the legend of 'the black dog of Newgate' on London's imagination

Hutton's experience inside the prison had inspired the thief briefly to swap his blunderbuss for a quill in order to compose a ballad, *The Blacke Dogge of Newgate*, which captured the public's imagination. In it, Hutton describes a shape-shifting ghostly monster, the Black Dog, which is now a gaoler, now a duplicitous coney-catcher: 'Then did I fixe mine eye upon this Beast', he wrote, 'Who did appeare first in the shape of Man':

> But in a trice he did transforme his shape,
> Which stroke a treble horror to my heart:
> A *Cerberus,* nay worse, he thrice as wide did gape,
> His haires all Snakes curling, they will not part.
> Cole-blacke his hew, like Torches glow his eyes,
> His breath doth poyson, smoke from's nostrils flyes.

His countenance ghastly, fearefull, grim, and pale,
His fomy mouth still gaping for his prey:
With Tigers teeth he spares none to assaile,
His lippes Hell gates, ore-painted with decay:
His tongue the Clapper, sounding wofull knell,
Towling poore men to ring a peale in Hell.

According to Newgate legend, Hutton's 'Blacke Dogge' had haunted the prison since the thirteenth century and continues, some say, to disturb the very ground on which The Gaol once stood. The story dates back to the reign of Henry III and a decision on the part of the Keepers to starve inmates who could not afford the extortionate prices that were levied for food. So desperate had one scrum of felons become that they conspired to kill a rotund German immigrant who had recently been gaoled on suspicion of performing alchemy, and cannibalise his flesh, which had been judged 'passing good meate'. Throughout the ensuing centuries, countless sightings were reported of a spectre of a rabid black dog, assumed by generations of inmates to be the vengeful reincarnation of the murdered mystic, prowling insidiously along the eastern wall of the prison that bordered the quiet cul-de-sac of Amen Court. On the eve of executions, the canine apparition proved an infallible omen of the arrival the following morning of the most menacing player in the unending drama of The Gaol: the hangman, 'Jack Ketch'.

6

Gape

'GAPE-Seed, *whatever the gazing Crowd idly stares and gapes after; as Puppet-shews, Rope danglers, Monsters, and Mountebanks; any thing to feed the Eye.*'

On 9 May 1662, Samuel Pepys stood transfixed in a rambunctious crowd as a pair of disjointed bodies dangled – every twitch of their lifeless limbs provoking great whoops of laughter and knee-slapping applause. Although the carnival atmosphere of belching and booze, of apprentice pickpockets plying their trade, and close brushes with winking whores was indistinguishable from what one could expect to find at one of the twelve 'Hanging Fairs' held annually at Tyburn, the performance that Pepys found himself in stitches watching in Covent Garden that balmy spring afternoon, while well executed ('the best I ever saw,' he said), was not in fact an execution at all. It was a marionette show put on by the celebrated seventeenth-century Italian puppet-master, Pietro Gimonde, and is thought to be the first ever staging of what became the enduring and endearingly violent hand-puppet pummellings of 'Punch and Judy'.

'I went,' Pepys wrote, 'into Covent Garden to an alehouse, to see a picture that hangs there . . . [t]hence to see an Italian puppet play that is within the rayles there, which is very pretty, the best that ever I saw, and great resort of gallants.' Egged on by the merry crowd, Gimonde hammed up his act in the guise of 'Signor Bologna', drooping his hand-carved characters out from behind a tent (or 'fit-up', as the portable-box would later be called) as he chomped on a metal 'swazzle' – the name given to the awkward mouthpiece that helped the puppet-master, or 'Professor', make the kazoo-like squawk by which the pointy-chinned Punch would forever be remembered. Almost instantly, Gimonde's comic 'theatre of cruelty' etched itself on to the imagination of Londoners – Pepys went again and again – and became a kind of cultural archetype for 'body' (if not 'bawdy') humour. After all, isn't the baton that Punch uses to whack the other puppets the veritable 'slap stick'? And what about his catchy catch-phrase, 'That's the way to do it!' – a 'Punch-line', no doubt.

At some unremembered moment towards the end of the seventeenth or beginning of the eighteenth century, the absurd stage of Punch and the noxious theatre of Newgate began to blur in urban imagination, reinforcing the allure and mystique of each. Where initially Punch's brutal antics culminated in a confrontation with Satan himself, whom Punch always manages to throttle – 'Huzza! Huzza! I have killed the Devil' – before long Satan is supplanted by a figure at once more fearsome and farcical, more loathsome and laughable than the default Devil: the legendary hangman called 'Jack Ketch'.

Jack Ketch made his career dangling convicts fresh from Newgate on the giant fit-up of the 'Triple Tree' at Tyburn, where he played the crowds like a travelling puppeteer. Many may find some comic cosmic justice in the thought of his puny effigy forever taking wallops from a shrill toy, swaying for eternity from flimsy strings at village fêtes and on seaside promenades. But what is his story? The actual life and times of the iconic executioner are as fuzzy as he was famous – his name thrust upon every one of his successors for the next two hundred years. Or was 'Ketch' even his name? Late-nineteenth-century historians tended to favour the speculation that 'Jack Ketch' was a corruption of Richard Jacquett, who once owned the manor of Tyburn, while more recent scholarship has surmised that he

14. *Newgate became known as 'Ketch's Theatre', after the colourful and cruel executioner who became a fixture in the British imagination.*

may have married a woman called Katherine 'and he and his wife are probably the John and Katherine Catch whose daughter Susanna was baptized on 1 June 1668 at St James's, Clerkenwell, the parish where he was buried eighteen years later'. Nothing of Ketch's birth or childhood is known and even the precise date when he took over as London's principal hangman is in dispute. No ledger of succession seems ever to have been kept, a gap in the historical record, which has proved frustrating. 'Is there any list extant,' one reader of the miscellany *Notes & Queries* asked in an issue of 1861, 'of the hangmen of London?' In compiling his *Chronicles of Newgate* twenty-two years later, Arthur Griffiths lists an egregious ingrate called 'Derrick' as 'one of the first names mentioned' in surviving literature. Derrick, we're told, had himself been sentenced to death but was pardoned by the Earl of Essex, an act of kindness that the executioner may have reflected on in 1601 when he raised his axe and chopped off the earl's head.

At the beginning of the seventeenth century, appointment to the position was hereditary. In 1611, the hangman Gregory Brandon narrowly escaped being condemned in Newgate for manslaughter by demonstrating that he could read, fittingly enough, the 'Neck Verse' from the Bible – that penal loophole known as 'the Benefit of Clergy', which had saved Ben Jonson's life some years earlier. Gregory Brandon left a lasting impression and it is a testament to just how memorably unmerciful Jack Ketch must have been that Ketch was able to eclipse him. During Brandon's tenure and long after he had handed down the noose to his son Richard (who is very likely the hooded executioner who decapitated Charles I), the gallows at Tyburn were known by the nickname 'the Gregorian Tree'. 'This trembles under the Black Rod, and he,' a popular couplet went, 'Doth fear his fate from the *Gregorian* tree.' The Brandons did all they could to establish a dynasty of hangmen and even managed to have a coat of arms bestowed on the family by the College of Heralds. This technically elevated them to the social rank of 'gentlemen', an absurdity seized upon by the raucous audiences who thereafter addressed hangmen facetiously as 'squires'.

The name 'Squire Ketch' first starts cropping up in popular broadsides in the late 1670s, ready made for caricaturing as the prototypical hangman, along with his sinister sidekick, 'Judge Jeffreys': 'When *Jeffreys* on the Bench, *Ketch* on the Gibbet sits,' wrote the poet John Tutchin in a well-known couplet, 'Some take ev'n them for Courages and Wits.' Ketch seems to have risen to prominence a few months earlier, as the hangman who presided over the execution of those convicted of involvement in the so-called 'Popish Plot' – that insidious scheme dreamt up by Titus Oates and Israel Tonge to discredit Catholics by alleging that there was a plan afoot to assassinate Charles II. Catholic conspiracy was soon seen as a cancer that Jack Ketch alone could eradicate. Broadsides appeared hailing Ketch's surgical skills: *The Romanists best doctor, who by one infallible remedy, perfectly cures all popish-diseases whatsoever in a quarter of an hours time, By an approved dose which never yet failed his Patients. Which approved remedy may once a month be had at Tyburn, near Paddington, of that famous physician of long practice, John Ketch, Esq; physician in ordinary to the pope* (1680). 'This *Remedy*,' the paper promised, 'will be Delivered to any *Patient* at *Thirteen-Pence-Half-Penny* the *Dose*; Provided they be legally-Condemned, but to *Roman-Catholiques*, Gratis, provided they can bring His *Holiness* Hand and Seal to Certifie they have been Actors in the late Treasonable Designs on Foot, in that Horrid Blood-Thirsty *Plot*.'

Macabre links between hanging and healing, which went back at least a generation before Ketch, were woven into his emerging myth as easily as hemp fibres into a noose. John Taylor, in his 1623 poem *The Praise of Hemp-seed*, had suggested a variety of natural remedies, including 'Tyburne hempen caudle' as a cure for love, before offering this handy herbal mnemonic:

> The name of Choakweed is to be assigned
> Because it stops the venom of the mind.
> Some call it neckweed for it hath a trick
> To cure the neck that's troubled with a crick.

The point is driven home further by John Dryden and Nathaniel Lee in a pair of quotable couplets from their play *The Duke of Guise: A Tragedy*:

> Lenitives, says he, suit best with our Condition.
> Jack Ketch, says I, s an excellent Physician.
> I love no Bloud—Nor I, Sir, as I breath,
> But hanging is a fine dry kind of Death.

By the late 1670s, the archetype of Jack Ketch had become so integrated into the very vocabulary of London life that songs celebrating his exploits were staples in public houses and slang dictionaries. Whole mythologies, complete with creation and destruction stories, sprang to life with Ketch at the centre of their spiritual cosmos. Take the bizarre title of this contemporary pamphlet: *The Tyburn ghost: or, The strange downfal of the gallows: a most true relation how the famous Triple Tree, near Paddington, was pluckt up by the roots and demolisht by certain evil spirits, with Jack Ketch's lamentation for the loss of his Shop* (1678). In 1676 a glossary 'of all sorts of thieves and robbers which go under these titles viz. the gilter, the mill, the glasier, budg and snudg. file-lifter, tongue-padder, the private theif' appeared under the title *A warning for housekeepers* and featured under the definitions for 'Budge' and 'Snudge' the following lyrics:

The Budge it is a delicate trade
and a delicate trade of fame
For when that we have bit the bloe
We carry away the game
But if the cully nap us
and the Lurres from us take
O then they rub us to the Whitt
And it is hardly worth a Make
But when that we come to the Whitt
Our Darbies to behold
And for to take our Penitency
And boose the water cold,
But when that we come out agen
as we walk along the street
We bite the Culley of his cole
But we are rubbed unto the Whitt.

And when that we come to the Whitt
For garnish they do cry
Mary faugh you son of a w—
Ye shall have it by and by
But when that we come to Tyburn
For going upon the Budge
There stands *Jack Catch* that son of a w—
That owes us all a grudge
And when that he hath noosed us
and our friends tips him no Cole
O then he throws us in the cart
and tumbles us into the hole.

So Ketch had already imprinted himself onto the fabric of London's consciousness when he was summoned to Lincoln's Inn Fields on 21 July 1683 to chop the head off William, Lord Russell. Russell had devoted himself to anti-Popish causes and had vociferously opposed the succession of James, Duke of York, a Catholic, over Charles II's illegitimate, though recognised, Protestant son, James Scott, Duke of Monmouth. When the Rye House Plot erupted in 1683, Russell was immediately suspected of supporting the insurrection to assassinate Charles, arrested, and marched to Lincoln's Inn Fields. An efficient enough hangman, Ketch had never wielded a hatchet and he arrived at the ceremony somewhat the worse for wear. Disturbed by the stench of ale on Ketch's breath and anxious at his inexperience, Russell tipped his executioner ten guineas, well in excess of the customary gratuity, a 'severance pay' he hoped would secure a quick and easy exit. It didn't take long for Russell to regret having refused the blindfold. Ketch's first swing missed Russell's neck entirely and split his shoulder. The following two strokes chopped loose an ear and only nicked the neck. 'You dog!' Russell raised his bleeding head and shouted. Witnesses could scarcely agree on how many blows it finally took, though few would ever extinguish from their minds the sight of Ketch stooping down to the block and finishing the job off with a short saw.

The image was still fresh when the crowds collected again on Tower Hill in July 1685 to watch Ketch take another swing with the axe. This time it was James Scott, who had enraged James II by declaring himself king after his father's death, who found himself on his knees, bowing to a stump. Before assuming this position, James produced a document forgoing all claim to the Crown. He then turned to Ketch and said, 'Here are six guineas for you. Do not hack me as you did my Lord Russell. I have heard that you struck him three or four times. My servant will give you some gold if you do the work well.' Yet again Ketch failed to strike the neck squarely, provoking such

intense outrage from the audience that a scuffle broke out. As
James lay writhing, royal guards kept the crowd from storming
the scaffold. In the end it took five strokes to separate the
head.

Ketch's fame was now assured and only grew in the ensuing
months with the fallout from the insatiable Bloody Assizes –
the systematic prosecution of Monmouth's supporters, which
kept the executioner busy drawing and quartering more than a
dozen men a day. His unique brand of incompetence and inhumanity was soon enshrined within the very fabric of Newgate's
structure. A room there that was devoted to dismembering
the bodies of executed traitors was thenceforth re-christened
'Ketch's Kitchen'. The religious dissenter and friend of John
Milton, Thomas Ellwood, who had been imprisoned for his
refusal to pledge the oaths of allegiance and supremacy, recalled
in nauseating detail what he witnessed there: 'When we first
came into Newgate, there lay (in a little by-place like a closet,
near the room where we were lodged) the quartered bodies of
three men, who had been executed some days before, for a real
or pretended plot . . . I saw the heads,' Ellwood remembered,

> when they were brought up to be boiled. The hangman fetched
> them in a dirty dust-basket out of some by-place; and, setting
> them down among the felons, he and they made sport with
> them. They took them by the hair, flouting, jeering, and laugh-
> ing at them; and then, giving them some ill names, boxed them
> on the ears and cheeks. Which done, the hangman put them into
> his kettle, and parboiled them with bay-salt and cummin-seed;
> *that* to keep from putrefaction, and *this* to keep off the fowls from
> seizing on them. The whole sight, as well as that of the bloody
> quarters first as this of the heads afterwards, was both frightful
> and loathsome, and begat an abhorrence in my nature.

With 'Ketch's Kitchen' percolating at one end and the Triple
Tree, or 'Ketch's shop' looming at the other, the psycho-
dimensions of London by the end of the seventeenth century

could be measured along the length of the well-trod route between Newgate and Tyburn, which had been wearing itself into the capital's soul since at least the twelfth century. The well-rehearsed ritual in which Ketch figured as the mirthless marionettist began the night before the scheduled hanging with a service for the condemned in the prison chapel. Those due to be executed were made to kneel around an empty black coffin, studded with yellow nails, propped up in a central pew while the 'Ordinary', or appointed prison chaplain, harangued the prisoners from the pulpit. Never ones to miss a trick, the Keepers used the occasion to line their pockets by charging admission to anyone anxious to witness the behaviour of men on the verge of death. Many of the condemned prisoners found it impossible to focus on the gravity of their situation, and endeavoured to endear themselves to the onlookers by pulling faces at the chaplain or mocking the other inmates. Some quietly sobbed.

An endowment left by a merchant-tailor by the name of Robert Dow in 1612 provided for a harrowing lullaby to be performed by the sexton, or bellman, of St Sepulchre's, on the eve of execution. Leaving £1 6s. 8d. a year until doomsday, Dow made certain that the condemned confronted their anguished thoughts against the ringing of the sepulchral bell, while the sexton recited a disturbing dirge:

> You prisoners that are within,
> Who, for wickedness and sin,

After many mercies shewn you, are now appointed to die to-morrow in the forenoon, give ear, and understand, that to-morrow morning the greatest bell of St Sepulchre's shall toll for you, in form and manner of a passing bell, as used to be tolled for those who are at the point of death, to the end that all godly people hearing the bell, and knowing it is for your going to your deaths, may be stirred up heartily to pray to God to bestow his grace and mercy upon you whilst you live. I beseech you,

for Jesus Christ's sake, to keep this night in watching and prayer,
to the salvation of your own souls, while there is yet time and
place for mercy, as knowing to-morrow you must appear before
the judgment-seat of your Creator, there to give an account of
all things done in this life, and to suffer eternal torments for
your sin committed against him, unless, upon your hearty and
unfeigned repentance, you find mercy through the merits,
death, and passion of our only mediator and advocate, Jesus
Christ, who now sits at the right hand of God to make intercession for as many of you as penitently return to him.

The routine began later the following day than one might
have expected. It was mid-morning before those sentenced to
die would be led from the Condemned Hold to have their
shackles hammered loose and to shake hands with the hangman,
who used the gesture to calculate the length of rope necessary
to fulfil his professional obligations. Bundled on to a back-
wards-facing 'sledge' or 'hurdle', sometimes referred to as a
'lurch', their heads inches from a horse's hindquarters, the condemned were scraped past St Sepulchre's, where the bell-
wielding sexton resumed his taunting:

All good people, pray heartily to God for these poor sinners,
who are now going to their death, for whom this great bell
doth toll. You that are condemned to die, repent with lamen-
table tears; ask mercy of the Lord for the salvation of your own
souls, through the merits, death, and passion of Jesus Christ,
who now sits at the right hand of God to make intercession for
as many of you as penitently return unto him.

> Lord have mercy upon you,
> Christ have mercy upon you,
> Lord have mercy upon you,
> Christ have mercy upon you.

So the sledge jerked onward, over Snow Hill and across
Holborn Bridge, past Lincoln's Inn Fields to present-day
Oxford Street. Only two and a half miles in length, the journey

could take as long as four hours, depending on the notoriety of the criminal concerned and the disposition of the crowds that would gather along the route. 'Every Monday morning the mob of London looked to have this brutal excitement provided for them; and more than one minister of the crown has been known to express the opinion, that, as a matter of policy, it was better, if possible, not to disappoint the many-headed monster.'

It was usual for the driver to pause at least once along the way, either at St-Giles-in-the-Field or, nearer to Tyburn, at Seymour Place, to allow the convict the opportunity to numb his senses with liquor, thereby bloating the bladder that, before long, would be letting go. Safely arrived at the gallows, the condemned were transferred to a special horse-hitched trundle designed to roll between the posts of the gibbet. Once the nooses were in place and whatever final confessions or speeches had been delivered, the hangman would slap the horse's flank, whiplashing the condemned into choking suspension, creating a space into which relatives might spill and grab hold of the twitching limbs or finish the job themselves.

As constituting the terrifying terminus for the countless pro-cessions that wound their way from Newgate to the Triple Tree, Tyburn and its grotesque geometry are worth pausing over. The name itself is fearsome, as if coupling violent restraint ('tie') with subsequent conflagration ('burn'). In fact, its origin is less grisly and merely comes from the small stream, or *burn*, that ran along the path of today's Marylebone Lane, crossed Oxford Street and spilled into St James's Park. According to legend, the banks were lined with elm trees, which, on the furthest fringes of the city, were considered a suitable place to hang criminals. The first recorded execution here, in 1196, was of the populist stirrer William Fitz Osbert, known as 'Longbeard', who, along with nine accomplices, was frogmarched from the Tower. This is also where Roger de Mortimer, Edward II's nemesis, was dragged and quartered in November 1330. Before long, Tyburn became the chief location for executions in London, though gibbets would continue to be erected from time to time across the capital, often close to the site where the alleged crime had been committed, earning it the infamous nicknames 'City of the Gallows' and 'Hangman's Town'. The noose itself had macabre monikers. There was the 'Tyburn Tippet' and the 'Horse's Nightcap', while having a noose fitted around your neck was 'to go up the ladder to bed' or 'take a leap in the dark'. 'Nothing on the social horizon of the English poor,' Robert Hughes has observed, 'produced more slang and cant than hanging.'

The design of the gibbet underwent occasional modernisation. The early hangman, Thomas Derrick, devised an ingenious buttress-like crane that could snap as many as twenty-three necks at one go, a feat of engineering that was soon adopted by shippers for lifting cargoes on to and off vessels, still in use to this day. The name of the inventor who outsmarted Derrick by creating the iconic Triple Tree, which could accommodate twenty-four convicts, has been lost to history. The structure got its nickname from the three crossbeams, each of which could hold eight bodies, supported by three legs – so that, from above, the apparatus formed a triangle. It would seem that this fearsome four-sided structure was a permanent fixture on the outskirts of London, put into play a dozen times a year:

> I have heard sundry men ofttimes dispute,
> Of trees that in one yeare will twice beare fruit;
> But if a man note Tyburn, it will appeare,
> That this is a tree that bears twelve times a yeare.

The Triple Tree was the favoured furniture of execution until the invention in 1760 of the scaffold-style platform with a collapsing trapdoor, or 'new drop' – the contraption that would stand in front of Newgate when executions were relocated there in 1783.

15. *Tyburn and the 'Triple Tree'. Notice, in the back left, a man is being 'drawn and quartered'. The artist has bizarrely warped London, so that the City is visible in the distance*

There has been much debate about where, precisely, in the neighbourhood of present-day Marble Arch the gibbet stood. One might have thought that William Hogarth's obsession with the site would be helpful in orientating the Tree in relation to other landmarks depicted in his drawings, such as the hills of Hampstead and Highgate visible in the distance of his famous panel from *Industry and Idleness*; *The Idle 'Prentice, Executed at Tyburn*. But the congested cityscape of today's London, bulldozed and obscured by buildings, is unrecognisable from the open countryside Hogarth recorded. Today, only a cracked concrete slab embedded into a traffic island at the intersection of Oxford Street, Park Lane, Bayswater and Edgware Roads – which can only be accessed by jaywalking and negotiating a steel rail – unceremoniously commemorates the supposed spot with the crumbling words 'THE SITE OF TYBURN TREE'. Strange to think that a place of such cultural consequence is now virtually inaccessible, all but erased from the memory of the urban landscape.

But there is reason to doubt the authenticity of this single official marking. A contributor to the Victorian journal *The Antiquary* in 1873 testified to having seen with his own eyes 'quantities of human bones' exhumed during the construction of nearby Connaught Square (a few hundred yards north along Edgware Road) in the 1820s, his uncle having lived and worked in that neighbourhood. The discovery dovetailed with recollections by members of the writer's family who insisted that the gibbet stood adjacent to 'the corner of Bryanston Street and the Edgware Road, nearly opposite Connaught Mews', where they had lived 'for many years'. Onlookers would hang from windows or purchase seats from one of the stall-keepers, or 'pew-openers', in charge of the wooden stands erected for each event. Even in the face of such convincing evidence, it is difficult to dismiss out of hand the silent testimony of surviving maps of London from the sixteenth and seventeenth centuries, with their fading doodles of a gallows where the stone marker sits today. It may be safest to conclude that the site was not a fixed one and that, in all likelihood, it shuttled back and forth along this now-bustling stretch of road where late-night shops and bars are now all that's swinging.

Though most malefactors who were brought to Tyburn accepted their fate with a minimum of fuss and often with remarkable composure, as though there were a quiet dignity in conforming to the established etiquette of execution, occasionally the crowd was treated to the kind of unrehearsed antics that would keep the coffee shops and taverns buzzing for weeks. In 1738 the hangman Thomas Turlis presided over a more animated performance than he had expected. On arriving at Tyburn, Hannah Dagoe, an obstreperous Irish thief, refused to play along and violently lashed out. Writhing loose from the cord that bound her arms, Dagoe struck Turlis in the face with her fist, knocking him off balance. Sensing that she now had the upper hand, Dagoe proceeded to taunt Turlis, daring him to follow through with his assignment, as she began stripping off her clothes before the gasping crowd. Hurling first her shoes, then her cloak and petticoat into the throng, Dagoe thus deprived the hangman of one of the few perks of his profession – the soiled clothes of the freshly executed, which, along with pieces of the rope used, could be sold for a hefty profit.

Twenty-two years later, 'Squire Berry' must have fared better after hanging Laurence Shirley, the fourth Earl Ferrers, whose plea of insanity for the murder of his business associate was rejected by the Old Bailey jury. 'His lordship was conveyed to Tyburn in his own landau,' remembered William Hickey, the famous memoirist, 'dressed in a superb suit of white and silver, being the clothes in which he was married, his reason for wearing which was that they had been his first step towards ruin, and should attend his exit.' Ferrers was the first to try the new and simpler 'drop' designed to replace the iconic angularity of the Triple Tree and it has been suggested, probably wrongly, that Berry was so delighted by the prospect of executing such a wealthy figure, with all the perquisites such a client brought, that he agreed to swap the customary hemp noose for one braided in silk.

The original Jack Ketch would have cringed at the thought of any such concession. Indeed, in the months following the boom in business brought on by the Bloody Assizes of 1685, Ketch found himself incapable of capitulating to anyone, including his superiors, the sheriffs. His insubordination earned him a brief interlude in Bridewell Prison and the humiliation of having to hand his axe and rope over to an upstart hangman and former butcher called Pascha Rose. Fortunately for Ketch, his successor was even less well behaved than himself. Rose had hardly measured his first neck before he found himself on trial for stealing a coat. His punishment was to endure a marathon of lashings from Rosemary Lane to the Hermitage and to relinquish the noose to Jack Ketch. And there it would remain for the next two hundred years, no matter who occupied the position. Though the crowds would come and go and the antics of the condemned might change from age to age, in the imagination of the capital, Jack Ketch's presence on a snap-apart scaffold, whether in person or as a puppet, was as reliable as that other recurring event of London life – the incineration of The Gaol.

II
BLAZE

7

Smoke

'SMOKE, *to suspect or smell a Design*. It is smok'd; *It is made Publick, all have Notice*. Smoke him, Smoke him again; *to affront a Stranger at his coming in.*'

When the last flames of the Great Fire of London were finally extinguished on 7 September 1666, over thirteen thousand houses, ninety-three parish churches and chapels, the Royal Exchange, Guildhall, the Customs House, four bridges, three gates, St Paul's Cathedral, and every prison inside the ancient walls of the city had been consumed by the greatest disaster ever to befall the capital. 'London was', the diarist John Evelyn wrote, 'but is no more.' Newgate itself was reduced to a smouldering uninhabitable husk. The stones along the eastern wall of The Gaol, which had separated the Press Yard from Warwick Lane, exploded in the heat. The slender statue of Richard Whittington's cat, which had adorned the structure's formidable façade, commemorating the former Lord Mayor's generosity in refurbishing the prison in the fifteenth century, had melted away.

Conventional history has it that the conflagration began in a bakery in Pudding Lane in the early hours of Sunday, 2 September. But a stack of neglected manuscripts and hidden diaries from the period tell a different story – that the catastrophe, which forever changed the face of London, may have begun with the friction between a pair of feuding astrologers fifteen years earlier in a gloomy cell inside Newgate gaol.

The years leading up to the execution of Charles I in January 1649 saw not only a brutal contest between Parliamentarians and Royalists on the battlefield, but a war between soothsayers and augurers over the meaning of the stars – over whom, in other words, God had predestined to prevail. The chief astrologer for the monarchists was Sir George Wharton, who was credited with having accurately predicted the sudden demise of the parliamentary leader John Pym in 1643. On the other side were the pugnacious prognosticators, John Booker and William Lilly (the self-styled 'Merlinus Anglicus' or 'England's Merlin'), who never shied away from a confrontation with their Royalist rivals. The 1640s witnessed a flurry of almanacs and counter-almanacs, each featuring complex rhombi and parallelograms, which were claimed to unlock the secrets of the heavens and foretell the triumphs and defeats that were soon to be enjoyed or suffered by the respective sides.

In March 1648, Wharton's attacks against Booker and Lilly had begun to take their toll on his enemies' patience and an arrest warrant issued by Parliament back in 1646 was acted upon with sudden urgency. Thrown into Newgate, Wharton refused to desist from his cosmic arithmetic and secretly composed another instalment of his controversial almanac. Propped against a mildewed wall with only the rustling of rats to divert his thoughts, Wharton prophesied a fiery end for the parliamentary leaders who had imprisoned him. Though he managed to escape from Newgate five months after entering The Gaol, Wharton was duly recaptured a year later and told that he now faced almost certain execution. Then suddenly, mysteriously, Wharton's fortunes changed. At the urging of their mutual friend, Elias Ashmole, Wharton's bitter enemy William Lilly interceded on the Royalist's behalf and arranged for his adversary's release in early 1650. Lilly's role in the freeing of Wharton coincides intriguingly with the compilation of Lilly's own most recent almanac. In it, Wharton's prediction of imminent immolation for his enemies, which he had calculated inside Newgate, is transmuted into one of the woodcuts that adorned his new pamphlet.

Though few took much notice of it at the time, Lilly's chilling illustration of a ferocious blaze, with flames licking at a dangling depiction of Gemini – the star sign said to rule London – while firefighters struggle hopelessly all around, would be called to mind fifteen years later when the apocalyptic image became an appalling reality. Following the four days of destruction between the second and fifth of September 1666, which were famously documented by Pepys and Evelyn in their diaries, the city was desperate for someone to blame.

But no sooner had a ragbag of Irish Catholics and petrified Scotsmen been rounded up as potential suspects than a Frenchman called Robert Hubert, the son of a watchmaker from Normandy, was caught in Romford, Essex, making arrangements to flee the country. With little urging, Hubert confessed to the crime and divulged a complicated plot, which he claimed had been hatched a year earlier in Paris and involved some two dozen secret cells. Few minded that Hubert was apparently mentally deranged or that his cloak-and-dagger account was riddled with inconsistencies and contradictions of known facts about the fire. Notwithstanding his claim that he had started it in Westminster, a part of the city where the blaze had never reached, on 27 October 1666 Hubert was executed at Tyburn before a ferocious crowd that ripped his still-twitching corpse to pieces.

Meanwhile, unconvinced by Hubert's confession, though content to allow the Frenchman's insanity to distract the masses, Parliament quietly pursued another line of inquiry – an extraordinary lead suggested by the woodcut in William Lilly's long-out-of-date almanac. Two days before the savage spectacle at Tyburn, Lilly was summoned to the Houses of Parliament to explain his foreknowledge of the fire. Once aware of the

16. *A 'hieroglyphic' from William Lilly's 1651 almanac,
which seems to predict a blaze engulfing Gemini, the sign
said to rule London. Fifteen years after the image was
published, Lilly was summoned to Parliament under
suspicion of having had a hand in starting the Great Fire
of 1666*

woodcut's existence, some members suspected that Lilly himself might have been involved in starting the blaze as a way
of rekindling his reputation as a formidable astrologer. Soon
every one of the horoscopist's equations was being scrutinised
for evidence of his complicity.

When asked whether his drawing, or 'hieroglyphic' as it was
called, contained any coded indication of the date on which
the fire would break out, or even of the actual year, Lilly said
that he had had no desire to ascertain such information. But
a manuscript draft of the 1651 pamphlet, now in the Bodleian
Library in Oxford, excavated by the historian Patrick Curry,

suggests that Lilly may not have told the whole truth. Alongside his cryptic drawing he had scrawled the words *'forsan* [either] 1666 *vel* [or] 1667'. Needless to say, had those interrogating Lilly been aware of the annotation, he would not have been dismissed as casually as he eventually was by a bewildered committee, which ultimately had little more to pin on him than a cryptic cartoon. Men and women in the seventeenth century had been made to suffer for less, however. Had the post-Fire committee known about the scribblings of an eccentric contemporary of Lilly's by the name of Arise Evans about fifteen years earlier, these would have earned him more than a few awkward questions. Born at Llangelynnin in Wales, Arise, it seems, began experiencing visions as an adolescent. In his early twenties, pursuing an apprenticeship in tailoring, he moved to London and started to attract attention after attempting to warn Charles I of certain prophecies he had heard of the King's imminent execution. While the eerie accuracy of some of Arise's prognostications won him a number of admirers, it also landed him in a selection of the city's prisons. Though the dates remain hazy, Arise could well have been in Newgate at the same time as Lilly's adversary, Wharton, at the end of the 1640s. Within a year of the publication of Lilly's risky hieroglyphic in 1651, Arise published his vision as *An eccho to the voice from heaven, or, A narration of the life, and manner of the special calling, and visions of Arise Evans by him published, in discharge of his duty to God, and for the satisfaction of all those that doubt.* 'At that time in a dream,' Arise recorded with chilling prescience, 'me thought I was on Islington hill by the water house, and London appeared before me as if it had been burnt with fire & that there remained nothing of it but a few stone walls.' What Arise himself might have made of the events of the late summer of 1666 and their connection to his disturbing dream will probably never be known; from the spring of 1660, this curious prophet had drifted into the smoke of history.

*17. A map of London from 1666, showing the extent of
the Great Fire*

Foretold or not, the fire had spread rapidly in the small hours
of 2 September, fanned by an easterly wind and fed by timber
homes left dry by an Indian summer. Immediate action to
contain the flames might have made a difference, but the decision by the risible Lord Mayor, Sir Thomas Bloodworth, to
return to his bed after being notified of the blaze demoralised
the concerned constables who had alerted him. 'Pish!' the
bloody-minded Bloodworth is recorded as saying, 'A woman
might piss it out.'

It would take six years to rebuild Newgate, which lay on
the westernmost edge of the fire's passage, and another thirty-
six before Christopher Wren would finish his lavish new St
Paul's Cathedral. 'Melting lead' from the roof of old St Paul's,
according to John Evelyn, percolated through the streets 'in

a stream'; 'the very pavements,' he said, 'glowed in a fiery redness':

> Thus lay in ashes that most venerable church, one of the most ancient pieces of early piety in the Christian world, besides near one hundred more. The lead, ironwork, bells, plate, etc., melted; the exquisitely wrought Mercers' Chapel, the sumptuous Exchange, the august fabric of Christ Church, all the rest of the Companies' Halls, sumptuous buildings, arches, all in dust; the fountains dried up and ruined, while the very waters remained boiling; the voragoes of subterranean cellars, wells, and dungeons, formerly warehouses, still burning in stench and dark clouds of smoke, so that in five or six miles traversing about I did not see one load of timber consume, nor many stones but what were calcined white as snow . . . The people who now walked about the ruins appeared like men in a dismal desert, or rather in some great city laid waste by a cruel enemy.

On the third day of the fire, under a pall of smoke, the prisoners were escorted from The Gaol and across the river to the relatively empty eleventh-century 'Clink' in Southwark, then a disused debtors' prison, the unnerving name of which is said to have derived from the sound of the manacles, or 'darbies', used there. Hubert's confession and subsequent execution meant that the fire would have to be regarded by the state as an act of war by a foreign power. As such, the tenants of the thousands of destroyed homes could not be held responsible for rebuilding them, as the law otherwise would have demanded. As for Newgate, it mattered little who was footing the bill for the reconstruction; The Gaol had long ago been marked out a site of irredeemable misery, despite a succession of ever more impressive, and expensive, façades.

When the new gaol was unveiled in 1672, it retained the basic form of a gatehouse, with two imposing towers flanking Newgate Street. On the eastern side of the gate, three stone statues, symbolising Justice, Mercy and Truth, stared with

LIVERPOOL JOHN MOORES UNIVERSITY
LEARNING SERVICES

disingenuous majesty in the direction of Cheapside. Under them, a grandiloquent Latin inscription became eroded almost as quickly as it had been etched: 'This part of Newgate,' it recorded, 'was begun to be repaired in the mayoralty of Sir James Campebell, Knight, Anno 1630, and finished in the mayoralty of Sir Robert Drury, Baronet, April, Anno 1631; and being damnified by the fire of London, was again repaired in the mayoralty of Sir George Waterman, Anno Dom. 1672.' To the west, four more figures representing Liberty, Peace, Plenty and Concord gazed out with grim austerity. The refurbishment cost the city a staggering £10,000, almost all of which was squandered on frivolous ornamentation – Tuscan pilasters, camp battlements and gratuitous gargoyles – intended to mask the enduring dilapidation inside the building. 'The sumptuousness of the outside,' according to one observer, 'but aggravates the misery of the wretches within.'

If the prison's ostentatious exterior was designed to assuage the public eye, little effort was made to appease the neighbourhood nose. The stench that wafted from the insalubrious conditions inside the new gaol, especially in warm weather, routinely forced adjoining shops to shut down. Just south of the prison, in the refurbished Sessions House of the Old Bailey, lawyers wore nosegays of Culpeperian herbs strapped to their upper lips, which were believed to offer protection against evil humours wafting in from next door. This practice gave rise to the solemn custom, still observed, of judges carrying posies on specific days in spring and autumn. Unwilling to expose themselves to rampant infection, physicians routinely refused to enter The Gaol, even for emergencies.

By the time that Newgate was gutted in the Great Fire, overcrowding had made conditions inside barbaric. 'Hell itself, in comparison cannot be such a place,' one condemned inmate speculated in 1662, after learning he was soon to be executed; 'there is neither bench, stool, nor stick for any person there; they lie like swine upon the ground, one upon another, howling and roaring — it was more terrible to me than this death.' Comparisons of Newgate with hell began to proliferate after the Great Fire. In 1683, the religious writer Richard Baxter published a list itemising 'The differences between this World, and that to which I am going', in which he merges the realms of earth and hell into a place of arbitrary fortune to be compared with The Gaol: 'This World is as *Newgate*, and *Hell*, as *Tyburn:* some are hence saved, and some condemned. The other World is the Glorious Kingdom of *Jehovah* with the Blessed.'

The new design did little to increase capacity. Intended to accommodate no more than a hundred and fifty people, before long five hundred prisoners, together with a great many of their family members, had been crammed into the half-acre of available space — each one bringing revenue to the Keeper. And then there were the animals. It was not until 1792 that dogs were prohibited from accompanying their owners and another two decades after that before pigeons, poultry and pigs were banned. The mingled stench of disease and faeces and the cacophonous din of wailing and screeching in the maze of unventilated wards was unutterably horrifying. According to one writer in 1714, Newgate was 'a Place of Calamity, a Dwelling in more than Cimmerian Darkness, an Habitation of Misery, a confused Chaos, without any Distinction, a bottomless Pit of Violence, and a Tower of Babel, where all are Speakers, and no Hearers.'

Among the first wave of inmates to measure conditions inside the post-Fire prison was the Quaker leader and founder of Pennsylvania, William Penn. An outspoken dissenter and rousing orator, Penn refused to be muzzled by the newly passed Conventicle Act, which had banned religious gatherings that were in any way doctrinally at odds with the orders of the Anglican Church. In August 1670 Penn was arrested for hosting such an illicit liturgy in Gracechurch Street, around the corner from the Friends' meeting house in White Hart Court. He and fellow preacher William Meade were dragged from their pulpits and lodged in Newgate, charged with 'terror' offences against 'His Majesty's liege subjects' for having subjected the public to a dangerously seditious harangue.

But when the trial took place in September, the jury members objected to such religious bullying by the prosecution and refused to be intimidated by the Lord Mayor's blustering insistence that they return a guilty verdict. When the foreman was asked by the Recorder, Thomas Howell, to read out the jury's decision to the court, he proclaimed, 'Guilty of speaking in Gracechurch Street.' No crime in that and the galleries grumbled in bemusement. 'Is that all?' Howell thundered in disbelief. 'That is all,' the foreman stated, 'that I have in commission.' 'Gentlemen, you have not given in your Verdict,' Howell insisted, 'and you had as good say nothing; therefore go and consider it once more, that we may make an end of this troublesome Business.' The jury disappeared briefly, and when it returned, the foreman once again addressed the court, his voice quivering as he read from a scrap of paper on which he'd scrawled the words, 'We the Jurors do find William Penn to be Guilty of Speaking or Preaching to an Assembly, met together in Gracechurch-Street, the 14th of August last, 1670. And that William Meade is Not guilty of the said Indictment.' The court was suddenly alive with gasps and guffaws and the sharp snaps of a gavel. 'Gentlemen, you shall not be dismist till we have a Verdict that the Court will accept,' an incandescent Howell fumed, 'and you shall be lock'd up, without Meat, Drink, Fire, and Tobacco; you shall not think thus to abuse the Court; we will have a Verdict, by the help of God, or you shall starve for it.' And so the jury was led, together with Penn and Meade, to the mildewed maze of The Gaol to reconsider its priorities. Only after an appeal to the Lord Chief Justice, who determined that such harassment of the jury was illegal, were the courageous jurors finally released.

Though glimpses of the interior of the prison can be cobbled together from the ever-growing number of pamphlets and alleged confessions of its inmates – often compiled by the prison's chaplain, or Ordinary, for a phenomenal sum – the most detailed and reliable description of The Gaol's layout comes from a man whose only tie to Newgate was idle curiosity. In 1724, a 28-year-old writer on architecture, Batty Langley, published *An accurate description of Newgate. With the rights, privileges, allowances, fees, dues, and customs thereof, which alone offers a detailed tour of the famous premises*. Langley was no criminal but had gained access to The Gaol through his brother, Thomas, who worked inside as a turnkey. Though inclined to cast the institution in as favourable a light as possible, even going so far as to characterise its administration as 'not inferior to that of a well-regulated Family', Langley is quick to reassure sceptical readers that, in leading them through the maze of fetter-ridden holds and noxious cells, he has not 'departed one Tittle from the naked Truth'.

Consisting of five levels – one subterranean, and devoted to dungeons, and four aboveground – the new layout made a more emphatic distinction between the Masters', Commons' and women's wards than The Gaol's previous incarnations had managed. These wards were in turn subdivided to accommodate felons on the one hand and debtors on the other in an area nicknamed 'Tangier', an allusion to the suffering of English captives at the hands of Arab pirates on the Barbary Coast. Inmates abandoned there, often for years or even decades over what amounted, in today's currency, to a few pounds, were known as 'tangerines'. Prisoners were admitted to The Gaol through a door under the archway in Newgate Street into a small lodge, where they underwent a rather unpleasant initiation.

Before being booked, it was not uncommon for prisoners to be taken first to the Condemned Hold on the other side of the arch, near the Keeper's house. For many, this offered the first offensive whiff of life inside, its 'Glimmerings of Light, tho' very imperfect' revealing, according to one observer, 'that you are in a dark, Opaque, wild Room. By the help of a Candle, which you must pay through the Nose for, before it will be handed to you over the Hatch, your Eyes will lead you to boarded Places, like those that are raised in Barracks, whereupon you may repose yourself if your Nose will suffer you to rest, from the Stench that diffuses its noisome Particles of bad Air from every Corner.'

Whether in the Condemned Hold or in the lodge, all inmates, irrespective of their alleged crime, were in due course clamped. As debtors were not required to be shackled for the duration of their detention, they remained in chains only until such time as they or their loved ones could purchase their release. Felons, however, were expected to be kept in irons throughout their imprisonment, and Keepers would initially weigh them down with the heaviest fetters on hand, allowing for the expensive option of replacing the chains with lighter ones later, a procedure known as 'easement'. Once registered, fresh arrivals were assigned to a ward – Masters' or Commons', depending on the depth of the prisoner's pocket – where they were expected to proffer a cover charge, or 'garnish', to the steward, for an allowance of candles and coal. The steward was typically a tenured inmate, whose good favour was necessary if one were to survive inside. Fall from the good graces of the steward, and a new inmate might find himself having to satisfy the unchecked wishes of the existing members of his new ward and forced, as the menacing expression went, conjuring the spectre of the beast that was thought to haunt The Gaol, to 'Make the Black Dog Walk'.

Behind the lodge, still at ground level, was the Hall Ward, a spacious dormitory for prisoners committed to the Masters' side. The room was twenty-five feet by fifteen, according to Langley, and it was abundantly clear what the extra rent bought those who could afford it. A window, five feet by six, facing south, offered a level of ventilation lacking anywhere on the Commons' side, while a large fireplace made certain that the space was kept consistently warm in the winter. Amenities such as benches and a decent table were more or less mirrored in the King's Bench Ward, which stretched above the Hall Ward on the first floor. Adjacent to the King's Bench Ward, just above the lodge, was the Stone Ward. Reserved for those who could afford greater comfort than was offered on the Commons' side, but who could not quite meet the rent in the Hall Ward, the Stone Ward, with its westerly aspect in the direction of Holborn, was said to have offered the best view in The Gaol, even if the lumpy mattresses provided there were left to sag directly on to the cold stone floors. Provided with their own ward, few women were ever assigned to the Masters' side, though a cramped and unventilated cell known as 'My Lady's Hold', equipped with two beds, was reserved for any that might be. 'This small Apartment,' writes Langley, 'is the very worst part of the Master Side.'

Rounding off the provisions for prisoners on the Masters' side were the Drinking Cellar and a curiously christened space called 'the Gigger'. Four feet below the level of the street and accessible from a spiral staircase leading to the lodge, the Drinking Cellar was divided into three areas – two reserved for male prisoners and one for women. A 'cellar man', who was elected from among the prison population to run the operation, was permitted to turn a profit on the sale of liquor and candles. Brandy sold for 4d. a quartern, wine for 2s. a bottle, and strong drink for 4d. a quart. Immediately above the Drinking Cellar, beside the lodge, was a hall reserved for interviews and visits with prisoners by family members and lawyers. Conversations were conducted through the grate in the door to the room – a feature known as a 'gigger'. Access to the Gigger by members of the public wishing to visit one of the prisoners could be arranged only through the Keeper, who profited by 1s. 6d. per visit – revenue, he insisted, that helped defray the considerable price he had paid for the position.

Felons and debtors who could not afford the exorbitant rates levied for a place inside the Masters' ward were committed instead to the warren of chambers that comprised the 'Commons' Side' on the second and third floors of The Gaol. In the cells that sprawled off these unkempt corridors, where skids of excrement and trails of lice competed with howling and what one inmate described as 'a solid stench', prisoners slept directly on the mildewed and splintered boards that lined the floor. Belligerent prisoners, or those deserving of special punishment, were separated from their peers and dragged to one of two detention chambers: 'The Bilbows' on the second floor, or a dungeon in the basement of The Gaol called 'the Stone Hold' – 'a most terrible stinking, dark and dismal Place, situated under Ground, in which no Day-light can come.' 'This Hold,' Langley records, 'is paved with Stone, on which the Prisoners lie without any Beds, and thereby endure great Misery and Hardship.' The Stone Hold may or may not have been synonymous with the hellish dungeon alluded to by some prisoners in this era as 'Limbo'.

While little expense was wasted on improving amenities in the common wards and holds in which destitute defendants would be held, some effort was made to up-grade the accommodation offered in the Press Yard and 'Castle'. This was looked upon as an investment, as lodgings in this wing of The Gaol continued to command some of the highest rents in all of London and were available only to the most affluent prisoners. Situated behind the notorious Stone Hold in the very back of the prison, the Press Yard was officially part of the Keeper's house and therefore not subject to the protocols that governed the rest of the institution. 'This Part of the Prison,' Langley attested, 'is composed of divers large spacious Rooms, which in general have very good Air and Light, free from all Ill Smells, with all necessary Appurtenances thereunto belonging. The Yard or Place for walking to take the Air, is situated between the Door which enters from Newgate Street, and Fabrick itself, the Dimensions whereof, are in Length about 54 Foot, and Breadth 7 Foot, being handsomely paved with Purbeck Stone.' 'The Persons imprison'd here,' we are told, are 'any Prisoners whatsoever, as are able to pay such a Premium at their Entrance, as shall be agreed on by the Gaoler thereof, and the Weekly Rent afterwards. The Praemuium [*sic*] is always in proportion to the Quality of the Prisoner, and is from 20 to 500 *l*.' The weekly rent of 11s. 6d. required by those living here included 1s. for 'a Woman call'd the Landress, for making Fires, cleaning the Rooms, &c.' It also included a bed, 'which of their kinds are very good'. The sheets were extra, as were the whores, who could be procured for twelve shillings a night.

Though the new gaol's layout was supposed to guarantee women prisoners, felons and debtors alike, some security from the male malefactors with whom they shared accommodation, in practice no such protection was enforced by the authorities. The women's ward was situated on the third floor of The Gaol, alongside the prison chapel. For a set fee of 6d. per visit, payable to the on-duty turnkey, male inmates from the wards below were permitted to mount the stairs. The practice was not always frowned upon by the female prisoners, some of whom appreciated the opportunity to earn a little money inside. On humid nights, the corridors and staircases of The Gaol, where the fetid air refused to move, wriggled with the unbodiced bodies of local whores and prowling felons. After a visit to Newgate in 1700, the Lord Mayor upbraided the deputy Keeper for having all but transformed the institution into a bordello where 'lewd women and common strumpets' are allowed to creep about at all hours.

For some desperate women, sex represented their only hope of avoiding execution, and many offered their services free in the hope of becoming pregnant before sentencing. A condemned felon who could 'plead her belly', so to speak, stood a decent chance of being pardoned or having her punishment reduced to either transportation or the pillory. Her condition, however, would first have to be verified by a 'committee of matrons' and the Proceedings of the Old Bailey that survive from this period are teeming with rejected applications for clemency by prisoners crudely deemed 'not quick with child'. In April 1684, the legendary highwaywoman Jane Voss (a.k.a. Jane Roberts) had her scheduled journey to Tyburn for stealing a silver tankard put on hold while a team of midwives corroborated her condition. But in processing Voss's subsequent application for an outright pardon it was discovered that, under a variety of disguises, she had been in and out of Newgate a dozen times in nearly as many years for capital offences. Taking no hostages to fortune, the Keeper decided to keep a close eye on the progress of Voss's pregnancy. In due course it was concluded that she was not 'quick with child' and her ticket to Tyburn was reissued.

Loopholes that might loosen the noose, such as pleading one's belly or 'the Benefit of Clergy' – the reading of the '*Miserere*' psalm or 'Neck Verse', which had saved Ben Jonson a century earlier – would slowly be tightened up in the years following the Great Fire as the era dawned of what became known as the 'Bloody Code'. When that biblical blaze engulfed the city in 1666, fewer than fifty offences were punishable by execution in England. But by the middle of the eighteenth century, serious crimes such as murder, treason and rape were matched in the lethal consequences that they brought by trivial transgressions, such as being caught with a blackened face after dusk and the filching of anything worth five shillings or more – the equivalent, in today's currency, of twenty-five pence. A century after the Great Fire, the number of crimes that carried a death sentence had reached over 150, and fifty years after that the figure stood at 225. Those who had hoped that such ruthlessness would serve as a deterrent to would-be felons watched in frustrated bemusement as the coining of new crimes merely resulted in an influx of newly christened capital criminals. No wonder that, for a time, to Newgate's nicknames (including

'Whittington's College', 'The Quod', 'Rumboe', 'The Start', 'The Stone Pitcher' and 'The Stone Jug') was added the curious sobriquet 'The Mint'. By the turn of the eighteenth century, Newgate cant was the common currency of the London underworld and the celebrities that The Gaol forged glittered like a fistful of stolen doubloons.

8

Whip

'**WHIP**-Jacks, *the* Nineteenth *Order of the* Canting Crew; *counterfeit mariners begging with false Passes, pretending Ship-wrecks, great Losses at Sea, narrow Escapes, &c. telling dismal Stories, having learnt* Tar-Terms *on purpose; but are meer Cheats, and will not stick to rob a Booth at a Fair, or an House in some By-road. They often carry their Morts or Wenches, which they pretend to be their Wives, whom they miraculously saved in the Shipwreck, altho' all his Children were drowned, the Ship splitting on a Rock near the* Lands End, *with such like Forgeries.'*

When the rope at the end of which Captain Kidd had been measured to die on 23 May 1701 suddenly snapped, the Ordinary from Newgate – who had escorted the infamous privateer from his cell to a desolate strip along the Thames east of the Tower known austerely as 'Execution Dock' – found himself unexpectedly back on duty. Accounts differ as to what exactly Reverend Paul Lorrain whispered when he bent down to steady Kidd, who was badly shaken by the sharp fall – flailing his head from side to side in bladderless bewilderment at the brief reprieve. Whatever was exchanged, the irascible sea-dog who had maintained, only moments before, an inebriated indiffer-ence in the face of oblivion, was now sobbing uncontrollably, begging the gasping throng for forgiveness, professing charity, and predicting the imminent return of the Redeemer.

Kidd's year-long stint in Newgate – from April 1700 to May 1701 – would prove crucial to the prison's transformation in cultural consciousness, from the beginning of the eighteenth century, into an insalubrious, if irresistible, centre of celebrity. Unlike most of the petty highwaymen and bungling pickpockets with whom Kidd would consort inside, his admittance to the prison had attracted unprecedented interest in England and abroad. News of his arrest the previous spring in Boston, Massachusetts, on charges of murder and piracy, and of his dramatic ferrying back to London on the King's yacht, ensured that his reception was a riotous horse fair.

Never before had the public taken such intense interest in the prosecution of a rumbled bluejacket. From the clattering coffee houses in Piccadilly to the smoke-fugged taverns of Shoreditch, for nearly two years London was abuzz with passionate debate over whether the prison's most recent resident was an incorrigible corsair or merely the scapegoat for a shady circle of untouchable Lords. So heavily has the legend of Captain Kidd been embroidered since he entered Newgate in the spring of 1700, it is difficult to unstitch the threads of biographical fact that have been woven into the tapestry of fiction. Even his Christian name is the source of some confusion. While most versions of the five-volume anthology of Crime, *The Newgate Calendar*, published in 1776/7, would insist on referring to him as 'John' (a few preferring 'Robert'), more reliable contemporary sources, including parliamentary papers and court records from the Old Bailey relating to his six eventual prosecutions, identify him as 'William'.

Of Kidd's childhood, almost nothing is known. He was born in either Greenock or Dundee, Scotland, perhaps around 1645. His father, who died when he was five, is said to have been a minister in the Church of Scotland. From there the trail is cold until the late 1680s, when Kidd surfaces in the Caribbean, captain of a ship called the *Blessed William* fending off the French in the West Indies. After a brutal mutiny by Robert

Culliford, which resulted in his vessel being wrested from him along with its hefty booty, Kidd resolved to hunt his ship down to New York City. Though *Blessed William* was never recovered, the pursuit would have lasting implications for his future, as it landed him in the midst of a formidable coalition of merchants in the colony, and in particular, face to face with Robert Livingston, a powerful landowner.

By the mid-1690s, Kidd – now a married father of two daughters – was jaded by the rough-and-tumble feast-or-famine life of a rented rover, combing the coasts of Massachusetts and New York. In cahoots with Livingston and the Governor of New York, Richard Coote, Earl of Bellamont, Kidd devised a scheme that promised to make all three parties appallingly wealthy. According to the plot, Kidd would be dispatched to the Indian Ocean with a special licence to devil the many pirate ships that threatened the financial interests of Livingston and his friends. In particular, he would be at liberty to harangue French vessels. Those whom Kidd apprehended would be prosecuted either back in the colonies or in London, and whatever treasure he managed to secure along the way would be split among the three principals and whomever else they could attract to the scheme. Invigorated by the enterprise, Bellamont set to work persuading his Whig cronies, including Lord John Somers and the Earls of Orford, Romney and Shrewsbury, silently to invest £1000 each in the anti-pirate partnership. If he could secure four-fifths of what was required to launch the operation, Kidd promised to make up the rest from some of his substantial property holdings.

Freshly fitted with a 300-ton ship christened the *Adventure Galley*, three dozen cannons, and a fearsome crew of over a hundred hand-picked veteran water-dogs, Kidd set sail first from Deptford in February, then from New York in September 1696 and reached East Africa the following January. According to legend, the most important weapon in Kidd's arsenal was a letter of marque, signed by the King, authorising him to seize ships. What occurred over the ensuing two years, however, has faded into the fog of fable, remaining to this day very much a matter of mystery and debate. Some historians allege that Kidd wasted little time in sliding insidiously from pirate-taker into pirate, ignoring the terms of his special licence and beating a path instead to the Red Sea where he mercilessly attacked pilgrim ships on their way back from Mecca. Others argue that the account offered later by the East India Company, which claimed that their own ship, *The Sceptre*, was called upon to defend pilgrim vessels against the aggressions of the *Adventure Galley*, was fabricated and merely reflected the Company's fury at not having been made partners in Livingston and Bellamont's secretive scheme.

Whatever transpired in the haze of cannon blast between clashing ships in the Red Sea, the chaos of these days was intensified when a dispute arose between Kidd and his bellicose gunner, William Moore, following a narrow escape that left the *Adventure Galley* and its crew rattled. In court, conflicting testimonies would eventually be aired as to what exactly precipitated Kidd's altercation with Moore, who was crouched down 'grinding his chisel on deck' when the captain approached him. Several overheard Kidd call Moore 'a lousy dog' and Moore retort, 'If I am a lousy dog, you have made me so; you have brought me to ruin and many more.' It was claimed that an incandescent Kidd poked tauntingly at Moore, provoking him with 'Have I brought you to ruin, you dog? Have I . . .?' over and over again before seizing a wooden bucket, 'hooped with iron'.

Afterwards, when his fellow crewmen took Moore's body down to the gunroom – his skull sagging above the right ear – the ship's ribs were said to echo with the whimper, 'Farewell, farewell, Captain Kidd has given me the last!'

From that point onward – and despite a string of successful seizures – Kidd's days were numbered. As his beleaguered ship capsized at Sainte-Marie, the East India Company began putting pressure on Bellamont in Boston to rein in this rapscallion. Returning to the Caribbean in a freshly stolen vessel, the *Quedah Merchant*, Kidd found himself skulking from island to island, selling off cargo where he could and monitoring the rumours that he was now a wanted man.

Determined that his only hope of remaining free was to enlist the support of his powerful partners, Livingston and Bellamont, Kidd, having abandoned the *Quedah Merchant* in the Greater Antilles, anchored himself in a new ship, the *San Antonio*, off the coast of Boston and waited for word that the charges against him would be dropped. In order to refute allegations that he had preyed neither on pirate ships nor on legitimate French targets but on defenceless vessels, Kidd forwarded to Bellamont from his floating exile a pair of French Passes, which had been seized during his raids. These documents, Kidd asserted, were crucial to his claim that he had kept to the strict terms of his licence.

Hoping to be cut some slack, but fearing the worst, Kidd attempted to buy time. He initiated a filibustering exchange of letters with Bellamont and even endeavoured to charm the earl's wife by sending her separately a diamond-studded gold box, opulently enamelled, in which he tucked two precious rings. But Bellamont was busy playing a game of his own. From his Governor's mansion, he tried to lure Kidd into a false sense of protection by claiming to have obtained testimony corroborating Kidd's innocence, sufficient to secure a royal pardon. 'I have to say in your Defence,' Bellamont wrote,

> that several Persons at New York, who[m] I can bring to evidence if there be Occasion, did tell me, That by several Advices from Madagascar and that Part of the World, they were informed of your Men's revolting from you in one Place; which I am pretty sure they said was at Madagascar; and that others of them compelled you, much against your Will, to take and rifle

Two Ships. I have advised with his Majesty's Council and shewed them this Letter, this Afternoon; and they are of Opinion, That if your Case be so clear as you . . . have said, then you may safely come hither, and be equipped and fitted out, to go and fetch the other Ship; and I make no manner of Doubt but to obtain the King's Pardon for you and those few men you have left, who, I understand, have been faithful to you, and refused, as well as you, to dishonour the Commission you had from England.

Eventually agreeing to come ashore and meet Bellamont, Kidd begged the Governor for patience while he prepared a full narrative account of his exploits, which, he promised, would substantiate his innocence. In the meantime, Kidd spent his last few hours of freedom tirelessly off-loading on to the passing boats of sympathetic seamen the hullful of booty that he was worried would be used as evidence against him if discovered.

With royal pressure mounting, Bellamont's patience eventually evaporated. On 6 July 1699 he ordered Kidd's arrest. When Kidd was finally apprehended and his quarters searched, gold and ingots were allegedly discovered between his two feather mattresses. When he was dragged back to London after ten months' detention in a Boston jail, Kidd was brought before a disdainful judge of the Admiralty Court who was singularly unpersuaded by the captain's protestations of innocence and specious allusions to the existence of 'French Passes' that could substantiate his story. The judge wasted no time in ordering that the prisoner's arms and legs be bound with iron fetters and that he should await trial, not in the relative comfort of the comfortless Marshalsea – where most pirates were taken – but in the slowly decaying pile of Newgate.

Though detention before trial was typically no longer than the sixty days' interval between assizes, it was determined that Kidd's was an extraordinary case, potentially implicating members of the House of Lords, and that prosecution should therefore be postponed until the next session of Parliament could be convened, the following spring. In all likelihood, Kidd's thirteen-month tenure in Newgate was hellish. After nine days inside, his petition to have the shackles removed from his limbs was grudgingly granted – though the manner in which they were knocked off, with a sledgehammer and crowbar, was itself the stuff of nightmares. Choking on the acrid air inside The Gaol with Kidd were a gaggle of scruffy villains. John and Thomas Bird were awaiting trial for allegedly stealing a gelding from John Hill in Whitechapel, while Bartholomew Allen waited to hear his fate for having stolen a silk petticoat from Henrietta Pen who, the court record-keeper was good enough to point out, was a 'spinster'. Huddled together in a cell reserved for women were an intimidating group of cutpurses and housebreakers. Rebecca Maud had helped herself to a pair of worsted stockings after slipping into the home of Thomas Meade of Stepney in the dead of night, while Anne Coffee (a.k.a. 'Clary', a.k.a. 'Mary Pool') had been caught lugging a sackful of pewter dishes from the dusty pantry of Joseph Meeling in Wapping.

Once back in session in March 1701, Parliament – then under the control of the Tories – was eager to humiliate the Whigs in whatever way possible. Subpoenaed to appear before a special committee appointed to investigate his case, Kidd was invidiously presented with the possibility of parliamentary leni- ence, perhaps even an outright pardon from prosecution, in exchange for his co-operation in naming the Whig lords who had encouraged him to undertake the vigilante venture in the Indian Ocean. But Kidd was at best combative, if not, in the estimation of many in attendance, actually drunk. He derided the offer of co-operation, provoking one member to exclaim, 'I had thought him only a knave; I now know him to be a fool as well!'

On 8 May 1701, William Kidd was led down the damp passage that connected Newgate with the Sessions House of

THE
Arraignment, Tryal, and Condemnation
OF
Captain William Kidd,
FOR
MURTHER
AND
PIRACY,
Upon Six several Indictments,

At the Admiralty-Sessions, held by His Majesty's Commission at the *Old-Baily*, on *Thursday* the 8th. and *Friday* the 9th.
of *May*, 1701. who, upon full Evidence, was found Guilty,
receiv'd Sentence, and was accordingly Executed at *Execution-
Dock, May* the 23d.

AS ALSO,
The TRYALS of *Nicholas Churchill, James Howe, Robert
Lamley, William Jenkins, Gabriel Loff, Hugh Parrot, Richard Barlicorn,
Abel Owens,* and *Darby Mullins,* at the same Time and Place
for PIRACY.

Perused by the Judges and Council.

To which are added,
Captain *KIDD*'s Two Commissions:
One under the Great Seal of *ENGLAND*, and the Other under
the Great Seal of the Court of *Admiralty.*

LONDON:
Printed for *J. Nutt*, near *Stationers-Hall.* 1701.

*18. Title-page of one of the many pamphlets devoted to the
case against Captain Kidd for piracy*

the Old Bailey and was placed in the dock to answer six indictments, to be treated sequentially in four separate trials. The first
charge – for the murder of his gunner, William Moore – he
faced alone. The other five charges were for piracy, which he
faced with nine members of his crew. When asked to enter a
plea, Kidd initially refused, demanding that he be provided
with counsel to prepare a proper defence and nominating the
services of a Dr Oldfish and a Mr Lemmon. At the beginning
of the eighteenth century, defendants were not permitted to
procure legal representation. Kidd's reluctance to repeat his

earlier performances before the Admiralty Court and Parliament, reveals that, however depressed and ill-tempered he may have been at this stage, he at last appreciated the severity of his situation. Having been denied his request for counsel, Kidd had little choice but to enter a plea or suffer the crushing consequences that he had more than once witnessed over the past year in the adjacent Press Yard. He pleaded not guilty to all six charges against him.

By now Kidd was convinced that the French Passes he had hastily entrusted to Bellamont were being wilfully withheld, or had already been destroyed, in a Whig plot designed to leave him twisting in the wind. Still, Kidd managed to persuade the judge to postpone the piracy trials until the question of Moore's murder was answered, in the hope that the passes might still materialise. Aware that all eyes were firmly fixed on the court proceedings, the Crown provided no fewer than six senior judges to preside over Kidd's prosecutions, including the colourful and reputedly fair-minded Justice John Powell, who once remarked to Jane Wenham, a woman charged with using witchcraft to help her fly, 'You may – there is no law against flying!'

Among the first witnesses called by the prosecution over the death of Kidd's gunner were crew members Joseph Palmer and Robert Bradinham, the ship's surgeon. Palmer testified to having placed his hand on Moore's head only to feel the skull 'give way' in the spot above the right ear where he said he saw Kidd plunge the rusty bucket. But it was Bradinham who stuck the knife in when he impersonated for the court Kidd's supposedly heartless reaction to Moore's death. 'Damn him!' Bradinham quoted Kidd as having roared, 'he is a villain!'

When it was his turn in the dock, Kidd insisted that his actions had been justified and argued that he was attempting to suppress a mounting mutiny. But when, during cross-examination, he implored one of the subpoenaed crew members, Hugh Parrot, to confirm his assertion that a revolt had been brewing on board,

Lord Chief Baron intervened. 'Captain Kidd, you are tried for the death of this Moore,' he cautioned. 'Now why do you ask this question? What do you infer from hence? You will not infer that if he was a mutineer that it was lawful for you to kill Moore.' Reading the writing on the wall, Kidd, in his closing remarks, endeavoured to sound a note of remorse. 'It was not designedly done,' he confessed, 'but in my passion for which I am heartily sorry.'

The jury took just thirty minutes to reach a unanimous verdict on the first indictment: guilty.

Had Moore's murder been the only count Kidd faced, he might well have been shown mercy by the court in light of his celebrated courage in fighting foreign foes of English interests. But less excusable charges of piracy were still pending and Kidd had exhausted the court's patience in waiting for the French Passes to be produced. As the proceedings unfolded, Kidd's only chance was to persuade the jury that the ships he had seized had been – or so he thought at least – legitimate targets. 'Did you not see,' he desperately pressed witness after witness, 'any French Passes aboard the captured vessels?' 'You told me you had French Passes,' the crewmen in turn would reply, 'but I never did see them.' On 9 May 1701, Captain William Kidd stood convicted of five separate counts of piracy and was sentenced to die along the marshy bank of the River Thames. When asked if he wished to add anything before being returned to Newgate to await his fate, Kidd replied, 'I have nothing to say, but that I have been sworn against by perjured and wicked people.'

On the morning of his execution, Kidd, after a sleepless night spent swigging smuggled rotgut, was made to attend a liturgy in which his fellow prisoners, kneeling around the empty coffin that had been propped up in the centre of the chapel, were asked to pray for the souls of the soon-to-be deceased (whose imminent dissolution, they were told, provided a poignant spiritual lesson). 'And they shall go away,' the

Ordinary, Paul Lorrain thundered tauntingly, 'into everlasting judgement.' After a brief meeting with his hangman, who failed to take proper notice of his subject's size, an abstracted Kidd, still hoping a pardon would be forthcoming, submitted to having his arms and legs tightly bound with strips of rope before his body was roughly bundled on to a hurdle for the mile-and-a-half journey to Wapping High Street and the Old Stairs there, which overlooked the place where he was going to die.

Unlike the procession west through the broad thoroughfares of Holborn and up a bustling 'King's Highway' to Tyburn, the journey east from Newgate to Wapping was negotiated through the narrow byways pinched between the old city wall and what Daniel Defoe would soon be describing as the 'deep, dirty, and unfrequented' lanes of Spitalfields and Whitechapel. 'Execution Dock' was situated off Wapping High Street between the 'New Stairs' and King Henry's Stairs. Used by the Admiralty since the middle of the fifteenth century, this stretch of the river was described a century earlier by the historian John Stow as 'a filthy straight passage' and 'the vsuall place of Execution for the hanging of Pyrates and sea Rouers, at the lowe water marke, and there to remaine, till thrée Tydes had ouerflowed them'. The procession through the thickening throng was led by a member of the Admiralty brandishing a silver oar to signify the seaborne nature of the crimes committed. Though it was customary for the condemned to bring along with them their uniforms and clothing for distribution to family and friends as mementoes, before mounting the ladder that was propped against the gibbet, Kidd was in no frame of mind to bestow hand-me-downs.

During the bumpy passage from Newgate the captain was nagged at by Pepys's former secretary, Reverend Lorrain, who would later write in a popular pamphlet that he 'was afraid the hardness of Capt. Kidd's heart was still unmelted.' 'I therefore applied myself,' Lorrain boasted, 'with particular exhortations

19. Convicted pirates were hanged at 'Execution Dock', Wapping, when the tide was low. The bodies were left suspended until three tides had washed over them

to him and laid the judgements of God against impenitent and hardened sinners . . . very plain before him.' And so it was with the insufferable haranguing of Reverend Lorrain ringing in his ears that Kidd – still three sheets to the wind – reached the makeshift platform on Wapping's soggy bank, was fitted with a flimsy noose, and, when the rope broke, was incompetently teased with the release of death before a heaving crowd. The scene would be repeated years later when the dangling body of another convicted seadog, John Gow, was yanked so violently by onlookers hoping to curtail his suffering that the tether split instead of Gow's neck, and the whole ritual had to be repeated. Unlike many of the pirates who had ascended the ladder in the previous two-and-a-half centuries, Kidd rejected the opportunity presented him to ask the jeering multitude for forgiveness. Pamphlets printed after the mass execution, a century earlier, in 1609, of nineteen convicted pirates emphasised the performance aspect of this part of the ritual, which many condemned corsairs curiously seemed to relish. Recalling the hanging of one of the men, a Captain Jennings, who was 'the first that was cald to goe vp to his death', one pamphlet described how

> he did now in soule repent him of his sinne, complayned of his lusts and ryots, as the causers of his ruine, confest that before this he had receiued pardon for his heynous transgressions, and had not the goodnesse to desist from ill: he desired God of his mercy to receiue his soule, & the world at his death to pardon his body, & so desiring the multitude of spectators to pray for him and sing a psalme with him . . .

By all accounts, there was no singing before either of Kidd's hangings.

9

Chive

'CHIVE, *a Knife, File or Saw;* To Chive his Darbies, *To saw asunder his Irons or Fetters.*'

On 14 October 1724, Jack Sheppard escaped from Newgate Gaol for the second time. It was his fourth prison break in seven months and as he let go of the knotted bed-sheet down which he had shinned from the Upper Leads of the towering structure, and slipped on to the roof of William Bird's adjoining house, he launched Newgate into a new era of cultural meaning. For centuries, The Gaol had slowly migrated from the margins of society on which it had been erected, to something more central, more culturally archetypal. As Sheppard disappeared down Holborn Bridge towards Leicester Fields, skulking in the shadows and clasping to his thighs the twisted fetters that were still attached to his aching legs, the prison was preparing to emerge as a mythic theatre at the epicentre of English con-sciousness – an existential stage without precedence in London's long history. For the rest of the eighteenth century and well into the nineteenth, Newgate was also seen by many as a sort of secular altar, and the miracle-performing Sheppard, a kind of cocky Cockney messiah.

'Oh that ye were all like Jack Sheppard,' so one preacher would thunder to his congregation after news of the 22-year-old housebreaker's escape had rippled across the country.

Mistake me not, my brethren – I don't mean in a carnal, but in a spiritual sense; for I propose to spiritualise these things. What a shame it would be if we should not think it worth our while to take as much pain, and employ as many deep thoughts to save our souls as he has done to preserve his body!

Let me exhort ye, then, to open the locks of your hearts with the nail of repentance! Burst asunder the fetters of your beloved lusts! – mount the chimney of hope! – take from thence the bar of good resolution! – break through the stone wall of despair, and all the strongholds in the dark entry of the valley of the shadow of death! Raise yourselves to the leads of divine meditation! – fix the blanket of faith with the spike of the church! let yourselves down to the turner's house of resignation, and descend the stairs of humility! So shall you come to the door of deliverance from the prison of iniquity, and escape the clutches of that old executioner the Devil!

John Sheppard, or 'Jack' as he was always called, was born in White Row, one of the cramped and narrow alleyways near Spitalfields Market, on 4 March 1702. His father, who was a carpenter, died when Jack was a boy. He and his older brother Tom received some education at Mr Garret's school in Bishopsgate before Jack went to work in the Strand for an avuncular woollen draper, William Kneebone, who made sure to equip him with basic skills – reading, writing and numbers. Jack was clever and before long he found himself apprenticed to a carpenter aptly named Owen Wood off Drury Lane in Wych Street, a popular haunt of actors. By his twentieth birthday, Jack seemed to have every prospect of becoming a respectable craftsman himself. What exactly served as the catalyst that derailed Jack Sheppard's future, and left him dangling variously from prison parapets on an improvised rope and a noose at Tyburn, is difficult to pin down, and may be little more than a case of bad company.

Around the corner from Wood's shop, in the insalubrious Lewkenor Lane, was the Black Lion alehouse, a favourite of

Sheppard's and his fellow apprentices. The Black Lion was situated in that slummy labyrinth around Drury Lane that Gay would evoke so memorably a few years later when trying to recreate the ambience of the world that Sheppard inhabited:

> O may thy virtue guide thee through the roads
> Of Drury's mazy courts and dark abodes!

It was here that Sheppard, according to the pamphlet that he helped prepare in time to distribute at his own execution, fell in with a clutch of unsavoury characters. 'After all I may justly lay the Blame of my Temporal and (without God's great Mercies) my Eternal Ruin on Joseph Hind, a Button-mould Maker, who formerly kept the Black Lyon Ale-House in Drury-Lane; the frequenting of this wicked House brought me acquainted . . . with a Train of Vices as before I was altogether Stranger to.' The Black Lion was where Sheppard first became acquainted with Elizabeth Lyon, a pudgy cutpurse and prostitute known on the street as 'Edgworth Bess'. Sheppard should have known from the start what sort of character he had met with in Bess, whose left hand was still livid from the brand she had received a year earlier after being convicted of stealing a piece of silk.

Egged on by Bess, Sheppard's criminal career began modestly with the sleeving of two silver spoons while on a building job at the Rummer Tavern in Charing Cross and it wasn't long before he had forfeited his apprenticeship with Wood altogether – with only seven months of his eighty-four-month indenture left to go – to pursue instead a full-time criminal partnership with Bess and his brother Tom. The chief obstacles that the gang faced in their ambition to thrive as thieves were the cheap liquor that swallowed their meagre booty and a basic incompetence that the three of them seemed to share in equal measure. By April 1724, an inebriated Tom Sheppard, his hand still blistered from where a 'T' had been branded after a conviction for stealing carpenters' equipment, was in custody for swiping linen from Mary Cook's stall in Clare Market. In exchange for a promise of leniency, Tom shopped his partners.

The evidence Tom provided brought Jack and Bess to the attention of Jonathan Wild, the self-styled 'Thief-taker General of Britain and Ireland', who, for over a decade, had walked a perilous tightrope between police informant, on the one hand, and grandmaster of the criminal underworld on the other. A buckle-maker by trade, Wild came from Wolverhampton to London in 1708. A brief stint in the Wood Street compter – a prison for debtors – awakened Wild to a new world of untapped opportunities. After trying his hand at running a brothel, he embarked on a devious enterprise whereby he would commission others to steal from people, and then charge the victims of the thefts a fee to have their property returned. On the surface, Wild would appear to be offering an invaluable service to society by rescuing otherwise unrecoverable goods. And by providing criminals with a guaranteed market for unloading stolen property – i.e. the rightful owners – Wild was the perfect partner for any thief. Before long, he had every pickpocket in London working for him, thus possessing incriminating evidence against them all. Whenever the authorities looked suspiciously in his direction, he pacified their concerns by helping them put handcuffs on another knave. Wild is thought to have helped fit some seventy ropes around the necks of others. It was a risky game and had its repercussions. By the time that he became acquainted with the Sheppards and Bess, Wild's skull was a squeaky kettle of mortises and dented plates from years of thumping comeuppances.

Always alert to the emergence of potential associates or rivals, Wild liked the sound of Jack Sheppard and sought him out. But according to Sheppard's own later recollection, which he entrusted to Defoe in Newgate in the days before his hanging, he resisted Wild's overtures and those of the proxies who were occasionally dispatched to bring him round:

I never corresponded with any of them. I was indeed twice at a Thief-Catcher's *Levee*, and must confess the Man treated me civilly; he complimented me on my Successes, said he heard that I had both an Hand and Head admirably well turn'd to *Business*, and that I and my Friends *should be always welcome to him*: But caring not for his Acquaintance, I never troubled him, nor had we any Dealings together.

Wild didn't appreciate being snubbed and he held grudges. Swapping his thief's hat for that of thief-taker, he set his sights on Sheppard and released one of his pit-bullish minions called James Sykes (a.k.a. 'Hell-and-Fury') to fetch him. Hell-and-Fury had a reputation for being the 'fastest-moving human being alive'. When he caught up with Jack in the Queen's Head alehouse in King Street, he challenged him to a game of ninepin 'skettles', which he said was getting under way in a pub at the Seven Dials. Jack was always up for a game, but what he didn't know was that a constable of St Giles's parish was waiting for him, armed with the evidence provided by his brother Tom for a string of thefts.

Remarkably, when Jack was thrown into the St Giles Roundhouse – a small house of detention in Soho – the incarceration awakened in him an agility of mind and steadiness of action that he seemed to lack on the outside. He was confined, he said, 'in the upper Part of the Place, being two Stories from the Ground'. With 'nothing but an old Razor in my Pocket', Jack immediately began whittling away at the damp ceiling. He placed a feather bed under the falling debris to muffle the noise as he chipped at the crumbling mortar. He was aware of people passing by outside when, suddenly, a 'Tile or Brick' prised loose and 'struck a Man on the Head, who raised the whole Place'. Within minutes the Roundhouse was a riot of shouting and confusion and crashing bricks. With no time to waste, Jack smashed a hole in the masonry and hoisted his slender, five-foot-four-inch frame through the jagged breach. Barely two hours after being admitted, amid cries of 'There's his Head!'

and 'There he goes behind the Chimney!', Jack Sheppard vanished into the night. 'I was well enough diverted with the Adventure,' he later recalled, 'and then went off about my business.'

News of Sheppard's escape spread quickly through the muddy lanes of St Giles and Holborn. By the following morning, he was famous. Sheppard's prising open the Roundhouse to public view can be read as a metaphor for the gradual opening up, in the eighteenth century, of hidden prison spaces into open diorama – places of scrutiny and entertainment. But however efficient Sheppard was in freeing himself from confinement, remaining free was another matter. Three weeks after his first prison break, on 19 May, Sheppard was casing Leicester Fields for ripe pockets with a friend by the name of Benson when the two of them came upon a mob gathered around a couple arguing. The man was accusing the woman of having attempted to steal his pocket watch. Benson saw an opportunity and slid in between the observers until he was in reach of the disputed watch. With a quick snap from the gentleman's waistcoat, Benson and Sheppard were off, passing the booty between them as they lost themselves in the crowded streets that spidered away from the open field towards Soho. Jack was caught almost immediately by a sergeant-of-the-guard in front of Leicester House and frogmarched to the nearby St Ann's Roundhouse. When news of the arrest reached Edgworth Bess, she tried to smuggle in 'the Spike of an Halbert' for Sheppard to use as a tool with which to free himself but was caught doing so and 'was put into the Dungeon of the Place fetter'd and manacled'. After their appearance before a justice, it was surmised that Jack and Bess were husband and wife and decided that they should be transferred to a shared cell in the New Prison in Clerkenwell, to await removal to Newgate.

Already household names after Sheppard's escape from St Giles, the pair were visited in Clerkenwell by a steady stream of well-wishers and awestruck admirers, several of whom suc-

ceeded where Bess had failed in slipping Sheppard sharp tools
– bits of broken–off saw and picks. Before long their cell was
strewn with iron filings and oak shards as Sheppard cut his way
through fourteen–pounds of fetters and the nine–inch wood
plank that barred the window. Strips from Bess's petticoat and
ripped–up sheets were knotted into a makeshift rope down
which the two abseiled into the adjoining exercise yard of the
Bridewell House of Correction. What happened next would
instantly enter local legend. Hoisting Bess – which was itself a
challenge – on to his shoulder, his feet groping in the moon-
light for a grip on the slippery bolts and hinges of a conveniently situated gate, Sheppard scaled the twenty–two–foot wall
that separated the couple from freedom and whirled his rotund
mistress down to the street below. Despite efforts to downplay
the escapade later – 'my Escaping from New-Prison, and carrying with me Elizabeth Lyon over the Wall of Bridewell Yard,
was not so wonderful as has been reported' – Sheppard had
pole-vaulted himself into unprecedented notoriety as the
greatest escape artist in history. 'It has been allow'd by all the
Jayl-Keepers in London,' one pamphlet would relate, an escape
'so Miraculous was never perform'd before in England; the
broken Chains and Bars are kept at New Prison to Testifie, and
preserve the Memory of this extraordinary Villain.'

But Sheppard's audacious escape only riled Wild, who saw
him as a loose cannon – a charismatic chancer who threatened
to undermine the thief-taker's dominion. From that point
onward, the former carpenter's apprentice was a marked man.
Rather than rethink his career in the light of recent hitches,
Sheppard seems to have been emboldened by his new-found
fame. 'Not warned by his admonition', so Defoe would later
write, Sheppard 'returns like a dog to his vomit'. Far from
giving up crime, Jack began thinking of ways to branch out
from housebreaking and he had plenty of willing tutors. 'Jack
was now become so eminent, that there was not a prig in St
Giles's, but thought it an honor, as well as an advantage, to be

admitted into his company.' It was around this time that Joseph Blake, a familiar face around Lewkenor Lane and the Black Lion alehouse, introduced Sheppard to the exhilarating life of highway robbery.

An incorrigible crook, Blake, or 'Blueskin' as he was called for his dusky complexion, had been a footpad since childhood. He was already in league with Jonathan Wild by the age of fourteen. A year before Sheppard and Blueskin took to the highways around Hampstead Heath, the latter had narrowly escaped hanging after his gang was rounded up and accused of committing a series of robberies. Shielded from prosecution by his 'stepfather' Wild, Blueskin was allowed to save his own neck by offering evidence against his fellow thieves, John Levee, Richard Oakey, Matthew Flood and his best friend William Blewitt. On the testimony provided by Blake, the four were executed at Tyburn, though it was well known that 'there was scarce a Robbery about the Town for some Tears [sic] but Blueskin was concerned in it'.

On 12 July a gang led by Sheppard and Blueskin descended on the home of the draper William Kneebone, who had not so many years earlier shown such generosity to Jack. Kneebone was aware of rumours circulating that his house was a target, but there was little he could do to protect himself against attack. After smashing the cellar window at the back of Kneebone's house, Sheppard and his men spent three hours inside piling up spools of woollen cloth, tye-wigs and beaver hats, penknives and handkerchiefs, not to mention a pair of sparkling silver spoons. Jack liked spoons. From there Blueskin took Jack hunting on Hampstead Way, a favourite haunt of highwaymen. The endless procession of ladies' coaches and drunken riders was like shooting fish in a barrel.

Devastated by his losses, Kneebone appealed to the Thief-Taker General for help in recovering his goods. Wild was already on the case. On a starless night in late July, his men waylaid Edgworth Bess as she ducked into a brandy shop in

Temple Bar and dragged her in for questioning. With hardly any persuasion, she began to rattle off to Wild a list of the places where Jack could most likely be found. A warrant for Sheppard's arrest was signed by a sleepy Justice Blackerby later that same night. Rechristened 'Royal Mint Street' in 1850, Rosemary Lane was once a rag-and-bric-a-brac fair more bustling even than Petticoat Lane. It was a place, one observer described, where 'ill-favour'd Mankins' were 'busie Raking into their Dunghills of old Shreds and Patches, and examining their Wardrobes of decay'd Coats, Breeches, Gowns and Petticoats, as so many Cocks upon a Pile of Horse-dung'. Above the mingled stench of mildew and stale sweat, Blueskin's mother kept a flat. Blake and Sheppard were busy dividing up their spoils when Quilt Arnold, one of Wild's heavies, burst through the door. Jack produced a loaded pistol and aimed it towards the intruder's chest, but the 'dag' misfired. Quilt tied up the two men and hauled them before an irritable Blackerby the next morning.

On 23 July 1724 Jack Sheppard was charged with robbing the home of William Kneebone and with breaking into two other houses. He was led away to Newgate to await trial at the Old Bailey. News of Jack's arrest was splashed across the broadsheets. 'Yesterday one Shepheard,' the *Daily Journal* for Saturday 25 July reported, 'a notorious house-breaker, who lately made his escape from New-Prison, and had impeach'd his own brother, was committed to Newgate, having been re-taken by Jonathan Wild; he is charged with several burglaries, &c.' Jack would have to wait three weeks before it was his turn to appear before a judge and jury in the Sessions House next door. In August, the air inside Newgate didn't move. Among those sweating it out in adjoining cells was a motley collection of London's least impressive coiners and crooks. John Heath was facing transportation for stealing a pair of hogs from Edward Taylor's yard. Anthony Upton was about to be found guilty of taking ten bars of iron from the house of Oliver Truelove, and, though he didn't know it yet, had only twenty nights to live. Upton would share the crossbeam at Tyburn with Joseph Ward who had mugged a mother and daughter in Bond Street and made off with a gold ring worth 20s. Across the prison, in the women's ward, Elizabeth Francis and Mary Clark stood accused of pinching George Frazier's leather shoes, while Mary Cyles was about to be acquitted for the theft of Daniel Guilt's rusty spurs.

When Jack's case was finally called, he was found not guilty of robbing the homes of William Phillips and Mary Cook, 'The Evidence against the Prisoner', according to Defoe, 'being defficient as to this Indictment'. But in the case involving the raiding of William Kneebone's fabric cellar, the sympathetic draper himself took to the stand. Observers of the trial report that Kneebone was heartbroken at having to testify against his former apprentice. Kneebone explained how he had visited Sheppard in prison in the hope of understanding 'how he could be so ungrateful to rob him, after he had shown him so much Kindness? The Prisoner own'd he had been ungrateful in doing so, informing him of several Circumstances as to the Manner of committing the Fact, but said he had been drawn into it by ill Company.' Wild made matters worse for Jack by producing a member of Sheppard's gang, William Field, who claimed he was present during the looting. Field insisted that the operation was Sheppard's idea from the start and that he and Blueskin had tried to persuade him against it. While there is little doubting Sheppard's involvement, according to Gerald Howson, in all likelihood Field's testimony was tailor-made by Wild to seal Jack's fate. 'I declare upon the word of a dying man,' Jack would later tell Defoe, 'that Will Field was not concerned with Blueskin and myself in the breaking and robbing of Mr Kneebone's house.' By that stage, Jack would have had little reason to lie.

On 13 August 1724, Jack Sheppard was convicted of robbing the home of William Kneebone and was told that he would have to hang by the neck until dead as punishment. Back inside

Newgate, he was moved to the Condemned Hold, the fabled waiting room of the doomed. Here, he was chained to a filthy floor with nine others while plans for his execution were finalised. But according to the author of the *Authentic memoirs of the life and surprising adventures of John Sheppard* (1724), Jack 'had other Thoughts in his Head': 'By G—d,' the habitual escapist promised, 'I'll do my best Endeavours to make Him [the judge] a false Prophet.' He knew it would be tricky, though, to keep his word. The Condemned Hold of Newgate made his former cells in Clerkenwell and in the St Giles Roundhouse seem like slippery turnstiles. For one thing, the only passage out of the Hold was in plain view of the Keepers' lodge. Above the door to the large cell was a narrow grate, barbed with iron spikes, through which prisoners were permitted to converse with visitors who stood outside.

To this day it is a mystery how sufficient tools were smuggled in with which Jack could file his way, not only through the shackles that bound him to the floor, but through one of the grate's iron spikes, without attracting attention. But four days before he was scheduled to climb the scaffold at Tyburn, he did just that. If the legend is to be believed, Edgworth Bess, racked with guilt for having betrayed Jack to Wild, came to visit him after news of his execution date had begun spreading across London. Bess brought with her a friend, Poll Maggot, who concealed under her long coat a wad of spare clothing. Whether the Keepers genuinely didn't notice the fierce tugging as the two girls helped Sheppard squeeze through the slender slot, or hear him tumbling into the corridor, or whether, as some have speculated, Jack had offered them a bribe to remain silent, will never be known. What is certain, though, is that on 31 August 1724, Jack Sheppard, clasping the frilly collar of a lady's nightgown to his chin, strode through the impregnable front doors of Newgate Prison, and hailed a coach to freedom.

Sheppard was not the first prisoner to escape from Newgate, nor would he be the last. Nine years earlier, the efforts of a Mr

Barlow to *drag* himself, as it were, out of the prison were considerably less successful. An imprisoned Jacobite in the days after a spate of successful escapes from their ranks, Barlow had made it as far as the Keepers' lodge 'close shaved and neatly dressed in female clothes' and insulated by 'a crowd of ladies' when a suspicious turnkey grabbed hold of his arm and spun him to the ground. As his entourage shrieked 'Oh my heaven!' and scolded the prison official for his barbaric behaviour, Barlow is said to have put on an impressive impersonation, patting his painted face and feigning faint-heartedness. The ruse would have worked had it not been for the ill-timed arrival, through the very door that Barlow was trying to reach, of the Special Commissioner appointed to oversee the rebels, Carleton Smith, who sensed that there was more to the rattled guest than met the eye. Rejecting Barlow's bribe, Smith shuffled the would-be escapee over to the Old Bailey, which happened to be in session, and had another count added to the reasons why he would hang.

News of Jack's escape met with general enthusiasm as well as disbelief that he had managed to break out of three gaols in a row. Inevitably there were those who suspected that it was an inside job. Collusion by prison staff was not unknown if the price was right. Sketchy records from 1593 suggest that an even more audacious escape than Jack's was pulled off when a 'corrupt officer' responsible for transporting a dead man from the prison was paid to switch the body in the coffin with that of a living prisoner.

Jack's movements in the nine days between his escape from Newgate dressed as a girl and the moment that he was recaptured in Finchley, near Highgate, dressed as a butcher, have been forensically traced by historians in the three centuries since the escapologist caught London's imagination. Contemporary notices in the press and the flurry of posthumous biographical sketches agree on a few particulars. Jack's getaway coach took off south down Old Bailey before winding along

Blackfriars Lane to the Embankment. 'The said Shepheard went off by water,' George Parker of the *London News* would report, 'between 7 and 8 o'clock on Monday night, at *Black-Fryers Stairs*, where his prostitute gave him the Meeting. The *Water-Man* saw his Irons under his Night Gown,' the bulletin continued, 'and was terrified thereat; he landed him at the Horseferry at Westminster, for which he rewarded him with a 7 pence.' According to Defoe, once Jack and Bess reached Westminster, the two felt deserving of refreshment.

> . . . at the *White-Hart* they went in, Drank, and stay'd sometime; thence they adjourn'd to a Place in *Holbourn*, where by the help of a Saw he quitted the Chains he had brought with him from *Newgate*; and then like a Freeman took his Ramble through the City and came to *Spittle-Fields*, and there lay with *Edgeworth Bess*.

It was the last time Jack and Bess would be together. Though she had assisted him in breaking out of Newgate, he could never forget her earlier betrayal to Jonathan Wild. 'There is not a more wicked, deceitful, lascivious wretch living in England,' he would later rage. 'God forgive her. I do.'

Before daybreak the following morning, Jack surprised his friend, William Page, by turning up at the butchery in the shambles of Clare Market where Page was an apprentice. The city was abuzz with news of the audacious escape and Jack knew that he was at risk of being rumbled at any moment. Swapping his mud-splattered nightdress for a blood-stained frock and woollen apron, Sheppard left London for Northamptonshire with Page to let the dust settle. After only three days, Jack could no longer tolerate being so far from the pulse of London, let alone from its watches and silver spoons. A cobbler spotted him in Bishopsgate. A milkman raised the alarm around Islington. Soon watchmen were standing guard outside shops, anxious for a glimpse of the living legend. From his headquarters in Old Bailey, opposite Newgate, in what used to be the Blue Boar

20. *Satirical invitation to the execution of Jonathan Wild, self-styled 'Thief-taker General of Britain and Ireland'*

tavern, Jonathan Wild kept his ear to the ground, measuring each reported sighting, biding his time. He'd had a word with Edgworth Bess the day after Sheppard's escape, but she was no longer of any use. Wild was confident, though, that Jack's luck would soon run out and that he would be the person to soak up the credit for his capture when it did.

But this wasn't to be. Across the street, in the prison's lodge, the humiliated Keepers were also keeping track of Sheppard's supposed whereabouts and were determined to rescue their reputations by being the ones to haul him in. On 10 September, reports reached them that two men wearing blue butcher's smocks had been seen swaggering through the markets around Finchley Common. A posse poured out of Newgate where a coach and horses were waiting. Whips cracked and the chase was on. Page was tackled first and a chisel found in his pocket. Jack ducked into a farmhouse but was quickly seized. Two watches were discovered tucked in his armpits.

Wild watched from his window as Jack was dragged from the coach and back into Newgate. He had received false information that morning and had goose-chased Jack to Sturbridge instead. Sheppard was marched past his former residence of the Condemned Hold – its grate, still missing an iron spike, like a gap-toothed grin. He was led through a dank labyrinth of human misery until he reached the central cell of the prison, 'the Castle'. The Keepers were taking no chances this time. Jack's limbs were clamped tight with two sets of heavy shackles as his body was roughly bolted to the floor of the Castle. News of his recapture spread fast and Newgate more than ever became the focus of intense interest – seeming at once the stage and the backstage between which Sheppard shuttled, donning disguises and extemporaneously performing a tragicomic masterpiece. Readers were hungry for every detail of Jack's adventures that could either be uncovered or concocted. 'He has hinted in dark terms,' the *Daily Journal* reported the following morning,

> that he hath committed robberies since his escape, and denies that he was ever married to the woman who assisted him therein, and who is now in the Compter for the same, declaring that he found her a common strumpet in Drury-Lane, and that she hath been the cause of all his misfortunes and misery; he takes great pains to excuse his companion Page of being any ways privy to his crimes, whom he says only generously accompanied him after his escape; he hath promised to clear his conscience as this day, and to be more particular in his confessions, as entertaining no hopes of life.

> This morning a Gentleman goes to Windsor to procure an
> order or warrant for his speedy execution, and 'tis thought that
> the same will be on Monday next.

From the flood of surviving contemporary anecdotes and
press reports devoted to Sheppard that appeared in the weeks
that followed, it is difficult to separate fact from myth. 'More
space,' according to Lucy Moore, 'was devoted to him in
London's newspapers than to any other single news item:
other stories might merit a sentence or a few lines, but there
was always a long paragraph about Jack.' From the moment of
his recapture, the Castle became a kind of peepshow for an
endless procession of priests and reporters desperate to catch
a glimpse of the caged exhibit. By charging admission to it,
the Keepers and turnkeys stood to make a packet. Three
weeks after Jack's re-incarceration, he was discovered strolling
about freely in the Castle cell, having shed his heavy chains,
which lay in a heap beside his bed. Once the fetters were refit-
ted, according to one report, the 'dumbfounded' Keepers
begged Sheppard to reveal how he had managed to free
himself. 'He reached forth his hand, and took up a nail, and
with that, and no other instrument, unlocked himself again
before their faces.'

Jack's real-world resourcefulness was, to many, a refreshing
antidote to abstract promises of other-worldly miracles and
salvation that they saw little evidence for in their everyday lives.
London has often been compared to a prison and so Jack's pre-
dicament inside Newgate, however much of his own making,
must have struck a swathe of society as a metaphor for lives that
they too wished passionately to escape. When a finger-wagging
Reverend Wagstaff visited Jack and asked him whether he
might stop putting his faith in rusty nails and turn his attention
to the scriptures instead, Jack is said to have replied, with envi-
ably irreverent verve, 'Ask me no such Questions; one file's
worth all the Bibles in the world.'

On 14 October 1724 public attention shifted briefly from the man in the Castle to the proceedings against Jack's former accomplice, Blueskin Blake, for his role in robbing William Kneebone. In a scene that today seems difficult to comprehend, before his arraignment, Blueskin – who had been led the short distance from his cell in Newgate to the Old Bailey next door – was allowed to enjoy a glass of wine with his former mentor, Jonathan Wild, outside the court. Hoping that Wild's decision to attend the trial meant that there was still some chance that the thief-taker might help him avoid the fate to which Sheppard had been condemned, Blueskin begged Wild to put in a good word for him with the judge. Since someone was already going to hang for the crime, perhaps Blueskin could be sentenced to transportation instead.

But Wild was still resentful of Blueskin for ever having mixed with the unmanageable and attention-seeking Sheppard. What exactly he said to Blueskin on that windy autumn morning will never be known, but it provoked Blake to produce the penknife that he had concealed in his pocket and slice through the heavy cravat around Wild's neck, leaving the thief-taker spurting blood and gasping for his life. Some insist that Wild had called the defendant 'a dead man' while others suggest that Wild taunted him by describing the Blueskin-shaped coffin that he had been designing.

As Wild was carted off to a nearby surgeon, news of the knifing raised Sheppard's spirits back in the Castle. He had always despised what he regarded as the inherent duplicity of thief-takers such as Wild. 'They hang by proxy,' he once rue-fully quipped, 'while we do it in person.' The near-fatal assault on Wild had whipped the inmates and Keepers inside Newgate into a stir. Blueskin was stapled back into his cell, and for the rest of the night attention was squarely focused on him and his continued ravings. 'I should be hanged with pleasure,' he was overheard seething, 'if Wild did but die before me.' Jack knew that the distraction created by the unfolding drama represented his best chance to operate in peace.

Shaking loose a bent nail that he had managed to hide in the hem of his sleeve, he jimmied the locks on his handcuffs. Having stared long enough at the chain that tethered his leg irons to the bolt in the floor, he had fantasised about how a few aerobic twists of his shins might just loosen the links. It worked. Within minutes he was pacing about his cell. He then prised loose a bar blocking the chimney flue and shoved himself up its sooty throat, dragging the bar with him as a tool. This brought him outside the Red Room, above the Castle. The room had not been entered for seven years, not since the Jacobites had been held in it en masse and executed following the 1715 Rebellion.

The locks presented little challenge to Jack, nor did a series of others on his way to the prison chapel. Finding the chapel door bolted from the inside, Jack rammed the door repeatedly with the crow bar that he had brought with him. Eventually, he had punched a hole large enough for him to slip his slender hand through and he was able to reach in and slide back the bolt. So he went, through door after bolted door without so much as a match to help him see in the darkness, anxiously expecting to hear the clatter of boots galloping after him at any moment. Eventually, Jack found himself standing on the ledge of the Upper Leads of the prison, too high above the roofs below to leap safely.

Teetering precariously on the brink of either freedom or death, Jack Sheppard made one of the most remarkable decisions of his short life. He climbed back inside the prison to retrace his footsteps to the Castle and retrieve the bedclothes from his cell, out of which to fashion a rope. Back down the chimney and up again, trampling broken door handles and bolts as he ran, Jack made it back to the ledge, tied the end of the ripped sheets to a pennant hook and lowered himself down on to the roof of William Bird. The night was strangely still. Jack was free, again.

10

Stag

'**STAG**, *a term (inverting Qualities) used for an Enemy, a Pursuer; as,* I spy a Stag, *used by that notorious young Robber* Shepherd, *lately executed, when he first saw the Turnkey of* Newgate, *who pursu'd and took him after his first escape from the* Condemn'd Hold.'

Throughout London the following morning and for several weeks, there was no other conversation than the apparent miracle that was Jack Sheppard's fourth spectacular prison break in seven months. Fed by front-page reports in all of the newspapers, every alehouse and ragstall rattled with speculation about how Sheppard could have pulled off the impossible. Newgate's warren of cramped corridors and bolted halls suddenly became the blueprint of the nation's imagination. Blacksmiths and cheesemongers who had never set foot inside the ancient gaol fancied themselves experts on the layout of the prison's chapel, the width of its chimneys, and the proximity of the Red Room to the Upper Leads. Cynics speculated that Jack had paid off the prison staff with proceeds from the Kneebone job, while others took a more darkly spiritual view, 'that the devil came in person and assisted him'.

Similar forces would be suspected of being at work twelve years later, when Daniel Malden, a seaman who had resorted to a life of crime after being discharged, managed to escape twice from Newgate. On the first occasion, the evening before

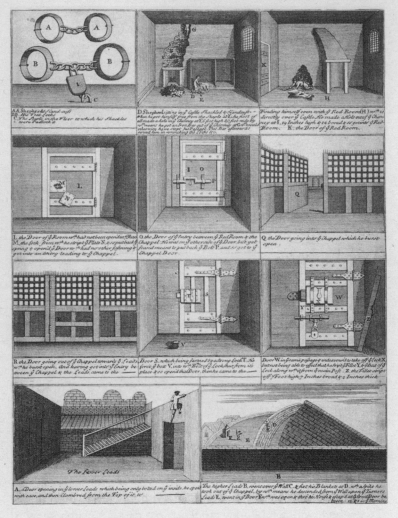

21. *Diagrams illustrating Jack Sheppard's miraculous escape from Newgate adorned many popular broadsheets*

his scheduled execution, Malden had been alerted by a fellow inmate to a loose plank in the floor of their cell. Left alone to contemplate his impending fate, Malden managed to snap the heavy gyves that bound his ankles to the floor, lift the wobbly plank with a broken stool leg, and slip into the empty cell below. From there he took off his shoes and tiptoed through the Press Yard, scaled the wall of the chapel, and inched 'all round the chimneys of the cells over the ordinary's house'. He then crawled in through a garret window, put his shoes back on, wrapped the dangling irons close to his legs as though he were 'gouty or lame', opened the door to Phoenix Court as though he had lived there all his life, 'and from thence' limped 'through the streets to [his] home in Nightingale Lane'.

Caught having tea with his wife in their living room two days later, Malden was brought back to Newgate and lodged in the Condemned Hold. With Sheppard having already exposed the vulnerabilities of the Hold, Malden soon went to work loosening stones in the cell's floor using a pocket-knife supplied by a visitor. Malden eventually removed enough of the stones to slide himself through the gap and drop down into a swampy funnel, which led to The Gaol's sewer. Allegedly dragging a hundred pounds of loose fetters behind him, Malden scraped and squeezed for eight hours through a cramped labyrinth of filth until he emerged in a ditch behind Christ's Hospital school. Malden managed to remain free for three and a half months, but was eventually picked up in Canterbury and escorted back to London 'guarded by about thirty or forty horsemen, the road all the way being lined with spectators'.

On the night of his fourth escape, Sheppard managed to make his way undetected through Holborn to a derelict cowshed in the quiet, open fields that once stretched through what has since become the Tottenham Court Road. Hungry and scared, he persuaded a sympathetic passer-by to fetch him a saw with which he could remove the remnants of the leg irons that were still clamped to his swollen ankles. The challenge now was to remain invisible in a city where he was the topic of every debate. Jack had had varying luck with disguises in the past and he decided that, given his dishevelled state – his unshaved face and tattered clothing – he might convincingly pass as a vaga-bond or beggar. So he went about London, with a soiled hand-kerchief wrapped around his head, the rips in his clothes exaggerated for effect, and feigning a congenital limp. Surreally, he crouched in front of public houses, shaking his woollen hat for donations, while inside raucous toasts to 'Jack Sheppard' were loudly punctuated with the thumping of wooden tank-ards and the rasping of homespun ballads in which he himself figured as the hero.

After two days of drifting, Jack was tired of skulking around the streets and managed to scrounge enough loose change to hire 'a Garrett for my Lodging at a poor House in Newport-Market'. Situated where Shaftesbury Avenue meets Charing Cross Road, near what is now the West End theatre district, Newport Market was a declining meat bazaar in Jack's day and there is something cosmically appropriate about the master disguiser and choreographer of his own stage exits gravitating to this dramatic spot. It was here that Jack was united with his mother, who pleaded with him 'to make the best of [his] way out of the kingdom'. He also had a messenger summon 'a sober young woman' called Kate Cook, whom Jack would later describe as 'the real Mistress of [his] Affections'. Rather than taking the risk of leaving London, Jack masochistically used his hard-won freedom to retrace the footsteps of his past, as if daring the city to take him again. 'I was oftentimes in Spittle-fields,' he would explain of these weeks, 'Drury-lane, Lewkenors-lane, Parkers-lane, St Thomas-Street, &c. those having been the chief Scenes of my Rambles and Pleasures.'

In the small hours of 30 October, Jack Sheppard committed his last robbery. Having abandoned 'a Design to open a Shop or two in Monmouth-street for some Necessaries', he trained his sights on a pawnbroker's in Drury Lane. To create the impression that he was not alone, he shouted instructions to himself to shoot 'through the Head' anyone who might interrupt the burglary as he stuffed his sack full of snuff-boxes and watches, a silk suit and silver sword, diamond rings, a wig, two pistols, and the obligatory pair of engraved spoons. He returned to his shabby garret, pleased with his haul and feeling invincible. The next day, he reached into his bag of loot and produced what would be his final disguise. 'I made an extraordinary Appearance,' Sheppard later boasted. 'From a *Carpenter* and *Butcher* [I] was now transformed into a perfect Gentleman.' It was, after all, Hallowe'en. With his lover, Kate Cook, on one arm, 'and another young woman of her acquaintance' on the other, Jack strode fearlessly back 'into the city, and were very merry together at a publick house not far from the place of [his] old confinement'.

Jack made every effort to call attention to himself. As if the expensive black suit, the precious rings, the gold pocket watch, the snuff-box and the wads of cash he waved at every opportunity weren't ostentatious enough, he slipped over his head a powdered peruke, or periwig – the sort worn by the judge in the Old Bailey whose sentence Sheppard had so far managed to dodge. As the trio slouched from alehouse to alehouse, Jack shouted heartily to all of the familiar faces in his old neighbourhood, who stared back gormlessly as if at an apparition. Having plied themselves generously with liquor, Jack and his companions hailed a hackney coach and clomped tauntingly past Newgate on their way towards Maypole Alley near Clare Market and the Sheers alehouse where they had arranged to meet Sheppard's mother. Three-quarters of a bottle of brandy later and the party was ready to move on to another public house, prowling the streets in their costumes like a band of drunken trick-or-treaters. In all likelihood, Jack did not remember his last hour of freedom as he slurred his way into an establishment that was owned by a constable:

22. *A chalk-and-wash sketch for James Thornhill's now-lost portrait of Jack Sheppard is all that survives*

. . . my Senses were quite overcome with the Quantities and variety of liquors I had all the Day been drinking of, which pav'd the Way for my Fate to meet me; and when apprehended, I do protest, I was altogether incapable of resisting, and scarce knew what they were doing to me, and had but two Second-hand Pistols scarce worth carrying about me.

Howling inanities behind him, Jack was dragged back to Newgate and lodged in a cell opposite 'Ketch's Kitchen', called the Middle Stone Room. As a precaution, a guard was positioned beside him night and day to keep an eye on the prison's most elusive guest. It has been said that hundreds of pounds' worth of irons were gratuitously piled on to his small frame. He could barely move. The extraordinary string of miraculous escapes by Jack Sheppard, the greatest prison-breaker in history, was at an end.

As news of Sheppard's arrest spread across the city, the relief felt by anxious shop-owners was mixed with a palpable sense of disappointment by those who had held out hope that Jack might remain at large for good. After all, as his biographers have pointed out, however obnoxious his thieving was, Sheppard had never physically harmed anyone. The Keepers of Newgate, twice humiliated for allowing Jack to slip through their fingers, knew that they were sitting on a gold mine. With the execution date now set for little more than two weeks hence, they would have to act quickly if they were going to capitalise on the outpouring of sympathy that his recapture had triggered. In the first week alone, we read that well over a thousand visitors were charged the inflated entrance fee of 3s. 6d. each to catch a glimpse of the caged wonder. Sheppard's performances on and off Newgate's insalubrious stage had propelled him and the prison alike into a shared celebrity status without equal in English history. The King's portrait painter, Sir James Thornhill, was granted a private session with Jack. Thornhill was tutor to the young William Hogarth, and would later become his father-in-law. In addition to royal portraits, Thornhill was best known for his decoration of the dome of St Paul's Cathedral, undertaken a few years earlier. Only a chalk-and-wash sketch for his portrait of Sheppard now survives, though it is possible to tell that it, like its subject, had relied principally on misdirection. In it, Sheppard's body leans to the viewer's right, in the same direction that his cuffed hands are pointing, while his eyes stare off to our left, where a barred window lets in sheets of light. The effect is strangely moving, in every sense. It is thought that Hogarth later cashed in on the public's affection for his father-in-law's likeness of Jack by using it as the basis for his depiction of Tom Idle in his popular picture-drama *Industry and Idleness*, which was 'calculated', Hogarth said, 'for the use and instruction of youth'.

On 11 November 1724, Sheppard was transferred from the Middle Stone Room, back to the Condemned Hold. The grate through which he had escaped on 31 August had since been repaired and a watchman was positioned outside the door. Until that morning, Jack's former colleague Joseph Blueskin

Blake had been resident there. Blueskin had been trundled off to Tyburn hours earlier, reaching the gallows roaring drunk and professing remorse for only one thing in his life – that he had failed to kill Jonathan Wild when he had had the chance. In the space of a few short months, the jaws of Newgate had ripped from Jack's life many of those who were closest to him. Blueskin was dead, William Page was awaiting trial for his role in abetting Sheppard, and his brother Tom, just weeks earlier, had been led out of The Gaol's doors and transported to Maryland for his role in some of Jack's first burglaries. The day before, 10 November, Jack had been escorted back into court at the Old Bailey and offered the opportunity to dodge the gallows altogether in exchange for divulging the names of those with whom he had operated, both during his robberies and his escapes. Jack refused to co-operate and took umbrage at the suggestion that his prison breaks were in any way staged. His only help, he exclaimed to gasps of horror from the bench, had come from God. Such sacrilege was the final straw. Jack Sheppard was going to die.

Monday, 16 November 1724 was a day unlike any before or since in London. Execution days, or 'hanging matches' as they were sometimes called, often attracted large crowds to the spots where the gibbets were erected, whether in St Giles, or on Kennington Common, or in Leadenhall. In 1701, tens of thousands of spectators had poured along the soggy banks of Wapping to witness the final throes of the irascible Captain Kidd and before that, in 1664, Pepys had joined a crowd fourteen thousand strong to watch the thief James Turner drag out his hanging with long orations. But Jack Sheppard was different. Though few doubted his involvement in the crimes of which he had stood accused, whole echelons of society had invested his escapes with meaning and hope. By the second quarter of the eighteenth century, between half a million and six hundred thousand people were living in the city, nearly a third of whom either followed the cart that dragged Jack the two and a half miles from Newgate to Tyburn or were waiting for him when he reached the scaffold. It was the largest crowd ever assembled for an execution in London.

A rumour had been circulating for days that Sheppard was planning another escape, which he would attempt somewhere along Holborn or Oxford Street. It was true. Aware that the tradition was merely to tie with rope, and not to cuff with irons, the hands of the condemned as they scudded in the hurdle towards Tyburn, Sheppard had managed even under intense observation to conceal in his coat pocket an open penknife, which he intended to rub his bound wrists against during the two-hour journey. Once his hands were free, and counting on a sympathetic crowd to assist him, Jack intended to leap a turn-stile near Lincoln's Inn Fields, forcing anyone then in pursuit on horseback to dismount. Once it was a man-to-man leg race, Sheppard fancied his chances. But his spirits were severely punctured when, just as the hurdle was about to set off from Newgate, the Under-Sheriff, a man called Watson, suddenly clamped a pair of irons around Sheppard's arms and confiscated the penknife he saw bulging in the prisoner's pocket.

After a brief stop along Oxford Street at a tavern that once stood near where John Lewis's department store stands today, so that the condemned men could be allowed a final drink, the cart carrying Jack Sheppard squeezed its way through the throng that fanned out around Tyburn and came to a halt beside the scaffold. It was a cold, windless autumn day. As he was helped off the hurdle, those who could reached out to brush from his shoulders and legs the soft bright petals that had been thrown at him by little girls in pretty dresses who had lined the procession route. Hopeful that the resuscitation efforts that would inevitably take place immediately after the hanging might actually succeed, Sheppard turned down the opportunity to address the crowd at length and invited those in attendance instead to purchase the pamphlet entitled *A narrative of all the robberies, escapes, &c., of John Sheppard, written by himself and printed by John Applebee of Blackfriars* (1724), which he said contained his final confession and which he stood to profit handsomely from if he were to be revived. Among those congregating at Tyburn were some who could still recall, fifteen years earlier, having witnessed the execution of a former soldier who, recovering after dangling for a full five minutes before a late reprieve was conveyed through the jostling throng, spent the rest of his life answering to the nickname 'Half-hanged Smith'. 'At first he felt great pain,' Smith is said to have related, 'but it gradually subsided, and the last thing he could remember was the appearance of a light in his eyes, after which he became quite insensible. But the greatest pain was when he felt the blood returning to its former channels.'

By all accounts Sheppard was calm when the horse's flank was slapped and the cart pulled away, leaving his body dangling from the noose that tightened around his throat. For those nearest the gibbet, who had waited the longest to witness the appalling event, Jack's writhing was intolerable to behold. Several standing by grabbed his short legs, dripping with urine, and began tugging violently at his convulsing body, hoping to snap his spine and hasten the end. When it finally came, a driver who had been asked by the publisher of Sheppard's memoir, John Applebee, to whisk the body away to where warm blankets and rehabilitating ablutions could be applied, reached his hand out to claim the gyrating corpse. However, he was mistaken by the crowd for a resurrectionist bent on seizing the corpse for dissection in the Surgeons' Hall and was mobbed while Sheppard's body bounced from shoulder to shoulder, with everyone eager to touch the skin of the dead, which was commonly thought to have healing powers. When the chaos finally subsided, the now stretched and juggled remains of Jack Sheppard were bundled off to the Barley Mow tavern in Long Acre, where he presided over a night of heavy drinking. From there, the corpse was carried off to the churchyard of St Martin-in-the-Fields, which once spread beside present-day

Trafalgar Square. There were rumours that Jack was buried clutching a pair of tarnished silver spoons.

Sheppard's execution was a spectacle that attracted people from every walk of life, though for most Londoners it was the first time that they had ever laid eyes on the famous criminal. There was, however, one individual who had met Jack before and who was instrumental in bringing the hanging about, but whose face was almost certainly not to be found among those jostling for position at the foot of the scaffold. That was Jonathan Wild. Blueskin Blake's assault on Wild outside the Old Bailey a month earlier had brought the notorious thief-taker to within an inch of his life, and some have speculated that he never fully recovered, either physically or psychologically, from the audacious knifing. But even if he had been fit enough to attend, it is unlikely that Wild would have risked being seen by a crowd most of whom he knew, held him responsible for having Sheppard convicted for the Kneebone robbery by suborning the testimony of William Field. By aggressively pursuing Sheppard, who had denounced the duplicity of thief-takers, Wild had hoped to quash the man he feared might emerge as a charismatic rival for control over the London underworld. But his heavy-handedness had backfired, and in a real sense the death of Jack Sheppard spelled the end of Jonathan Wild.

From the moment that Blueskin dragged his knife across Wild's throat, balladeers began composing vivid libretti for the fiery opera that was unfolding around Newgate:

> When to the *Old-Bailey* this *Blueskin* was led,
> He held up his Hand, his Indictment was read,
> Loud rattled his Chains, near him *Jonathan* stood,
> For full Forty Pounds was the Price of his Blood.
>> Then hopeless of Life,
>> He drew his Penknife,
>> And made a sad Widow of *Jonathan*'s Wife.
> But Forty Pounds paid her, her Grief shall appease,
> And every Man round me may rob, if he please.

Wild's stranglehold on the criminal ranks of London was slipping. Where once the authorities were prepared to look the other way – however glaring Wild's involvement in vice might have been – provided he continued to supply the courts with plausible defendants, following Sheppard's death in November 1724 the once untouchable thief-taker became the object of relentless scrutiny. On 15 February 1725 Jonathan Wild was arrested and committed to Newgate Prison. He was charged with having assisted a one-time forger by the name of Roger Johnson in evading a constable who possessed a warrant for Johnson's arrest. Johnson was the captain of a secret vessel that Wild used to ferry stolen goods from England to Flanders. Fearing that once the authorities began snooping around Johnson's affairs, it would not be long before he too would be implicated in wrongdoing, Wild helped Johnson slip out of the back door of an alehouse where he had been detained, by starting a fistfight with the constable.

Once Wild was put in Newgate, a 'Warrant of Detainder' was issued against him, which would give the court the time it needed to begin unravelling the complex criminal web that he had been weaving for over a decade. The warrant itemised a dozen crimes for which Wild was now under investigation, and accused him of having established 'a kind of Corporation of Thieves of which he was the head or director'. These were vague charges and while everyone knew that they were true, finding prosecutable evidence to ensure a conviction in court was another matter. Wild had always been masterful at covering his tracks and it soon seemed likely that he would be released from gaol without facing trial for any charge. Convinced that he inhabited a privileged sphere in which the tawdry laws that ensnared others did not apply, Wild contemptuously continued to orchestrate his criminal empire from inside The Gaol.

On 10 March he was visited in his cell by Katherine Stetham, an elderly dealer in fabrics. Stetham had met Wild some months earlier, before his arrest, about some fifty yards of lace that had been stolen from her shop. She had relied upon Wild in the past to recover stolen merchandise. On her visit to Newgate, Wild informed the old lady that he had managed to track down the lace and that, if she were prepared to pay ten guineas to a messenger at a place and time to be agreed, she could have it back. While it was common knowledge that fencing stolen property had been the bread-and-butter of Wild's operation, connecting Wild with the robberies them-selves had always proved difficult. Rarely would he take the risk of actually coming into contact with the burgled goods, prefer-ring instead to choreograph transactions from a distance. After the passage of the second Transportation Act in 1718, which made the receiving of stolen goods itself a felony punishable by death, Wild had learned to be especially cautious. Though he had never been charged or convicted under it, the legislation quickly became known as 'the Jonathan Wild Act'. Perhaps it is an indication of how much his game had slipped since being attacked by Blueskin that on this occasion he had foolishly maintained possession of the valuable lace that he had commis-sioned Henry Kelly and Margaret Murphy to steal.

When Wild was brought to trial at the Old Bailey on 15 May, Kelly and Murphy provided the most damning evidence by rehearsing before the bench Wild's own words. 'In January last I went to see Mrs Johnston,' Kelly explained to the court:

who then lived at the Prisoner's House: Her Husband brought me over from Ireland; upon which Account I wanted to speak with her. I found her at home, and we drank a Quartern of Holland's Gin together. By and by in comes Mrs Murphy with a Pair of Brocaded Shoos and Clogs, and makes a Present of them to Mrs Wilde. The Prisoner was in Company. We drank two or three Quarterns more, and then I and Mrs Murphy got up to go away together. The Prisoner ask'd me which way I was going? I told him to my Lodgings at the Seven Dials. I suppose you go Holborn Way, says he. We answer'd, Yes. Why then, says

he, I'll tell ye what; – There's an old Blind Bitch that sells fine
Flanders Lace just by Holborn-Bridge; her Daughter is as blind
as herself; and if ye call there, you may speak with a Box of Lace,
(that is, steal a Box) – I'll go along with ye, and shew ye the
Door. So the Prisoner and I and Murphy went together, till we
came within Sight of the Door: He pointed and shew'd us
which it was, and said he would wait for us, and bring us off,
if any Disturbance should happen.

Sensing the direction in which the jury's sympathy was now
drifting, Wild attempted to ingratiate himself with the court by
producing a roster that he had compiled the previous night of
all the highwaymen, burglars and transportees he had either
delivered to the court or testified against. It was a pathetic ploy,
which many read as a shopping list of cruelty and hypocrisy. It
took the jury only thirty minutes to find Wild guilty of violating the law prohibiting the handling of stolen goods, which had
colloquially been christened after him. Less than a year after
promising to fit Blueskin Blake for a coffin, Jonathan Wild, 'the
Thief-taker General of Great Britain and Ireland', was being
measured for his own.

Wild's last few nights in Newgate were ghastly. His wife's
messy attempt to hang herself had failed, as had his appeal to the
King for a pardon. Doubled over with gout and harassed if ever
he set foot inside the prison chapel to pray, Wild attempted to
cheat the hangman by flooding his system with a large dose of
laudanum. Though he vomited up most of what he had swallowed, enough had sunk in to render him all but catatonic for
the jerky cart ride to Tyburn. There was some mercy in that.
The triumphant cheers with which Sheppard had been greeted
by the crowd had now curdled into vicious caterwauls. In place
of the flower petals that had drifted down on Jack from the
hands of little girls, like confetti on a returning hero, rocks and
excrement hailed from the fists of enraged women and men.
Not since the quartering of Guy Fawkes over a century earlier
had the city revelled so bloodthirstily in an execution.

Elaborate invitations were circulated on which the figure of Death, in the shape of a skeleton leaning on a spade, draws back the curtains of a stage to reveal a coffin and the words 'To all Thieves, Whores, Pick-pockets, Family Fellows &c. in Great Brittain & Ireland, Gentlemen & Ladies, You are hereby desir'd to accompany yr worthy friend ye Pious Mr I— W—d from his Seat at Whittingtons Colledge to ye Tripple Tree, where he's to make his last Exit . . .' There wasn't much left of Jonathan Wild, mentally or physically, by the time the hurdle finally reached Tyburn. The projectiles that had battered the night-dress that had been slipped over Wild's head before setting off from Newgate had left him cut and bleeding and gibbering nonsense. Though he was initially told to wait his turn behind a pair of highwaymen and a coiner called Robert Harpham, the crowd demanded that Wild be brought to the front of the queue. Having endured the thief-taker's puppet-mastering of crime and punishment for so long, few were willing to wait even another minute to see his string pulled. Though the hangman had already started on Harpham, he began to sense a riot brewing and cut the coiner down before he had finished. He then grabbed a new piece of rope and went to work on Wild.

The death of Jonathan Wild brought the curtain down on an astonishing drama starring a larger-than-life cast of characters whose very names look forward to delicious Dickensian inventions – from Blueskin Blake to William Kneebone, from Edgworth Bess to Hell-and-Fury Sykes. It is not surprising that to many contemporary writers, poets and bawdy balladeers, the unfolding events constituted a real-life morality play that was too compelling to resist. Within hours of their executions, salacious pamphlets documenting the careers and alleged confessions of Jack Sheppard and Jonathan Wild were being flogged from every street corner. Just two weeks after Sheppard's hanging, a play entitled *Harlequin Sheppard; A Night Scene in Grotesque Characters*, composed by a dancing instructor called

John Thurmond, was performed at the Theatre Royal in Drury Lane, yards from where Jack had turned his back on Owen Wood's apprenticeship to pursue a life of crime. *Harlequin Sheppard* was a bizarre balletic reconstruction of Jack's final and most athletic escape from Newgate and the playbill proudly promised 'Scenes Painted from the Real Places of Action'. The actor who impersonated Sheppard made every effort to research the role and when he visited Jack in Newgate days before his execution, the condemned housebreaker is said to have quipped from under a mound of irons, 'I should be glad to have it in my power to play my own part.'

Having performed so many miracles before his execution, it is not surprising that there was a great hunger for stories of Sheppard's resurrection. Rumours began to circulate that an ingenious body-swap had been engineered amid the clamour on the scaffold, and that Sheppard had somehow managed to slip away. In the months after the hanging, a pamphlet was published, purporting to be by Sheppard himself, extending his extraordinary adventures into the afterworld: *Sheppard in Ægypt, or news from the dead.* 'Dear Sir,' the work opens,

> Notwithstanding the great Care and Pains, taken by your self, and my Confessor, here I am: Though 'tis no more than I expected; after I found the last Effort discover'd, and prevented by the plaguy Hand-cuffs. However, I acknowledge my self much oblig'd, to those Hearty Cocks, who waited at the Turn-stile for me with their Truncheons, and likewise to Houssare for his Pen-knife, though it prov'd as useless to my Purpose as Blueskin's did. My Thanks and a good Fortune attend the kind Soldier, who with his broad Sword, did so expeditiously fever me from the Gallows.

At first, the reader is teased into thinking that perhaps the narrator has cheated death and managed to sneak away from Tyburn and the confines of London. Soon, however, it becomes clear that the Sheppard of the pamphlet is on a journey in the hereafter. 'New and strange Objects, appear'd every Moment to my View; and I found that I had nothing of a real Substance left.' Sheppard is then ferried across the River Styx by a boatman 'far more dreadful to behold than a Keeper of Newgate'. Eventually, he is brought to a hell-like realm where an endless procession of murderers and highwaymen and housebreakers pay homage to him – a realm for which Newgate has satirically served as the preposterous prototype.

> A Legion of Limners and Sculptors, had environ'd me in an Instant, all of them fell to nibbling at my Phyz, with their Pencils, which made me incline to believe, I had gotten back into the Middle-Stone-Room of Newgate.

In the popular imagination of early-eighteenth-century London, hell has been re-imagined as a place of crass celebrity where one's condemned 'Phyz' is sketched and sculpted before being dragged down a road and snapped with a rope – a place which in every respect resembles Newgate Prison.

Foremost among those who had squeezed their pens to satisfy the public's insatiable appetite was the veteran novelist Daniel Defoe, author of *Robinson Crusoe* (1719), whose first-hand biographical sketches of the celebrated prison-breaker and notorious thief-taker – *A narrative of all the robberies, escapes, &c. of John Sheppard* (1724) and *The true and genuine account of the life and actions of Jonathan Wild from his birth to his death* (1725) – were hurried into press to meet the extraordinary demand. Defoe had well over three hundred titles to his name by the time that Sheppard filed his first fetter. His long interviews with the escapologist in Newgate awakened memories of his own stint inside The Gaol. Defoe had been committed to Newgate in 1703 after publishing a satirical tract entitled *The shortest way with the dissenters* – a mock sermon that lampooned intolerant High Church attitudes. Although Defoe counted himself among those whose opinions he was poking fun at, such irony was lost on the newly crowned Queen Anne, who took

23. *Daniel Defoe in the pillory at Temple Bar for sedition.*
The adoring crowd spared him from abuse

umbrage at the satire and had Defoe arrested for sedition. He
was sentenced to three sessions in the pillory and to however
long in Newgate that it took to secure from him a bond against
subsequent wrongdoing.

Before the heavy wooden yoke of the stocks could be
clamped around the novelist's neck and raised wrists, Defoe had
prepared a charming 'Hymn to the Pillory', which was distrib-
uted among the gathering mob. Suggesting that the author
had been 'an Example made / To make Men of their Honesty
afraid', the hymn won over the members of the crowd who
swapped their projectiles for garlands of flowers, which were
adoringly draped around Defoe. His experience in Newgate,
however, was considerably less fragrant. Years later, around the
time that Sheppard first met Edgworth Bess in Lewkenor Lane,
this inspired him to write one of the works for which his name
is still remembered, *Moll Flanders*. The novel was published
under a pseudonym in order to bolster the impression that it was
an authentic journal chronicling the triumphs and tribulations

of a woman who was born inside the prison. ''Tis impossible to describe the terror of my mind when I was first brought in,' Defoe has Moll confess,

> and when I looked around upon all the horrors of that dismal place, I looked on myself as lost, and that I had nothing to think of but of going out of the world, and that with the utmost infamy, the hellish noise, the roaring, swearing, and clamour, the stench and nastiness, and all the dreadful crowd of afflicting things that I saw there, joined together to make the place seem an emblem of hell itself, and a kind of an entrance into it.

For Defoe, Newgate was a fascinating moral stage. Through animating the lives of Sheppard and Wild, he hoped to sound a warning about the tragic consequences of following a life of crime. It is for this reason that he objected to the glamorising of criminals in what became by far the most popular work to be based on The Gaol ever written, John Gay's *The Beggar's Opera*. Gay's masterpiece ran to a remarkable sixty-two performances in its first season. Taking a comic swipe at aristocratic tastes in Italian opera, the story seeks also to lampoon the Prime Minister, Robert Walpole, whose alleged corruption had often been likened in the press to the affairs of the underworld. In Gay's work the central character is a jaunty highwayman called Macheath – a clever farrago of celebrated felons, from Jack 'Mulled Sack' Cottington to Jack Sheppard – while Macheath's nemesis, Mr Peachum, was presumed to have been based on Jonathan Wild.

Gay had begun thinking about transforming the persona of Wild into a stage character almost a decade earlier, when he first met the thief-taker at the races. This coalesced with a comment made by Jonathan Swift a few years earlier to their mutual friend Alexander Pope about the possibility of composing 'a Newgate pastoral among the thieves and whores there'. Gay began work on the project in 1726 and made frequent visits to Newgate in order, he said, to create an authentic atmosphere. When Gay informed Swift that he had finished a draft of the work, which he had initially entitled 'The Newgate Opera', Swift advised him to be careful not to squander whatever modest proceeds he might make. 'I beg you will be thrifty,' he told Gay, 'and learn to value a shilling'. He persuaded his friend John Rich to produce the opera and the German composer Johann Christoph Pepusch to arrange the music. *The Beggar's Opera* opened on 29 January 1728 at Rich's Lincoln's Inn Fields Theatre. It was a runaway sensation. The role of Peachum's daughter, Polly, was played by an enchanting 19-year-old, Lavinia Fenton, who was quickly hailed as the most beautiful girl in London. Before long she was the Duke of Bolton's mistress and later his wife. *Beggar*-crazed memorabilia – from fire screens to fans – flew off the shelves.

After three years, Gay had pocketed somewhere between three and four thousand pounds, more than enough to justify the quip that the opera had made 'Gay rich and Rich gay'. *The Beggar's Opera* became the most successful theatrical work of its time and continued to be produced annually, without exception, for over a century and a half. At a mid-week performance in April 1782, a Mrs Fitzherbert began laughing uncontrollably when the popular actor John Bannister burst on to the stage in drag playing Polly, and had to be escorted from the theatre after having infected the entire audience with the giggles. She continued to laugh outside the Theatre Royal and for the rest of the evening. After two days of non-stop laughter, Mrs Fitzherbert died.

Not everyone, however, was so amused by Gay's outlandish success. The crowds queuing up outside Rich's theatre for the first run of *The Beggar's Opera* were siphoning off support for competing productions the very titles of which have faded like thin applause into the empty concert hall of history. In Drury Lane, a hapless 20-year-old dramatist, who had been hoping to attract some notice with his debut comedy, *Love in Several Masques*, was among those who suffered from the competition.

Gay's masterwork had sucked all the available air out of the London theatre scene, sending the bruised playwright, a young man by the name of Henry Fielding – the future literary giant and pioneering magistrate – off to Leiden to study literature instead. Years later, when Fielding tried his hand at writing fiction, Gay's agility in transposing the salacious story of Jonathan Wild into an independent work was foremost in his mind. Though not the first novel that he published, *The History of the life of the late Mr Jonathan Wild the great* is very likely the first that Fielding worked on.

Like Gay, Fielding saw in Wild an archetype of political corruption and used the criminal legend as an allegory for lampooning the retiring novelist Horace Walpole. By then, Fielding had developed a reputation as an acerbic stage satirist, taking aim at the Prime Minister in such plays as *Tom Thumb* (1730) and *The Covent Garden Tragedy* (1732). Along with *The Beggar's Opera*, these works provoked Walpole to devise ways of clamping down on subversive performances, resulting eventually in the Theatrical Licensing Act of 1737, which made all productions subject to the approval of the government. Fielding's greatest literary achievement, however, would come some six years after the publication of *Jonathan Wild*, with the appearance of *Tom Jones*, a work often heralded as a landmark in the birth of modern fiction. That same year, 1749 – and also at the hand of Fielding – marked the inception of another great English institution: the police.

Just as the first edition of the six-volume *Tom Jones* was enthralling the reading public in early 1749, Fielding, a trained lawyer and ambitious prosecutor, was skilfully manoeuvring his way through the complicated echelons of judicial power in Middlesex, whose jurisdiction still included Newgate Gaol. In a matter of months, Fielding found himself promoted from the duty-less appointment of 'high steward of the New Forest' to chief magistrate of metropolitan London. Devoting himself to the challenges of his new role, Fielding resolved to reform the climate in which the disciples of Jonathan Wild continued to control the streets of London. From his office in Bow Street, Covent Garden, Fielding marshalled a team of professional agents committed to enforcing public order. Called 'Runners', the squad aimed to eliminate the loose network of thief-takers who, by playing both ends against the middle, had control of both. After Fielding's death from dropsy five years later, the responsibilities of the legendary Bow Street Runners – now generally regarded as the first police force in Britain – were professionalised by the magistrate's brother, John, whose diminished eyesight and alleged ability to sense a man's guilt or innocence merely from the sound of his voice, earned Sir John Fielding the nickname 'the Blind Beak of Bow Street'.

Though the friction between the charismatic characters of Jack Sheppard and Jonathan Wild may only have lasted a matter of months in 1724, the clash ignited a cultural blaze the flames of which would continue to lick at London's imagination long after Newgate itself had disappeared.

Snaffle

'*To* SNAFFLE, *to steal, to rob, to purloin. A* Snaffler *of* Prancers*; a* Horse-stealer*.* Snaffle*, is also a Highwayman that has got Booty.*'

It takes roughly ten minutes to walk from where the church of St-Giles-in-the-Fields sits at the junction of Charing Cross Road and New Oxford Street to where jugglers and mimes work the bustling piazza in front of St Paul's Church in Covent Garden. Though it is but a short stroll – past the posh perfumeries and smart shoe shops of Neal's Yard, the cafés and Balti houses of Seven Dials – in London terms the walk bridges the murky divide between fact and fiction. Under the foot-worn marble slabs that line the elegant nave of St Paul's Church lie the imagined remains of Claude Duval, the flamboyant seventeenth-century footpad who helped mould the archetype of the dashing English highwayman on which John Gay's comic invention Macheath depended. Meanwhile, back in St Giles, under an unmarked patch of turf, are deposited the real though unremembered bones of Claude's historical alter ego, 'Peter de Val' – a less gallant thief, perhaps, and one whose life story will doubtless remain buried forever under a smooth slab of myth.

The Duval who swaggers down the centuries to us, whose 'debonair' demeanour was as devastating as his blunderbuss, is stitched together from a collection of unreliable and often contradictory sketches and poems published just after the celebrated

thief's execution in 1670. Few of these pamphlets agree even
on what his first name was: this is variously given as 'Peter' or
'Lewis' or 'Claude'. To further complicate matters, Duval is said
sometimes to have assumed the blasé alias 'John Brown'. Some
early obituarists had it that Duval was born in Normandy to
well-to-do parents in 1643, while others claimed that he started
life a world away in the rather less salubrious Smock-Alley,
Bishopsgate, the son of a cook who 'sold boil'd Beef and
Pottage' on the side. There is talk too, in early English pamphlets from the period, of a 'scabby' 'Bawdy-house' in Paris,
where he is said to have 'run errants', and it is easy to see how
some biographers, such as Barbara White, have come to regard
these publications more as 'extended satires on French manners'
than reliable records. What is clear is that by the time Charles
II returned to the throne in 1660, a man, if not French himself,
at least of French extraction, and roughly answering to the
name of 'Duval' or 'Du Vall', was living in England sharping
cards, seducing women and unburdening unwary travellers of
their watches and gold rings on the empty heaths around
London.

To the legend of Duval were attached picaresque tales of
ingenious robberies involving everything from elaborate disguises to alchemical quackery. What seems to have qualified an
anecdote for inclusion in the growing canon was evidence of
the extraordinary chivalry and panache in some of the crimes
he pulled off. A favourite one among pamphleteers in the 1670s
was an incident on Blackheath, that windswept stretch to the
south-east of London where Wat Tyler's forces had once gathered and a regular haunt of Duval and his bandits. Having heard
rumours that a passing lady's coach was transporting £400 in
cash, Duval's 'squadron', so the pamphlets put it, set its sights
on intercepting the booty. Whether to calm her own nerves or
to demonstrate to the half-masked hijackers her refusal to be
intimidated, the lady unsheathed a seven-finger flageolet, a
kind of slender recorder, and began whistling through it defi-

*24. A likeness of the debonaire 'footpad' Claude Duval,
from a colourful contemporary portrait,* Devol's last farewel:
containing an account of many frolicksom intreigues
[sic] and notorius robbers which he committed:
concluding with his mournful lamentation, on the
day of his death *(1670).*

antly. Rather than asserting his control over the proceedings,
Duval is said to have ridden up to the lady's window, produced
a 'fipple flute' of his own, and joined her in an impromptu
duet.

What allegedly followed embossed itself so firmly on the
English imagination that two hundred years later it was still
providing inspiration for nineteenth-century artists, most
notably William Powell Frith, whose impressive painting
Claude Duval (1860) is among his most accomplished works. In
it, the mesmerised lady, leaving her instrument behind, has
been helped down from her carriage to the scraggly heath to
dance in her white silk slippers a French courante with the
dashing Duval, while her serving maid, overtaken by the
excitement, faints in the background. When the dance is over,

Duval is said to have turned to the dumbfounded knight who had escorted the coach to request a donation to the afternoon's entertainment. Charmed by the highwayman's refined manners, the knight responded by reaching into a leather satchel and producing one hundred pounds. Though Duval was aware that four times that amount was there for the taking, he was nevertheless impressed by the gentleman's generosity. Not wishing to spoil the convivial atmosphere that the music and dancing had created, the refined footpad cordially responded, 'Sir, you are liberal, and shall have no cause to repent your being so; this liberality of yours shall excuse you the other Three Hundred Pounds.'

By the late 1660s, White says, Duval was the most celebrated and, according to the *London Gazette*, most wanted highwayman in England. Advertisements offering £20 for his arrest began appearing in the press, only adding to the accelerating notoriety. As one by one his band was seized and sentenced at the King's Bench by Judge William Morton, who prided himself on the number of footpads he had hanged, the noose slowly began to tighten around Duval's neck. On Christmas Eve, 1669, he was spotted by a bailiff in the Hole-in-the-Wall tavern in Chandos Place, Covent Garden, so drunk as to render meaningless the sword and three pistols that dangled at his side. Committed to Newgate, Duval was convicted of six charges of robbery at the Old Bailey on 17 January, and returned to his gaol cell to await execution. According to Walter Pope's spirited sketch *The memoires of Monsieur Du Vall: containing the history of his life and death* (1670), the news of Duval's condemnation wrenched the hearts of the many women his manners had seduced:

> There were a great Company of Ladies, and those not of the meanest Degree, that visited him in Prison, interceded for his Pardon, and accompanied him to the Gallows; a Catalogue of whose Names I have by me, nay, even of those who when they visited him, durst not pull off their Vizours for fear of shewing their *Eyes swoln*, and their *Cheeks blubber'd* with *Tears*.

On 21 January, a hurdle bearing Duval's trussed-up body was dragged across London to Tyburn where, from the scaffold, he was permitted to address the heaving crowd of hysterical girls and weeping women who had been waiting in the bitter cold since the previous night.

I Should be very ungrateful (which amongst Persons of Honour, is a greater Crime than that for which I die) should I not acknowledge my Obligation to you, fair *English* Ladies. I could not have hoped that a Person of my *Nation, Birth, Education*, and *Condition*, could have had so many and powerful *Charms*, to *captivate* you all, and to tie you so firmly to my interest; that you have not abandon'd me in *distress* or in *prison*, that you have accompanied me to this place of *Death*, of *Ignominious Death*.

From the Experience of your true *Loves* I speak it; nay I know I speak *your Hearts*, you could be content to die with *me now*, and even *here*, could you be assured of enjoying your beloved *Du Vall* in the other world.

How *mightily* and how *generously* have you rewarded my *little* Services? Shall I ever forget that *universal Consternation* amongst you when I was taken, your *frequent*, your *chargeable Visits* to me at *Newgate*, your *Shreeks*, your *Swoonings* when I was *Condemned*, your *zealous Intercession* and *Importunity* for my *Pardon*? . . .

A 'mourning Coach' was waiting to take Duval's body from Tyburn after it had hanged for the mandatory fifteen minutes. It was whisked away to the Tangier tavern in St-Giles-in-the-Fields, 'where he lay in State all that Night', according to a contemporary chronicler, 'the Room hung with black Cloth, the Hearse cover'd with Scutcheons, eight Wax-Tapers burning, as many tall Gentlemen with long black Clokes attending'. One wants to believe the climax to the tale: that Duval's body was then transferred to the elegant St Paul's Church in Covent Garden, which had been designed by the virtuoso architect Inigo Jones some twenty-five years earlier, and lowered into a space reserved for him in the nave under a marble slab that bore 'the family arms, curiously engraved' and inscribed with the irresistible epitaph:

> Here lies *Du Vall*: Reader, if *Male* thou art,
> Look to thy *Purse*; if *Female*, to thy *Heart*.
> Much havock has he made of both: For all
> *Men* he made *stand*, and *Women* he made *fall*.
> The second Conquerour of the *Norman* Race,
> *Knights* to his *Arms* did yield, and *Ladies* to his *Face*:
> Old *Tiburn*'s Glory, *England*'s Illustrious Thief,
> *Du Vall* the Ladies *Joy*, *Du Vall* the Ladies *Grief*.

Alas, a few hard facts stand in the way of that version of events. While neither gravestone nor record of Duval's interment survive in St Paul's Church – an erasure that one could attribute to the fire that gutted the structure in 1795 – there is, rather more conclusively, an entry in the registry of St-Giles-in-the-Fields (where a few years earlier nearly fourteen hundred plague victims had been buried) of a burial on 22 January, the morning after the Tyburn fair and the sombre lying-in-state, recording the interment in the frosty churchyard, a short walk from the Tangier tavern, of a 'Peter du Val', one of the highwayman's more pedestrian aliases.

A rash of ballads and poems written in the wake of Duval's death, including a popular elegy by the poet Samuel Butler, celebrating Duval's elegant swindling, added to the growing canon of literature glamorising English highwaymen – a tradition that extends back at least as far as the fourteenth-century tales of Robin Hood. For years, every apprehended footpad invoked the name of Duval as a way of ennobling his trade. In 1677, a balladeer hailing the career of the thief Thomas Sadler, a frequent visitor to Newgate, made reference to the 'brisk Du Val that French Latroon / Who put the ladies in a swoon'.

In a very real sense, the history of Newgate Gaol is woven inextricably into the history of the highwayman. It was only after Bishop Mauritius's rebuilding of the cathedral church of

St Paul's in the eleventh century – forcing Londoners to under-take detours around the fortressed city and into the clutches of waiting highwaymen on the periphery – that the need for a fifth gate was recognised. Like the very class of criminal it sought to protect against, Newgate, from the first, operated on the fringes of society. Hovering on the margins of the imagina-tion, The Gaol became England's subliminal theatre and the swashbuckling brigands, with their Venetian masks and care-fully choreographed courantes, the actors who refused to conform to the rules of society.

Among the most colourful characters to haunt the heaths between the era of Robin Hood and that of suave Duval, was a handsome chimney sweep, or 'flue-faker', called John Cottington. The nineteenth, and youngest, child of a humble haberdasher from Cheapside, Cottington's preference for spiced white wine earned him the appellation 'Mull Sack'. His favourite drinking hole was a public house at No. 1 Fleet Street, between Temple Bar and Middle Temple Lane, called the Devil Tavern. Still harbouring the ghost of Ben Jonson, who once 'held forth' there, this is where Mull Sack fell for a 'noted person' called Aniseed-Water Robin, whom 'he took to be a real woman'. Convinced that his happiness lay with Aniseed-Water, the two courted their way to the chapel in Fleet Prison – 'the common place', according to the contemporary chron-icler Captain Alexander Smith, 'for joining all rogues and whores together'. On their wedding night, Mull Sack discov-ered Aniseed-Water's secret, or in the words of his subsequent biographer:

> he soon found Nature's impotence by reason her redundancy in making the supposed bride both man and woman had, in effect, made the party neither, as having not the strength nor reason of the male, nor the fineness nor the subtlety of the female.

Disorientated, Mull Sack left both Aniseed-Water and his sweep's kit behind and set out on a life of crime. Before long, he was carousing with a notorious quintet of 'women shavers' near Covent Garden, who were so well known for their abusive demeanour towards customers that they inspired a contemporary ballad:

> Did you ever hear the like,
> Or ever hear the fame
> Of five women barbers
> That lived in Drury Lane?

But his association with 'these five termagants' ended when three of them were forced to flee to Barbados and the other two were pilloried after an especially vicious attack during which the group stripped, whipped and shaved bald a girl they suspected of having flirted with one of their husbands. Mull Sack next found himself entangled with the beautiful and promiscuous wife of a merchant in Mark Lane, near the Corn Exchange, who fell fatally ill not long after their affair began. On her death-bed, so the pamphlets reported, she summoned her husband, twelve children, and lover to her side for an extended confession: 'This eldest boy is truly yours,' she explained to her husband, 'no man ever having to do with me until after his birth; but this next to him is such a knight's son; that such a merchant's; that such a nobleman's; that such a doctor's,' and so on until, one by one, her entire family melted away, bewildered by the relentless cuckolding to which she had blithely admitted.

Having been left £120 by his prolific mistress, Mull Sack resolved to fend for himself and soon became a proficient pickpocket, despite an appearance so absurdly ostentatious that it is inconceivable he could have slipped himself unnoticed into any situation. A floppy velvet headpiece with a spray of cascading plumes complemented his long plush garment and embroidered collar, the garter and streamers that hung from his knees, the cape-like pleats of flowing fabric that winged his shoulders, the silk stockings, the boots and spurs that were finished, not with a buckle but with rosettes. Perhaps determined never again, after his experience with Aniseed-Water, to be left wondering what lurks beneath a lady's frock, Mull Sack perfected an adroit ruse whereby he would escort a woman from her carriage to a church or a shop without her ever suspecting that he had managed to negotiate her jumbled garments and unfasten a necklace or gold watch. 'The many various neat tricks Mull-sack played upon Ludgate Hill by making stops of coaches and carts and the money that he and his consorts got there by picking pockets, would have been almost enough to have built St Paul's cathedral.'

Mull Sack's luck nearly ran out after a bungled attempt to rob Oliver Cromwell on Hounslow Heath, and finally did so after a short spell in Germany where he stole £1,500 worth of plate from Charles II, who was then in exile in Cologne. After returning to England in 1659, Mull Sack tried to negotiate immunity by claiming to have seized incriminating correspondence from Charles II. The authorities seized the flamboyant sweep at the Devil Tavern. He was sent to Newgate before being shuffled up Giltspur Street to Smithfield, where his plumes were plucked for good.

Though Charles II may have fallen victim to Mull Sack's sleight of hand, his relationship with highwaymen may not always have been altogether negative. In the second half of the seventeenth century, a legend grew around the bespoke figure of Captain James Hind – a Royalist soldier with a peculiar penchant for pinching – that he had helped hide the fugitive King. In 1651 a broadside appeared with a title that removes the need to quote from the work itself: *Another victory in Lancashire obtained against the Scots by Major General Harrison, and Collonel Lilburn. With, the taking of Lievt. Gen. David Lesly, Maj. Gen. Middleton, and other eminent officers and commanders, with six hundred private souldiers, horse and arms; and a list of the particulars. Also, the death of Maj. Gen. Massey and Duke Hamilton, and the Scots Kings going with Hind the great robber.*

When he wasn't 'sculking about' with the Scots King, Hind was busy prowling the outer-lying heaths of the city. His attempted robberies displayed a quick-wittedness that earned him many admirers. During one incident in the wooded Enfield Chase, the unlucky victim appealed to what he hoped might be a latent religious sensibility lurking somewhere inside Hind, saying, 'The eighth commandment commands that you should not steal; besides, it is said by Solomon, Rob not the Poor, because he is poor.' Not to be out-quoted, Hind is said to have replied, 'Pray Sir, make no reflections on my profession, when Solomon plainly says, "Do not despise a thief."' Therefore deliver your money at once, or else I shall send you out of the world in a moment.' Rumours of such exchanges were capitalised on by enterprising pamphleteers who produced such picaresque titles as *No jest like a true iest being a compendious record of the merry life and mad exploits of Captain James Hind the great robber of England (1670)* and *An excellent comedy, called, The Prince of Priggs revels: or, The practises of that grand thief Captain James Hind, relating divers of his pranks and exploits, never heretofore published by any* – a work that was scarcely out of print from 1651 until the nineteenth century.

In November 1651, Hind was finally apprehended and lodged in Newgate to await trial at the Old Bailey. Again, the queues of impatient visitors, eager to catch a glimpse of the gentleman highwayman with royal connections, helped line the pockets of the Keepers and encourage broadsheet hacks to continue spinning ever taller tales of the captain's adventures and capture. The pithily titled *The True and perfect relation of the taking of Captain James Hind: on Sabbath-Day last in the evening at a barbers house in the Strand neer Clements Church. With the manner how he was discovered and apprehended: his examination before the Councel of State; and his confession touching the King of Scots. Also, an order from the Councel of State concerning the said Captain Hind; the bringing of him down to Newgate (yesterday) in a coach; and his declaration and speech delivered in prison* was quickly followed by

25. James Hind, Royalist soldier and highwayman

*The declaration of Captain James Hind (close prisoner in New-gate)
and his acknowledgment, protestation, and full confession at his examination before the Councel of State, on the 10. of this instant Novemb.
1651.* More than one pamphlet boasted exclusive publication of
Hind's 'real portraiture' and 'actual words'.

Hind was eventually executed for treason in Worcester in
September 1652, after having been dragged back and forth
between Reading and Newgate while the authorities worked
on a fail-safe strategy for prosecuting him that would guarantee he would never be released as a Royalist hero. Hind's
brutal dismemberment after hanging did little to ease the
appetite for stories of the captain's supposed exploits. Invariably,
the pamphlets were obsessed with the highwayman's elaborate
costumes. One work, entitled *A pill to purge melancholy: or
merry newes from Newgate*, promised in its subtitle fresh instal-
ments of the masquerade ball for which the prison had
become a kind of backstage changing room: *How Hind, putting
on a bears skin, attempted to rob a committeeman at Oxford of 200
l. and how he had like to have been worried by a mastiff dog ... How
Hind disguising himself in womens apparel, gul'd an old lawyer in*

the temple of 14 l. shewing him such a trick in the law, that he never knew before.

In the end it was Hind's politics (his allegiance to the future King) rather than his glamorous robberies that cost him his life. It would be another forty years before a highwayman's political and criminal personas were in such colourful competition for regard. On New Year's Eve 1692, James Whitney – a Jacobite conspirator and notorious highwayman – was betrayed by the owner of a whorehouse off the Strand, where he regularly roughed up staff. A mob gathered outside Madam Cosen's in Milford Lane to tackle the former butcher as he tucked in his shirt-tails, and pack him off to Newgate. In spite of offers to name his comrades in exchange for a pardon, on 16 January 1693 Whitney was sentenced at the Old Bailey to hang at Tyburn the following week.

Defying the gravity of his situation, Whitney was curiously relaxed in the intervening days, summoning a well-known tailor to the Condemned Hold where taking his leg measurements was hampered somewhat by the forty-pound leg irons that anchored him to the floor. While he was being fitted frivolously for a plush 'embroidered suit with perug and hatt', which 'the Keeper refused to let him wear', Whitney began rehearsing in his head the letter that he would address to Chief Justice Holt, confessing to having been party to an elaborate plot to assassinate William III. The conspiracy was still moving forward, Whitney claimed in the urgent missive that he passed to Lord Capell on the morning that he was scheduled to die, and it involved some eleven other Jacobites whose identities he was prepared to reveal to the Crown should a pardon be granted. As the hurdle bearing the exquisitely turned-out footpad lurched its way over Snow Hill and down Holborn, hurtling towards Tyburn, Lord Capell raced to find Chief Justice Holt and present him with the convict's extraordinary confession. Whitney had already ascended the scaffold, addressed the large crowd that had been waiting to catch a glimpse of the famous 'jacobite robber', and had the coarse fibres of the noose cinched tight against his Adam's apple when the exhausted messenger shoved his way through the throng to the foot of the Triple Tree, waving a sheet of parchment, and presented the hangman with Whitney's royal reprieve.

As Whitney clambered back on board the lurch, a severed hoop of rope still drooping from his neck, many in attendance felt hard done by, having given up part of their day to attend the aborted spectacle, and began hurling rocks and discarded apple cores at the hurdle as it disappeared towards Whitehall. During an inquisition conducted by a syndicate of the King's private counsellors, Whitney refused to shed any more light on the alleged plot without first being promised an outright pardon. After four days of questioning, the authorities decided that his story was little more than a desperate scheme. Rather than dignify him by dedicating another full Tyburn fair to his fate, the arrangements for which took days, on 1 February 1693 Whitney was instead shuffled the short distance up Giltspur Street to Smithfield. A makeshift gallows had been erected in front of the butcher's shop where he was once apprenticed. And so, in front of his former friends, 'he was tumbled out of this world into another'.

Whitney knew that reported rumours of an assassination plot would buy him, at most, a few extra days to flounce around his cell in his embroidered suit. As one scours the thousands of pamphlets published at the end of the seventeenth century and throughout the eighteenth, devoted to the final actions and words of condemned footpads, it is impossible not to be struck by the carnivalesque absurdity of human behaviour when facing the prospect of oblivion. In the summer of 1722, an Irishman called James Carrick was wrestled to the ground outside a tavern in Lincoln's Inn Fields by the dog of a man he had tried to rob moments before around the corner in Little Queen Street. Already sporting a brand on his thumb for stealing a sword a year earlier, Carrick was caught the following day in a 'slop shop' trying to buy an expensive suit with the proceeds from the gold 'repeating' watch, crystal snuff-box and 'silver hilted sword' he had recently pawned. Carrick's vanity and frivolousness is what stuck most in the minds of subsequent pamphleteers. 'He signaliz'd himself,' so one sketch reported,

> by several Engagements with the Spanish Ladies of Pleasure, and was not a little proud of his Success; for he fancy'd every Surrender was a Proof of his own irresistible Charms. He was, indeed, a brisk young Fellow, and well shap'd; but his Stature was a little below a middle Size, and his Complexion pale. The Extent of his Understanding may be guessed at, by the Defence he made at his Trial. He overflow'd with Impertinence, and was so vain of his Person, his Dress, and what he mistook for Gallantry, that it seem'd his chief Ambition to merit the Character of the most petty, gay, smart and dissolute Fellow in the Army. In a Word, he was a Fop, a Coxcomb, and a Rake, and squander'd his Time and his Money in Dressing, Gaming, Drinking, and Whoring.

Broadsheet hacks marvelled at Carrick's unperturbed disposition – his 'foppish Airs' and 'Levity' and 'Unconcern' – as he awaited execution, while the Keepers raked in inflated admission fees for a chance to see the prison's latest celebrity. Recognising that he had 'increas'd the Number of Visitors, and the Profit of the Keepers', Carrick is said to have advised the queues, 'You pay your Money, good Folks, to see me in Newgate, but, if you'll go to Tyburn To-morrow, you may see me for nothing.' James Carrick spent his last hours alive 'with some Whores of his Acquaintance, who were almost continually with him in Newgate'. Not even when he had reached the scaffold at Tyburn did a more sober tone emerge. 'He employ'd that time' instead, according to one account, 'in Giggling, taking Snuff, making Apish Motions to divert himself and the Mob', and after rejecting the overtures of the Ordinary to reflect on the significance of his situation, he adjusted 'the Halter about his Neck' and folded into silence as 'the Cart was drawn away'.

For some highwaymen, the element of disguise went well beyond vanity or fashion to something more existentially defining and unsettling. This was certainly true for William Davis, a farmer from Surrey who, for over forty years until he was caught and hanged in 1689, concealed from everyone his double identity. So complete were Davis's physical transformations that in one instance he was, apparently, able to hold up his landlord, shortly after having handed over £80 worth of rent, and steal back the money without the landlord being any the wiser. Intriguingly, given his penchant for role-playing and dressing-up, Davis would target members of society whom he deemed in some sense to be two-faced. When the Duchess of Albemarle refused to surrender her jewellery during an attempted robbery on Salisbury Plain, Davis is said to have yanked the rings off her fingers, one by one, while admonishing her for her 'painted face': 'You Bitch incarnate, you had rather read over your face in the glass every morning, and blot out pale to put in red, than give an honest man, as I am, a small matter to support him in his lawful occasions on the road.' Not that the duchess was easy to deal with, even under civilised circumstances. Pepys, who dined with her and the duke in November 1666, referred to her as 'Dirty Besse' for her 'nastiness' and 'bad meat'.

If for some, like Davis, the guise of highwayman was a bizarre second nature to which he would routinely revert, for others it was an altogether repressed or undiscovered identity waiting to be expressed. Such was the case with the seemingly successful Irish grocer, James Maclaine, who owned a profitable shop in the newly built Welbeck Street in the 1740s. Described by one recent biographer as 'the black sheep of an otherwise unexceptionable family', little is known of Maclaine's upbringing in Ireland. While there are indications in his past that he would not always take the honourable path in life, such as the time he was dismissed from his position as footman to a Richard Tonson of Dunkettle for taking liberties with his employer's cellar, there is little to suggest that he would emerge as one of the jauntiest footpads of the eighteenth century. But following his wife's sudden death in 1748, Maclaine changed. He abandoned his children to his in-laws and relocated to smarter digs in Dean Street, Soho. After exhausting most of his savings on expensive suits and dubious women, he found himself at the mercy of a charitable scheme arranged by his brother to move him to Jamaica. But on the evening before he was scheduled to depart for the West Indies, Maclaine bought his way into a masquerade ball and embarked on a gambling binge.

Within hours he had lost everything. That evening he made the fateful acquaintance of another luckless cardsharp, a persuasive young apothecary called William Plunkett, who convinced him that his future happiness was to be found not in the West Indies, but in the riches and fame that were there for the taking along the highways and heaths that surrounded the city. For the next eighteen months, armed with a pair of pistols and painted opera masks, the legendary duo Plunkett and Maclaine terrorised the desolate byways in and out of London like caricatures of John Gay's comedic hero, Macheath. 'They agreed upon a Co-partnership,' according to *A complete history of James Maclean, the gentleman highwayman*, published shortly after his execution in October 1750,

> and hired two Horses; Plunket furnishing Pistols, for this was not his first Entrance upon Business of that Kind, and set out the Evening after the Masquerade, to lie in Wait for Passengers coming to Smithfield Market. They met on Hounslow-Heath, with a Grazier, next Morning, between three and four o'Clock, from whom they took, without any Opposition, between sixty and seventy Pounds.
>
> In this, and all other Expeditions of the same Kind, they wore Venetian Masques; but this thin Covering could not stifle Conscience in Maclean, nor animate him to Courage. He accompanied Plunkett it is true, was at the Robbery, but strictly speaking had no Hand in it; for his Fear was so great, that he had not Power to utter a Word, nor draw his Pistol.

By the autumn of 1749, Maclaine had overcome his initial nerves and by all accounts was as comfortable as his mentor at shoving a blunderbuss through the windows of unsuspecting carriages and swiping purses from the laps of petrified ladies. The serendipity of one unexpectedly lucrative robbery on 8 November was so brazen that, ironically, it nearly cost the English language the very word 'serendipity'. When the two footpads spotted a coach trundling through Hyde Park, Maclaine galloped to the side and thrust his pistol into the speechless face of none other than Horace Walpole. As the terrified passengers scrambled to collect whatever watches and silver they had on them, Maclaine's finger slipped against the trigger, launching a scorching ball of lead across the cheek of the genteel politician and out through the corner of his carriage. Walpole, who five year later would coin the word 'serendipity' in one of his famous letters, narrowly survived the accidental shooting.

The following day, Walpole took out an advertisement offering a reward of twenty guineas for the safe return of the items that were taken. Maclaine, however, wrote directly to Walpole sneering at the public offer and demanding twice that amount:

Sir friday Evening [Nov. 10, 1749].

seeing an advertisement in the papers of to Day giveing an account of your being Rob'd by two Highway men on wedensday night last in Hyde Parke and during the time a Pistol being fired whether Intended or Accidentally was Doubtfull Oblidges Us to take this Method of assureing you that it was the latter and by no means Design'd Either to hurt or frighten you for tho' we are Reduced by the misfortunes of the world and obliged to have Recourse to this method of getting money Yet we have Humanity Enough not to take any bodys life where there is Not a Nessecety for it. we have likewise seen the advertisem[en]t offering a Reward of twenty Guineas for your watch and sealls which are very safe and which you shall have

BLAZE

with your sword and the coach mans watch for fourty Guineas and Not a shilling less as I very well know the Value of them and how to dispose of them to the best advantage therefor Expects as I have given You the preference that you'll be Expeditious in your answering this which must be in the daily advertiser of monday; and now s[i]r to convince you that we are not Destitute of Honour Our selves if you will Comply with the above terms and pawn your Honour in the publick papers that you will punctually pay the fourty Guineas after you have Reced the things and not by any means Endeavour to apprehend or hurt Us I say if you will agree to all these particulars we Desire that you'll send one of your Serv[an]ts on Monday Night Next between seven and Eight o clock to Tyburn and let him be leaning ag[ain]st One of the pillers with a white hankerchif in his hand by way of signall . . .

A:B: & C:D:

P:s: the same footman that was behind the Chariot when Rob'd will be Most Agreeable to Us as we Intend Repaying him a triffle we took from him −

Walpole refused either to accept the inflated price or to send a servant to Tyburn at the appointed hour. Nevertheless, Plunkett and Maclaine's string of thirty-odd robberies became the talk of the town. The two became prominent fixtures in polite society and pamphleteers began remarking on the narrowing distance between crass and class. By the spring of 1750, Plunkett and Maclaine had succeeded in rattling the social sensibilities of the city every bit as remarkably as the bizarre earthquake that struck London early that March. Before long Maclaine was lodging in fashionable St James's Street, passing himself off as an Irish gentleman and courting 'a young Lady of Fortune'. The romance was quickly scuppered, however, when 'Captain M——', according to Andrea McKenzie, revealed to the naïve Chelsea girl 'Mac's Character and Design'. The split marked the beginning of the end for Maclaine's brief career as a highwayman.

*26. James Maclaine became, briefly, the epitome of the
dashing highwayman in the middle of the eighteenth
century. Note the signature Venetian mask, at his feet,
which he wore during robberies*

On 26 June 1750, as the summer sun was just beginning to
mount, Plunkett and Maclaine hijacked a stagecoach from
Salisbury and made off with several trunks of expensive clothing.
Later that evening, the brazen pair assaulted Lord Eglinton
on Hounslow Heath, confiscating his blunderbuss and wallet.
Ultimately it was Maclaine's own stupidity, though, that cost him
his freedom. In attempting to dispose of some of the stolen
goods from the Salisbury coach, he left his name and address
with a shop owner who had earlier in the day been alerted to
the robberies. Brought initially to the Westminster Gatehouse,
Maclaine was eventually transferred to Newgate to await his trial
at the Old Bailey while his accomplice, William Plunkett,
managed to remain at large. Not since the extraordinary escapades of Jack Sheppard had the public become so captivated by

Newgate's outrageous theatre of thieves. Among the thousands who waited to see the 'gentleman highwayman', as Walpole nicknamed him, was a steady stream of 'ladies of distinction', including Lady Caroline Petersham, who had become infatuated with the host of 'likenesses' that had flooded the streets. In the weeks after Maclaine's arrest, Walpole monitored the highwayman's progress from conviction to execution in a series of letters to his friend Horace Mann in Arlington Street, Piccadilly:

Sept. 1, 1750

My friend M'Lean is still the fashion: have I not reason to call him my friend? He says, if the pistol had shot me, he had another for himself. Can I do less than say I will be hanged if he is? They have made a print, a very dull one, of what I think I said to Lady Caroline Petersham about him,

Thus I stand like the Turk with his doxies around!

Sept. 20, 1750

M'Lean is condemned, and will hang. I am honourably mentioned in a Grub ballad for not having contributed to his sentence. There are as many prints and pamphlets about him as about the earthquake. His profession grows no joke: I was sitting in my own dining-room on Sunday night, the clock had not struck eleven, when I heard a loud cry of 'Stop thief!' a highwayman had attacked a post-chaise in Piccadilly, within fifty yards of this house: the fellow was pursued, rode over the watchman, almost killed him, and escaped.

Oct. 18, 1750

Robbing is the only thing that goes on with any vivacity, though my friend Mr. M'Lean is hanged. The first Sunday after his condemnation, three thousand people went to see him; he fainted away twice with the heat of his cell. You can't conceive the ridiculous rage there is of going to Newgate; and the prints that are published of the malefactors, and the memoirs of their lives and deaths set forth with as much parade as Marshal Turenne's — we have no generals worth making a parallel.

In the end, the vast number of visitors to Newgate were not enough to distract Maclaine from the reality of his situation, and he was seen more than once breaking down in his cell in the days prior to his execution. On 3 October 1750, before a sobbing throng that lined the route from the prison to the gallows, a rather more dignified Maclaine, though deprived of his signature stage prop, his Venetian mask, took his final bows at Tyburn.

Overseeing Maclaine's melodramatic 'Exit, stage down', was a colourful figure whose animated antics loomed as large in London's imagination as the saucy highwayman of Welbeck Street. John Thrift, a.k.a. 'Jack Ketch', first came to notoriety in 1736 when he was arrested and thrown into Newgate for assaulting a girl called Mary White on his way home from an execution. Public opprobrium had hardly diminished when, three months later, Thrift attempted to drag back up to the scaffold a condemned thief called Thomas Reynolds who, lying in his coffin after having endured the obligatory quarter of an hour at the end of his tether, suddenly regained consciousness. Remarkably, crowds of people who, only moments before, had relished the prospect of watching someone die became fiercely protective of a criminal's right to life, should he withstand the fifteen-minute dangle. Thrift survived the drubbing he received, though he left Tyburn with more bruises and fewer friends than Reynolds.

The easy access that the public had to criminals of every class in the eighteenth and nineteenth centuries is a phenomenon for which there is no obvious parallel in contemporary society. Migrating, as it had for over half a millennium, from the margins of London life to its very centre, Newgate became a kind of living morgue of social history, a platform of ceaseless entertainment that did not so much compete with as complement the more respectable stages of Haymarket and Drury Lane. The *dramatis personae* of its endlessly rehearsed sagas – from Mull Sack Cottington to Claude Duval and Jack Sheppard

– bled into the operatic inventions of Gay's Peachum and Macheath as seamlessly as those characters bled into such real-life replicas as Plunkett and Maclaine. Thirteen years after Maclaine made his exit before a heaving audience, its wealthier members using ivory monocles to help them see each jerk and grimace, yet another highwayman, Paul Lewis, managed to capture the city's imagination.

Lewis's colourful past included a stint as a naval officer in the West Indies during which he participated in the capture of Guadaloupe in 1759. Once an unruly student, Lewis had risen to the rank of lieutenant, but his reputation for bravery in battle was damaged by accusations of robbery. In 1761, Lewis was banned from his ship for stealing his fellow sailors' pay and was forced to return to England where he resolved to pursue a life of highway robbery. In a crowded field of aspiring footpads, Lewis gradually came to public notice not because of any talent he possessed for stealing, but for his dashing attire, his enviable confidence, and his finesse in winning himself acquittal during trial. Over the course of a single year, Lewis was brought before a judge and jury in the Old Bailey four times to answer charges of highway robbery and on each occasion, sniggering at the noose, he walked free.

Lewis's luck finally ran out, however, in the spring of 1763 when he pulled a pistol on the seemingly unmuggable Joseph Brown: 'I was going home on the 12th of March last to the parish of Wilsden,' Brown would later testify in court, 'within about a quarter of a mile of my own home, the prisoner at the bar came up, and clapped a pistol to my breast, and bid me stop; I said for what? I shall not stop, this is my way home; he cried stop again. I said, it is not my intent to stop to you, neither will I be stopt.' Flabbergasted by Brown's insolence, Lewis fired a shot at him, but missed. Thrown from his horse in the com-motion, Brown 'clapt [his] knee on Lewis's breast' until the gunman 'begged for mercy'. Lewis then pleaded with Brown that 'he was a gentleman bred', and was eventually allowed to stand up. 'After which,' Brown explained with disgust, 'he clapped another pistol to my breast, and said, now d——n you, I'll shoot you dead.' Enraged, Brown knocked the pistol from his body and returned Lewis to the floor, where he 'clapt' another knee 'upon his breast, and with garters tied his hands, and took his pistols; after which delivered him into the custody of the constable'.

Paul Lewis was convicted of attempting to rob Joseph Brown and removed to the Condemned Hold in Newgate to await execution by hanging. Lewis's preference for fine clothes earned him the nickname 'Captain' from his fellow inmates, an allusion to Gay's Captain Macheath. Nor was the resemblance lost on the voyeuristic public outside. The young writer James Boswell, for whom the grim dramas of Newgate and Tyburn were to become a lifelong fascination, paid Lewis a visit on the eve of his execution. His journal entries for that day and the following are vivid and moving and help us to reconstruct the sombre stage on which these scenes were enacted:

Tuesday 3 May 1763

I walked up to the Tower in order to see Mr Wilkes come out. But he was gone. I then thought I should see prisoners of one kind or other, so went to Newgate. I stepped into a sort of court before the cells. They are surely most dismal places. There are three rows of 'em, four in a row, all above each other. They have double iron windows, and within these, strong iron rails; and in these dark mansions are the unhappy criminals confined. I did not go in, but stood in the court, where were a number of strange blackguard beings with sad countenances, most of them being friends and acquaintances of those under sentence of death. Mr Rice the broker was confined in another part of the house. In the cells were Paul Lewis for robbery and Hannah Diego for theft. I saw them pass by to chapel. The woman was a big unconcerned being. Paul, who had been in the sea-service and was called Captain, was a genteel, spirited young fellow. He was just a Macheath. He was dressed in a white coat and blue silk vest and silver, with his hair neatly queued and a silver-laced hat, smartly cocked. An acquaintance asked him how he was. He said, "Very well"; quite resigned. Poor fellow! I really took a great concern for him, and wished to relieve him. He walked firmly and with a good air, with his chains rattling upon him, to the chapel.

Erskine and I dined at the renowned Donaldson's, where we were heartily entertained. All this afternoon I felt myself still more melancholy, Newgate being upon my mind like a black cloud. Poor Lewis was always coming across me. I felt myself dreary at night, and made my barber try to read me asleep with Hume's *History*, of which he made very sad work. I lay in sad concern.

Wednesday 4 May 1763

My curiosity to see the melancholy spectacle of the executions was so strong that I could not resist it, although I was sensible that I would suffer much from it. In my younger years I had read in the *Lives of the Convicts* so much about Tyburn that I had a sort of horrid eagerness to be there. I also wished to see the last behaviour of Paul Lewis, the handsome fellow whom I had seen the day before. Accordingly I took Captain Temple with me, and he and I got upon a scaffold very near the fatal tree, so that we could clearly see all the dismal scene. There was a most prodigious crowd of spectators. I was most terribly shocked, and thrown into a very deep melancholy.

Though highway robbery would continue to plague the fringes of London well into the nineteenth century, the public's fascination with individual offenders seems to have peaked in the second half of the eighteenth century. With the move towards a paper-based economy, white-collar crimes came more to the fore, creating a different kind of intrigue. The shift in interest from robberies on the periphery of society to cloistered scheming within its walls was mirrored by Newgate's own stationary voyage in social consciousness. But in the murky period of transition, when forgers began to rival footpads for control over the public imagination, one flamboyant figure managed to keep alive the link between Newgate Prison and the evaporating romance of highway robbery, and that was Sixteen String Jack.

John Rann, as Jack was initially christened, began his brief career as a footpad with an extraordinary string of luck. After being arrested for one of his very first outings – the commandeering of a stagecoach in November 1773 – he managed to escape conviction at the Old Bailey when neither the coach driver nor any of the passengers could identify Jack's gang of Hampstead hijackers. Jack's acquittal set in motion a series of judicial farces, which included the jury's reaching a verdict of not guilty in what should have been an open-and-shut case of theft. When he appeared in court, 'his irons were tied up and decorated with blue ribbons, and he had an enormous bouquet of flowers affixed to the breast of his coat.' With greater 'audacity than was ever observed in any other person in the like circumstances', he insisted that the chief witness in the case, Eleanor Roache, who could connect him with the stolen watch, had testified against him merely because he had declined to take her on as a mistress. With each acquittal, Jack's fame grew. He was soon seen flaunting his freedom in fashionable society, picking fights, and discovering deep inside himself an unlikely fondness for foppish finery. 'Our hero appeared at Bagnigge-Wells,' remembered the author of a contemporary pamphlet,

> elegantly dressed in a scarlet coat, a tambour waistcoat, white silk stockings, laced hat, &c. and publickly declared himself to be a highwayman. Having drank very freely, he became extremely quarrelsome and abusive, and several scuffles ensued, in one of which having lost a ring from his finger, he appeare quite indifferent, saying in a careless manner, 'it was but an hundred guineas gone, which one evening[']s work would replace.' He became at length so turbulent, that some of the company proposed turning him out of the house; but they met

with so obstinate a resistance, that they were obliged to give up their design.

According to John Villette, author of the *Annals of Newgate*, compiled a couple of years later, Jack cut a dashing figure despite his gauche manners. 'Five feet five inches high', he 'wore his own hair, of a light brown colour, which combed over his fore-head, remarkably clean, and particularly neat in his dress . . . always having sixteen strings to his breeches knees, always of silk (by which he acquired his fictitious name) and a remarkable hat with strings, and a button on the crown'. Jack soon set a gold standard of excellence. Dr Johnson once remarked that '[Thomas] Gray's poetry towered above the ordinary run of verse as Sixteen-string Jack above the ordinary footpad.' But Jack's sartorial fame would prove short-lived. In September 1774, Princess Amelia's chaplain, Dr William Bell, was assaulted in Middlesex on his way home to Gunnersbury. A watch, 18d. in cash, and a stone seal were taken by a man Bell 'believed, but would not swear' looked like Jack. Having patched things up with Eleanor Roache, Jack, the pamphlets claimed, foolishly entrusted the watch to her. Once the watch was spotted by Mr Cordy, an alert pawnbroker, linking Jack to Roache was easy. His lucky string had finally snapped. 'When Rann had received his sentence,' according to one witness, 'he attempted to force a smile; but it was evidently the smile of a man whose heart was tortured with grief and vexation.' On the day of his execution, Jack dressed himself in a stylish pea-green coat, 'new buckskin breeches, ruffled shirt' and his signature 'silver strings' dangling from his knees and hat. As the sledge rolled past St Sepulchre's, one of the clutch of whores, or 'Fair Sisterhood' as they were called, who gathered there presented him with a large nosegay, which was inserted into his button-hole as though he were a groom.

Clack

'CLACK, a *Woman's Tongue.*'

There can be little doubting that the tragic deaths in infancy of thirteen of her sixteen children left Elizabeth Brownrigg's wretched soul reverberating with tortured shapes and voices. But when the 47-year-old midwife was discovered in June 1767 to have subjected a number of young girls entrusted to her care by the Foundling Hospital to systematic abuse of the most horrifying kind, Brownrigg emerged into public view from the labyrinth of her private torment as among the most reviled villains of the eighteenth century.

Her story – which held the public in thrall during the eventful summer that marked the introduction of the piano into England and the opening of Dr William Hunter's famous Theatre of Anatomy in Great Windmill Street – would be enshrined for posterity along with the trials, alleged confessions and gruesome executions of hundreds of other convicts ten years later in a five-volume compendium known as *The Newgate Calendar*. It was said that by the end of the eighteenth century, *The Newgate Calendar* had joined the King James version of the Bible, the Book of Common Prayer, *Pilgrim's Progress* and Foxe's *Book of Martyrs*, as being the five titles 'most likely to be found' in even less well-read households. For a work full of assumed identities, it is not surprising to discover that *The Newgate Calendar* was itself an alias for the book's official title:

*MALEFACTORS' BLOODY REGISTER containing: Genuine and circum-
stantial narrative of the lives and transactions, various exploits and
dying speeches of the most notorious criminals of both sexes who
suffered death punishment in Gt. Britain and Ireland for high treason
petty treason murder piracy felony thieving highway robberies forgery
rapes bigamy burglaries riots and various other horrid crimes and misdemeanours on a plan entirely new, wherein will be fully displayed the
regular progress from virtue to vice interspersed with striking reflexions
on the conduct of those unhappy wretches who have fallen a sacrifice to
the laws of their country.*

For three-quarters of a century, anthologies of the lives and
deaths of the nation's most notorious criminals had been compiled from the barrage of broadsheets and uncorroborated
confessions that would hit the streets within hours of almost
every hanging, burning or quartering, and keep the capital
entertained. The first of these collections appeared in 1705
under the title *The Tyburn Calendar* (the word 'calendar' in its
legal sense referred to the roster of prisoners scheduled for trial
at an assize) and relied heavily on the hastily published accounts
of Newgate's Ordinaries. Enjoying unrivalled access to inmates,
these moonlighting clergymen routinely trebled or quadrupled
their paltry salaries by divulging and embellishing the condemned's version of events. *The Tyburn Calendar* proved an
unprecedented publishing phenomenon, sales of which outdis-
tanced those of more respectable literary works. Its success
triggered innumerable imitations by writers unencumbered by
copyright prohibitions; these were only just beginning to figure
in the consciousnesses of authors, booksellers and legislators,
and culminated in the 1709 Copyright Act.

The Tyburn Calendar was followed in 1714 by Alexander
Smith's wildly popular three-volume *Complete history of the lives
and robberies of the most notorious highwaymen, footpads, shoplifts, &
cheats of both sexes*; soon after by Captain Charles Johnson's
derivative *A complete history of the lives and adventures of the most
famous highwaymen, murderers, street-robbers & etc.*; and in 1768 by

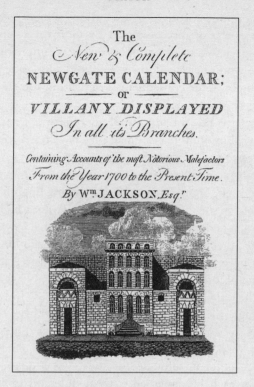

The

New & Complete

NEWGATE CALENDAR;

or

VILLANY DISPLAYED

In all its Branches.

Containing Accounts of the most Notorious Malefactors
From the Year 1700 to the Present Time.
By W.ᵐ JACKSON, Esq.ʳ

27. *Title-page from one of the many editions of the so-called*
'Newgate Calendar' – a publishing phenomenon in the late
eighteenth century

The Tyburn Chronicle: or villainy display'd in all its branches.
Shameless regurgitations of each other, with rampant disregard
for accuracy, these works established an effective and affecting
formula and could scarcely keep pace with public demand.
Starting with whatever was known or could be invented about
the birth and upbringing of the convict concerned, the works
would go on to detail the spiced-up circumstances surrounding the criminal's supposed transgressions, the predictable
denials of responsibility after being apprehended, his or her
confinement and subsequent remorse, last-minute appeals for

redemption, and fortitude in execution, which served as an example of the dignity bestowed by God on a supplicating soul. A species of what became known as 'improving literature', the works belonged, many believed, alongside the Bible as a reminder of the consequences of drifting too far from the teachings of Scripture.

As a generic title for any anthology of crime, irrespective of which penal institution a criminal may have been confined to, *The Newgate Calendar* to this day is responsible for creating considerable confusion about just who was incarcerated in Newgate itself. Some of the most notorious English felons to be featured in such works, including the famous highwayman Dick Turpin and the sixteenth-century cannibal Sawney Bean, committed their crimes and suffered their prosecutions far from London, never actually setting foot inside Newgate. Just as Jack Ketch had become shorthand for executioner, Newgate was in a sense the only gaol.

Although the narratives, which rehashed the outlandish escapades of countless felons, including Jack Sheppard and Jonathan Wild, Claude Duval and Captain Kidd, rarely differed from each other in substance or style – as a quasi-canonical version of each life emerged – what did tend to alter from edition to edition were the accompanying illustrations. These did as much to impress on contemporary imaginations the centrality of Newgate as a psychological space as any other cultural contour relating to The Gaol. As criminal biography established itself over the course of the eighteenth century as a discrete species of literature, more and more respectable artists were accepting lucrative commissions to adorn editions of *The Newgate Calendar*.

Among the most celebrated illustrators to tackle the tricky task of revitalising oft-told episodes of murder and assault was Samuel Wale, a distinguished Fellow of the Royal Academy who had studied drawing at the St Martin's Lane Academy in the 1740s, and been apprenticed to a goldsmith. Wale had already established a reputation as a draughtsman of London's seamier side with several studies of the city's hospitals and a series of majestic views of the grand 'New Spring Gardens' in Vauxhall – that favourite haunt of Dr Johnson, Goldsmith and Walpole – before turning his attention to books. Taking on a broad range of subjects, from literary to religious, historical to allegorical, Wale would eventually illustrate over one hundred works, from Thomas Percy's influential *Reliques of Ancient English Poetry* (1765) to various histories of England, which flooded the bookshops in the second half of the eighteenth century. Wale's prolific output can be explained by his decision, unusual for the period, to hand over the time-consuming task of engraving his works to such artists as Pierre-Charles Canot and, increasingly, Charles Grignion, so freeing his hands to embark on other commissions. There is little doubting that the works that brought Wale and Grignion their greatest notoriety were the illustrations they undertook in the early 1770s for the five-volume *Newgate Calendar*.

Accustomed to the challenges of reconstructing scenes of iconic familiarity, whether biblical or Shakespearean, Wale had an eye for compelling composition and his surviving illustrations are laced with powerful visual codes to which he knew readers were likely to respond, emotionally if not intellectually. This is particularly apparent in his renderings of the unholy actions of Elizabeth Brownrigg. In 1759, when the Foundling Hospital began sending teenaged girls to Brownrigg as apprentices in midwifery, no system had been established to monitor the well-being of its charges, despite suspicions of widespread mistreatment of adolescents by guardians. Such laxity was all that Brownrigg's sadistic streak needed, and though stories of domestic cruelty were not uncommon in the eighteenth century, there was something about the Brownrigg case that unsettled the public imagination and brought focus to Wale's illustrations. The three girls that she was eventually found to have tortured, by cramming them naked into a coal hole after sessions of unmerciful whipping and the slicing of their tongues, shared the Christian name 'Mary': Mary Jones, Mary Clifford and Mary Mitchell. As someone entrusted to help nurture young women in the skills of bringing innocents into the world, Brownrigg's actions seemed especially demonic – the trinity of Marys lending the case a disturbing religious dimension. Seizing on precisely that aspect of the horrible tale, Wale's illustration of the Brownrigg case in *The Newgate Calendar* comprises three panels in the manner of a Byzantine triptych or altarpiece. The gold relief of timeless spiritual space in which one would expect the figures of Christ and Mary to be sitting is replaced by the hellish, blackened interiors of Newgate, a torture room, and the infamous coal hole, or anti-womb, with which Brownrigg's story would forever be associated.

In the middle panel, Brownrigg sits alone in her austere cell in Newgate Gaol. Where in a medieval triptych, the baby Jesus would prototypically be sitting in the Madonna's lap, the wrinkled hands of the abusive midwife wring endlessly, emphasising the empty childless space. In the panel on the left, where one would expect to find a Christian crucifixion scene, Wale depicts the dangling arms of the naked Mary Mitchell, who eventually died from her injuries. Behind her, Brownrigg holds a sharpened switch in mid-swing, while all around lie whips and canes and other implements of torture. In the foreground, Mary's ripped garments echo the wadded shroud found at the foot of the cross in Christian iconography. Behind Brownrigg, the bars of a heavy screen stretch across the opening of a charred fireplace, foreshadowing the incarceration and hellfire that await her. The third panel shows the cramped coal hole in which the apprentices were imprisoned, with one of the three Marys kneeling in prayer at the centre, her left arm raised delicately to her breast as though holding a suckling child.

Without reading the adjacent account of Brownrigg's cruelty, perusers of *The Newgate Calendar* absorbed a powerful religious lesson through the images alone, which added to the work's enormous popularity. Illustrators such as Wale helped to elevate events and individuals almost to the level of spiritual icons, suspending them in a timeless psychological space that transcended particularities of time and place. Though the incidents collected in the *Calendar* stretched back centuries, to an earlier incarnation of Newgate, the volumes succeeded in establishing an eternal present in which the crimes, punishments and ultimate redemptions were, in a sense, forever unfolding.

Original artwork converted into engraved plates was an expensive frill for the volumes and it was not affordable to complement every story with an illustration. Since artists and publishers had to be selective, it is telling to compare, across editions, which figures consistently attracted attention. In virtually every version of the *Calendar* to appear after 1726 could be found a depiction of the disturbing events that unfolded on Tyburn Road (the present-day Park Lane) on the evening of 1 March 1726. This is where and when 36-year-old Catherine Hayes persuaded her burly lodgers, Thomas Wood and Thomas Billings, to hack to pieces her allegedly abusive husband, John Hayes. The redoubtable Thomases took considerable convincing, and not a little liquor, before they agreed to club Catherine's husband to death. Dizzy beyond reason with hooch, the trio persuaded itself that the most efficient way to dispose of the body was to bend it into a wooden box. 'We wanted to get him into an Old Chest,' Catherine would later testify to a horrified courtroom in the Old Bailey, 'but he was too long, and too big. We thought to have done it with only cutting off his Head, and his Legs, but we were forced to cut off his Thighs and his Arms, and then the Chest would not hold 'em all.' The three spent the following day concealing the pieces that until recently had comprised John Hayes throughout the city. His limbs and torso were scattered like chopped wood in Marylebone Fields. His head was tossed like a stubbled buoy into the Thames, near Westminster.

When, one scrap at a time, the remains of Catherine's husband began to reassemble themselves with the help of disturbed passers-by, it wasn't long before the now-sober trio were rounded up and deposited in the city's prisons. Catherine Hayes spent her final days in Newgate in the spring of 1726, before becoming the last woman in England, on 9 May, to be burned at the stake for the crime of 'petty treason', or the betrayal of a superior by a subordinate, which typically took the form of spousicide. Perhaps sensing the imminent obsolescence of that punishment, the executioner had already begun to lose his touch. Customarily, when burning a convict alive, he would, as a gesture of mercy, lasso the condemned's neck with a rope just before the flames could inflict excruciating pain. Missing his target with every toss, the executioner conceded the task of curtailing Hayes's suffering to the horrified onlookers who, hurling chunks of wood at her head, eventually put an end to the unimaginable misery.

The scene from the Hayes dismemberment that illustrators frequently depicted was one where Catherine, having just entered the room, discovers that the deed is done and the three begin to divide up the spoils. In most early editions of the *Calendar* (in the 1730s and 40s), the body of John Hayes is shown spreadeagled on the floor, while over him hover the inebriated conspirators. But a version of the incident to appear in a volume of 1826 reveals just how agile artists were in adapting even the most familiar stories to the evolving visual vocabulary of their day. In the illustration of the scene published by Andrew Knapp and William Baldwin, in their hugely successful *The Newgate Calendar; comprising interesting memoirs of the most notorious characters who have been convicted of outrages on the laws of England since the commencement of the eighteenth century; with anecdotes and last exclamations of sufferers*, the murder occurs, bizarrely, in a kind of Turkish tent, with heavy drapes all around. Elevated from its usual position on the floor, the limp body of John Hayes now lounges on the dishevelled bed, while the three partners-in-crime begin the gruesome job before them. By the first quarter of the nineteenth century, a print by the Swiss-born Romantic artist Henry Fuseli, entitled *The Nightmare* (1781) had become the single most reproduced image in Europe. Famously depicting a swooning girl in an exotic, velvety interior, on whose stomach squats a mischievous imp while the ghoulish head of a horse rams itself through the folds of the tent, the work was as much parodied as admired and there is little doubt that the artists commissioned by Knapp and Baldwin were intentionally echoing the almost farcical power of the mysterious image. By merging the horror of Hayes's butchery with the eroticism of Fuseli's vision, *The Newgate Calendar* was operating on a level its publishers knew would keep readers hooked.

Skrip

'SKRIP, *Paper; as,* The Cully did freely blot the Skrip, and so tipt me forty Hogs; *i.e. One enter'd readily into Bond with me for forty Shillings.*'

Like many of the con-artists it accommodated, The Gaol was forever forging for itself a fresh identity. As new crimes were added to the penal code and out-of-fashion offences fell into disuse, the complexion of this chameleon castle ceaselessly shifted. Where once it lurked, like footpads, on the outskirts of society, by the second half of the eighteenth century Newgate lay at the centre of a swelling metropolis. As a result, it is not surprising it gradually took on an aspect of urban vice, where the crimes were caused by *papier* not *rapière*, and the blood was ink . . .

On a bitterly cold morning at Tyburn in mid-January 1776, a crowd of over thirty thousand spectators trampled the thick blanket of snow that had briefly knitted the rolling fields of Hyde Park to the tail-end of Oxford Street, eager to enjoy the merrymaking that made execution days among the most festive of the year. Jostling for a favourable position, the throng watched impatiently as a pair of mounted city marshals, carrying staves, were followed in ceremonial style by a cart draped in black cloth bearing three convicted thieves. Two of the men, who were Jewish, Saunders Alexander and Lyon Abrahams, looked up from the halting hurdle to see the special crossbeam from which non-Christians were separately hanged. They had travelled the two and a half miles from Newgate with George Lee, a teenager who was caught picking pockets and convicted even though it was his first offence. Lee, it is said, wore a bright crimson coat and had spent the bumpy journey working the crowd that had lined the streets from Holborn. But Lee's desperate antics were merely the warm-up act for the main event – the arrival in a covered carriage of identical twin brothers of Huguenot descent whose story had captured the interest of the English public in a way that not even the escalating conflict with the American colonies could.

The 'unfortunate Perreaus', as they came to be known, were taken into custody on 9 March 1775, after Robert – a distinguished apothecary and the slightly older of the two – attempted to borrow £5,000 from a bank using, as collateral, a bond bearing a forged signature. When it emerged that the promissory note had been passed on to Robert by his feckless brother Daniel – a louche socialite, who in turn claimed it had been manufactured by his lover, the high-society Irish courtesan Margaret Caroline Rudd – the three colourful figures were rounded up and brought before the magistrates. Initially, the questioning was to take place in Bow Street, but the crowd that surrounded the Runners' entrance in anticipation of catching sight of the defendants ensured that the proceeding would have to be moved to the Guildhall.

There, Caroline retracted the confession that she had let slip when first apprehended – which she would later insist had been elicited under duress – and was granted protection from prosecution in exchange for her co-operation in testifying against the twins. Caroline claimed that her hand in the affair had been forced by Daniel, who threatened to cut her throat if she refused to falsify the bond, and that she could substantiate the twins' involvement in a long string of similar scams. In the weeks leading up to the trials of Robert and Daniel, the newspapers and the public hung on every newly excavated detail.

Many believed that the seemingly respectable Robert had been duped by his playboy brother, whose lascivious lifestyle lent the case added lustre. For others, suspicion centred on Caroline, who, it emerged, had years earlier abandoned a young husband, an Irish soldier, in favour of a life of lewd adventures. In the eyes of many, she was the ruthless *femme fatale*, the scheming seductress who cunningly secured an immunity for herself at the first opportunity, thereby ensuring that the person responsible for orchestrating the scam would be the only one to walk away from the affair.

Once in court, the brothers stood little chance of acquittal and even less of leniency if found guilty. Since the turn of the eighteenth century, the Crown's attitude towards forgery had steadily hardened. In May 1689, when John Ingham was convicted of falsifying a warrant to help secure the release from Newgate of Edward Williams, a pickpocket facing execution, by stencilling in the signature of a Justice of the Peace – in exchange, it was established in court, 'for a few guineas' – his punishment was merely to spend an hour in the pillory. The same relatively mild fate was faced by Robert Young (alias 'Smith the Minister') when he was found to be 'Guilty of a Cheat' in manufacturing a false 'Bill of Exchange' from which he and his wife had profited by £20. Though it was established during the course of the trial that Young was in fact a congenital counterfeiter, the court was satisfied that a brief session of public humiliation, which involved being on the receiving end of rotten fruit and bedpans of excrement, was sufficient comeuppance.

But by the middle of the eighteenth century, the Crown's attitude had altered dramatically. While there is no record of the death sentence being handed down in the Old Bailey for the offence of forgery in the years between 1700 and 1719, the count jumps suddenly to six in the 1720s, nine in the 1730s, twelve in the 1740s, and two-score capital convictions in the 1750s. Use of the pillory, on the other hand, declined, with twenty people being sentenced in the 1710s, half that figure in the 1720s, and only two during the entire two decades stretching from 1730 to 1749, when the punishment was discontinued altogether. The change in the law came about in 1729. Whereas, before, the Crown was concerned chiefly with protecting 'the paper of the Bank of England', thereafter 'a large addition' was made to the criminal code, which eventually accommodated some 120 separate statutes, almost half of which prescribed execution. The shift in judges' attitude towards forgery suggests the changing world that now confronted Newgate, one increasingly dependent on paper. 'The development of banks, trading houses, and systems of credit in the eighteenth century,' according to Frank McLynn, 'made the entire financial system vulnerable to the arts of the forger.'

Taking the stand in his own defence, Robert Perreau made an eloquent appeal. He passionately protested his innocence, and drew a distinction between his own upstanding character and that of the woman whose evidence threatened to bring him and his brother to the end of their tethers. 'I have followed no pleasures,' he insisted,

nor launched into any expenses: there is not a living man who can charge me with neglect or dissipation. The honest profits of my trade have afforded me a comfortable support, and furnished me with the means of maintaining in a decent sort, a worthy wife, and three promising children, upon whom I was labouring to bestow the properest education in my power; in short, we were as happy as affluence and innocence could make us, till this affliction came upon us by surprise, and I was made the dupe of a transaction from whose criminality I call God, the searcher of all human hearts, to witness, I am now as free as I was at the day of my birth.

Robert and Daniel Perreau were convicted of forgery on 31 May 1775 and sentenced to hang by their necks until dead. Their trials were conducted separately, the jury taking only ten minutes to decide their fate. But the drama was far from over.

Before their sentences should be carried out, it was decided that, because Caroline's immunity extended only to those instances of forgery for which she had been called upon to provide testimony against the twins, nothing in law prevented her from facing a separate prosecution for the one forgery to which she had unguardedly confessed. In prosecuting the Perreaus, therefore, Henry Howarth, the lead prosecutor, had been careful to resist calling Caroline as a witness in that particular case. Immune from immunity, Caroline was returned to Newgate along with the Perreaus to await trial.

From June to December 1775, all eyes were on Newgate. Though other alleged forgers circulated through the system, such as Joseph Bereau and Margaret Abbot, London remained focused on the fate of the inscrutable threesome. From opposite sides of the prison, Caroline and the Perreaus attempted to shape public opinion. Robert and Daniel knew that their only chance of survival was to have their death sentences commuted – to transportation, say, or prolonged sessions in the pillory – and that was only likely if Caroline were to be found guilty in her separate trial. The race was on to influence the public pool from which Caroline's jury would be summoned. By some means or other, Caroline managed to secure a private apartment on the women's side, in which she was able to receive her legal council as well as merchants eager to capitalise on her notoriety. Every sartorial decision that she made was scrutinised and in the autumn of 1775, Caroline was responsible, according to her biographers, for making black silk 'polonaise' overdresses fashionable again. When she wasn't setting trends, she spent her days writing open letters, which the newspapers were all too happy to print, attempting to project a sympathetic persona that would serve her well in the coming trial. 'I rest my defence,' she asserted in a letter to the *Morning Post* on 12 June, 'on stubborn facts and plain-told truths, and have no doubt but that will yet prevail over all the fallacies of a fine dress'd tale, and the power, perjury, and bribery which has been exerted to destroy my character, and take away my life.'

Across the prison, in the dismal Press Yard, Robert and Daniel were endeavouring to make the best of an intolerable situation and also to cast themselves in as favourable a light as possible. While Daniel spent his time in solitude revising for publication a pamphlet entitled *Mr Daniel Perreau's narrative of his unhappy case*, Robert, we read, was allowed to have visits from his wife and children. Heartbreaking accounts of the reunions were widely reported in the press, raising the emotional stakes when the public's sympathies were already heatedly divided. A reporter who witnessed one of these family visits remarked that 'he never beheld any thing half so moving':

> the wretched objects beheld each other with speechless anguish for several minutes, not being able to address each other till many floods of tears had fallen from both, and those gave them the power of utterance: the keeper himself acknowledged at the same time . . . he never beheld a scene so affecting.

Margaret Caroline Rudd was brought to trial at the Old Bailey on 8 December before an expectant audience, most of which had long been convinced of her innocence. The jury took thirty minutes to concur. Caroline's release from custody signalled the end for the twins. A series of heart-rending appeals were pointlessly lodged with the King, mostly on Robert's behalf, by distressed colleagues. On 7 January, ten days before the scheduled execution, Robert's wife Henrietta braved severe weather to make a wrenching personal plea to the Queen for intercession. It was, according to one witness, 'a picture of distress which surpasses imagination'.

By all accounts, Daniel and Robert appeared smart and com-posed on the morning of their execution. Dressed 'in new suits of deep mourning, their hair dressed and powdered, but without any hats', they paid a brief visit to the prison chapel before meeting and shaking hands with their hangman, Edward

Dennis, to whom they presented the customary gift of a guinea each in exchange for the promise of swift service. It was eleven-thirty when the covered carriage carrying the brothers came to a halt behind the hurdle dragging the three thieves, Alexander, Abrahams and Lee. As a rabbi ascended the special scaffold erected for the two Jews, the ropes were removed from the twins' wrists. They then bowed to the audience, 'embraced and saluted each other in a most tender and affectionate manner', clasped each other by both hands, and, thus bound almost as tightly as they had been at birth, were 'launched into eternity'.

The composure with which the twins took their leap of faith was by no means characteristic of the demeanour of the condemned. Johann Wilhelm Archenholz, a Prussian historian who witnessed a London hanging in 1778, captures movingly, and with an alien's eye, the desperate appeals for regard, which those in attendance had come to expect: 'A young man of twenty years of age,' Archenholz wrote,

> was condemned to death on the evidence of a highwayman, who accused him of being an accomplice . . . the unhappy wretch was in consequence of this conducted in a cart to Tyburn, with some other criminals. He remained with the rope about his neck, according to the permission which the law allows, one whole hour at the foot of the gibbet. During that hour the culprit is permitted to say whatever he chooses; were he to utter high treason against the sovereign, or inflame the people to a revolt, it would be illegal to prevent him. They think humanity requires that such an alleviation should be permitted to one who is about to be launched out of the world by a violent death. There are actually a great many men, who on this sad occasion experience a certain pleasure in communicating those sentiments with which they are affected.

Anxiety surrounding the safety of the Perreaus' convictions fed a growing uneasiness with execution as an appropriate penalty for a crime that had, until recently, been punished with an hour in the pillory. Such squeamishness was magnified a year later when the well-known preacher William Dodd confessed to forging a bond in the name of his friend and former pupil, the Earl of Chesterfield, in order to borrow £4,200 from Lewis Robertson, a broker. Admired as a mesmerising speaker in the 1760s, Dodd had fallen on hard times by the mid-1770s after a series of failed enterprises, which he had embarked upon to finance his expensive tastes in clothes and furnishings. Mocked by many as the 'Macaroni Parson', Dodd had all but abandoned a lifelong ambition to be taken seriously as a writer, which had begun inauspiciously as an undergraduate at Cambridge when he published a poem on foot-and-mouth disease entitled *Diggon Davy's Resolution on the Death of his Last Cow* (1747). Indulging for decades a dangerous habit of living beyond his means – moving from one lavish lodging to another, from a house in Wardour Street to a mansion in Mayfair – Dodd was being hounded by impatient creditors when he succumbed to the temptation to fabricate the bond.

Unlike with the Perreaus, there were no mysterious ladies to complicate the matter, and on 22 February 1777, William Dodd was tried on charges of deception and forgery and faced execution if found guilty. 'My lords and gentlemen of the jury,' Dodd addressed the court:

> Upon the evidence which has been this day produced against me, I find it very difficult for me to address your lordships; there is no man in the world, who has a deeper sense of the heinous nature of the crime for which I stand indicted than myself . . . My lords, oppressed as I am with infamy, loaded as I am with distress, sunk under this cruel prosecution, your lordships and gentlemen of the jury, cannot think life a matter of any value to me; no, my lords, I solemnly protest that death of all blessings would be the most pleasant to me after this pain. I have yet, my lords, ties which call upon me; ties which render me desirous even to continue this miserable existence: I have a wife, my lords, who for 27 years has lived an unparalleled example of conjugal attachment and fidelity, and whose behaviour during

28. William Dodd, parson and forger

this crying scene would draw tears of approbation, I am sure, even from the most inhuman. My lords, I have creditors, honest men, who will lose much by my death; I hope for the sake of justice towards them some mercy will be shewn to me.

Though, for many, Dodd's materialism and lavish lifestyle were the object of intense derision as being hypocritically at odds with the spiritual life that he so robustly advocated, few had the stomach to witness a repeat of the tragic scene of one year earlier for a transgression so seemingly petty as falsifying the signature of a friend. The Methodist icon John Wesley, whose religious principles Dodd had once ferociously attacked in a sermon, came forward to offer pastoral support to the condemned clergyman. Dr Johnson, who made no secret of his contempt for Dodd's duplicitous demeanour, agreed to lend his gravitas and skill to the formidable appeals that were being launched, in the desperate hope of winning clemency for the 'unfortunate divine'.

SKRIP

From the dank confines of the Press Yard, Dodd oversaw the efforts to save his life, summoning some of the zeal for which he had made his name as a fiery exegete. 'Depend upon it, Sir,' Johnson remarked of Dodd's disposition in these grim weeks, 'when a man knows he is to be hanged in a fortnight, it concentrates his mind wonderfully.' From across the country, petition after petition poured in bearing tens of thousands of signatures begging the King to exercise his royal prerogative and show mercy. But the effort was wasted. 'If I pardon Dodd,' a perplexed George III is quoted as saying, 'I shall have murdered the Perreaus.' Before a hundred thousand spectators – the largest crowd ever to have assembled at Tyburn – Dodd was hanged to death on 27 June 1777.

After his body was cut down, amid the nauseated hush that overcame the uncharacteristically subdued audience, John Hunter, a physician, in desperation attempted to reverse the course of events and resuscitate Dodd by pumping spirit of hartshorn, or volatile alkali, into his lungs with double bellows while hot balsam was 'forced up his anus'. Peppermint water, horseradish juice and turpentine, according to contemporary accounts, were also applied, but to no avail. Beside Hunter as he worked was a recent edition of *The Newgate Calendar*, open at the page featuring the murderer 'William Duell' who had preceded Dodd to the scaffold by thirty-seven years: 'His body was brought to Surgeons' Hall to be anatomised,' an underlined sentence read, 'but after it was stripped and laid on the board, and one of the servants was washing it, in order to be cut, he perceived life in him, and found his breath to come quicker and quicker, on which a surgeon took some ounces of blood from him; in two hours he was able to sit up in his chair, and in the evening was again committed to Newgate.'

Though Dodd's execution began to breathe life into the debate over the use of capital punishment for white-collar crimes, forgery continued to be a hanging offence well into the next century. So ruthless had the courts become in deterring any form of paper fraud that merely to be accused of the crime was enough to make one feel the chill of the gibbet's shadow. When, in 1783, the virtuoso engraver William Wynne Ryland was suspected, wrongly, of having been party to a pair of forged bills written against the East India Company, he panicked and went to ground. In the ensuing manhunt, the public was put on alert for a man of 'about fifty years of age, [and] about five feet nine inches high', with 'a black complexion' 'wearing a wig with a club or queue'. Ryland's face, it was said, was 'thin' 'with strong lines; his common countenance very grave, but, whilst he speaks, rather smiling, and shows his teeth and has great affability in his manner'. To his supposed administrative misdemeanours were added rumours of tawdry personal entanglements and that 'he supported a mistress in a very extravagant manner'. Ryland's seemingly guilty behaviour proved his undoing. Though never actually accused of perpetrating the forgery itself, he was sentenced to hang until dead at Tyburn on 29 August that year, depriving England of one of its most talented engravers.

Ryland's execution may have been among the last to take place at Tyburn, but it was far from the final one faced by convicted forgers. Though the severity of the penalty continued frequently to be challenged in Parliament over the course of the following decades, it was still the expected punishment forty years later, when over a hundred thousand people forced their way into the cramped strip of land in front of Newgate to watch the final scene of one of the most sensational legal dramas of the nineteenth century. On 11 September 1824, a warrant was issued for the arrest of Henry Fauntleroy, a partner in the banking house of Marsh, Sibbald & Co. Two of the bank's trustees accused Fauntleroy of having forged their signatures in what would soon be exposed as a complicated recipe of book-cooking and personal excess. While Fauntleroy stewed in Newgate, every aspect of his indulgent lifestyle was revealed to a hungry public. Fancying himself a dead ringer for Napoleon

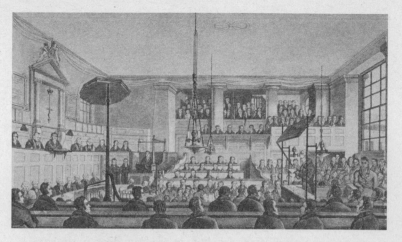

29. Henry Fauntleroy on trial for forgery in the Old Bailey in 1824

Bonaparte, whose bust he was never far from posing near, he purchased a preposterous Grecian villa in Brighton in which he constructed a replica of Napoleon's war tent. But the real trouble started when another lover of Fauntleroy's mistress Mary Bertram, who was known to most by the appellation 'Mrs Bang', began demonising Fauntleroy in the press.

Pandemonium reigned outside Newgate on the morning of 30 November 1824. The railings that were customarily erected around the 'drop' to prevent the crowd from interfering were 'strengthened by strong iron spars driven into the ground'. To avoid sudden stampedes, barriers were constructed dividing the Old Bailey into a series of human pens, 'fastened with spikes to posts', according to one paper, 'and bound round with iron hooping'. Executions were also popular events for aspiring pickpockets and whores and over four hundred constables had been assembled by the city's sheriffs, who expected trouble. When the condemned man appeared, dressed 'in a black coat, waistcoat, and trousers, with silk stockings, and shoes', flanked by the prison's Ordinary, a Mr Cotton, and the two sheriffs, the expectant crowd had barely time to gasp before the executioner 'pulled the cap over the prisoner's face and over that', according to the reporter for *The Times*, 'tied his neck cloth across his eyes, which we believe is not usually done'. So rehearsed in every nuance of the grim ritual of execution had the hardened crowd become, that the hangman's deviation from tradition, which deprived the audience of a proper look at the doomed man's countenance before the knot slipped, led to rumours that one of the crazed proxies who had begged to die in Fauntleroy's place, such as the language teacher Edmund Angelini, had been slipped in at the last minute; or that Fauntleroy's neck had been fortified with a steel splint and that Napoleon's doppelganger, whose body was frantically whisked away after being cut down, was thriving off ill-earned riches somewhere deep in the south of France.

III
SMOULDER

14

Twig

'**TWIG**, *to disengage, to sunder, to snap, to break off;* To twig
the Darbies; *To knock off the Irons.'*

By the time the knock came – as the bells of St Sepulchre's,
a few yards away, were striking seven in the evening –
Richard Akerman had already lowered the iron bar across the
solid oak door, slid the heavy bolts into their sleeves along
the seam of the door jamb, and chained the windows of the
Keepers' house shut.

As he peered through a slit in the shutters at the throng that
was assembling in front of The Gaol with menacing military
discipline – three abreast as far back as the eye could see down
Holborn – Akerman was struck by the jaunty appearance of
the leading rioter still hammering his fist against the barricaded
door. Dressed in a stylish brown coat and donning a round
wide-brimmed hat like an evangelical minister witnessing
doom, the caller suddenly stopped his insistent rapping, turned
to the legion of anti-Papists snarling behind him, pointed to
the very shutter behind which Akerman was squinting, and,
with a short sharp whistle through broken teeth, let loose the
dogs of destruction.

The first salvo was a rock, hurled through the mullioned
mosaic of glass above Akerman's door, sending splinters raining
down into the face of the maid who was cowering below it. Out
in front were columns of men armed with chisels, battering rams

and crowbars, while behind revved an engine of 'innumerable' agitators wielding daggers and 'the spokes of cart wheels'. Waving blue flags stitched with the words 'NO POPERY', they waited their turn. Then, with instinctive precision, like pirañhas swarming over a capsized elephant, the rioters split into angry groups, striking the massive bulk of Newgate at its weakest points. One faction remained at the Keepers' house and went to work with mattocks, while another pack descended on the Debtors' Door and still another on the sealed entrance to the Felons' Wing.

Whatever the religious or political motivations behind such a ferocious surge, there was little disguising the sheer animal pleasure that the rioters took in savaging a structure as lavish and expensive as The Gaol. For on the evening of 7 June 1780, when over a thousand Protestants who had followed Lord George Gordon in violently protesting against Catholic emancipation, smashed Newgate open – releasing all of its prisoners and gutting the interior with brickbats and lamp oil in a conflagration more destructive than the Great Fire of 1666 – the building was no longer the crippled shell that had limped hellishly through the eighteenth century.

In 1757 the Common Council of the Corporation of the city of London had been forced to appoint a special committee to investigate complaints lodged by neighbourhood groups about the abominable stench that emanated from the prison. The inquiry was merely the latest in a seemingly endless series of task forces whose conclusions had met with nodding approval by the Council when presented, only to be set aside later – their recommendations for full-scale refurbishment permanently postponed or ignored. When, five years later, a blaze broke out in the room of a mentally deranged murderer, Captain Ogle, which adjoined the Press Yard, killing both its inmate and a suspected corn thief, Thomas Smith, the city resolved at last to take action. Allocating, in stages, the unheard-of sum of £100,000 to build from scratch both a new gaol and a new Sessions House next door, Parliament appointed the 29-year-

30. Newgate engulfed by fire during the Gordon Riots in June 1780

old architect George Dance the Younger, who two years earlier had succeeded his father in the prestigious post of Clerk of the City Works. Newgate Prison would be Dance's first major commission and on 31 May 1770, the Lord Mayor, William Beckford, laid the first stone.

Taking nearly a decade to complete, the new Newgate was the first structure in The Gaol's history not to be towered over by an actual gatehouse. Shifting slightly south along Old Bailey, thus alleviating growing concerns over congestion clogging the artery east and west between Holborn and Cheapside, Dance's prison was a massive monolith of windowless brick. Whereas the arched gateways of its predecessors implied some semblance at least of coming *and* going, Dance's design was unmistakably that of a hulking terminus, a place of coming, *not* going – the end of the line. The young architect's demolition of The Gaol's iconic arch over Newgate Street smashed one of the oldest apertures into the ancient city of London.

Among the first to survey Dance's handiwork was the philanthropist and tireless penal reformer John Howard, who had
recently returned to England from a lengthy tour of European
prisons. Howard's celebrated obsession with prison conditions
had been ignited by an alarming turn of events in 1755, when
the sickly 29-year-old widower, and heir to a substantial uphol-
stery fortune, resolved to travel to Lisbon in the aftermath of
the devastating earthquake there, in the hope of assisting in any
way that he could. When Howard's ship, the *Hanover*, was
seized by French privateers, and its crew locked in a castle in
Brest where they 'lay six nights upon straw', his eyes were suddenly opened to the silent suffering of prisoners. After years
spent chasing warm weather and European spas throughout
Italy and the Netherlands in the hope of alleviating the discomforts of recurring gout and fatigue, Howard was appointed
High Sheriff of Bedfordshire in 1773, which provided him with
a platform from which to raise public awareness of the plight
of prisoners. Among the chief responsibilities of the High
Sheriff was that of Keeper of the local gaol, and Howard was
appalled to discover the depraved quality of life that prisoners
in his jurisdiction were made to suffer. Within a year of his
appointment, Howard was appealing passionately to Parliament
for a reassessment of the nation's protocols in the treatment of
inmates and an end to the tradition of prisoners remunerating
gaolers for their confinement. It was in order to appreciate
more fully contemporary attitudes towards incarceration that
Howard had embarked upon his exhaustive tour of European
prisons, visiting in turn institutions in Ireland, France, the
Netherlands, Flanders, Germany, Scotland and Wales.

Howard gained access to the construction site in 1777 and in
an eviscerating exposé of prison conditions in Britain, entitled
The state of the prisons in England and Wales, with preliminary obser-
vations, and an account of some foreign prisons, he offered his own
views on what life would be like inside the rebuilt Newgate.
'Many inconveniences of the old Gaol,' he conceded, 'are

avoided in this new one; but it has some manifest errors . . . It is now too late,' Howard writes, as if resigned to the inevitable endurance of Newgate as a site of untold misery, 'to point out particulars . . . All I will say, is, without more than ordinary care, the prisoners in it will be in great danger of the Gaol-Fever.'

Tipped into Howard's book is a blueprint of the new gaol along with a spreadsheet detailing everything from the salaries of prison staff to the intended capacity for each of the three principal 'Quadrangles' around which the cogs of the prison's administration were to turn: the Debtors' Quadrangle to the north, the Male Felons' Quadrangle in the centre, and the Women Felons' Quadrangle to the south. Howard fastidiously recorded not only the physical dimensions of the cells ('full nine feet by near six'), but also made reference to their psychological parameters. 'I was told by those who attended me, that criminals who had affected an air of boldness during their trial, and appeared quite unconcerned at the pronouncing [of] sentence upon them, were struck with horror, and shed tears when brought to these darksome solitary abodes.' Never before had the prison's architectural, financial and emotional co-ordinates been so painstakingly plotted for the public eye. Where The Gaol once loomed in the London imagination as a Piranesian maze of confused corridors and subterranean dungeons, which only a shadowy escapologist like Jack Sheppard could hope to negotiate, in the waning years of the 1770s, largely thanks to the efforts of John Howard, Newgate looked destined to enter its final era of existence as an arena of relative transparency.

That is, until the summer of 1780 and the bloodcurdling shrieks attested to later by witnesses to the uprising that began to foment outside Westminster. 'Ahoy for Newgate!' an anonymous rioter thundered. Within hours, all that was left of Dance's decade-long labour was a smouldering shell. The trouble began on 2 June 1780 when the President of the Protestant Association and Member of the House of Commons,

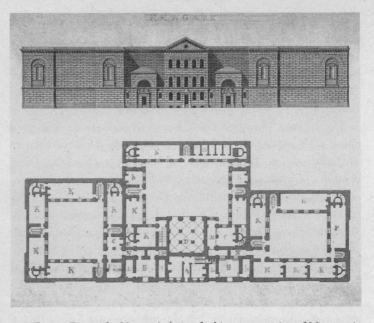

31. *George Dance the Younger's design for his reconstruction of Newgate in the 1770s*

Lord George Gordon, announced his intention to present to Parliament a petition demanding the immediate repeal of the 1778 Relief Act, which had permitted Catholics to own property, inherit land and join the military. Gordon said he was only prepared to sponsor such an action, however, provided that a crowd of sufficient size would gather to show support for him. When nearly seventy thousand snarling anti-papists gathered in St George's Field, south of the river, armed with makeshift weapons and sporting the blue cockades with which the Protestant Association had equipped them, it became clear that Gordon had awakened a sleeping fury, which no mere legislative gesture was likely to pacify.

Rolling towards Westminster, the mob surged across the city's bridges, picking up strays, and pinned itself against the

Houses of Parliament. In the days that followed, pockets of agitation flared up across the city, burning a chapel here and sacking a Catholic household there. By 5 June, the hotspots had begun to merge. The homes of Irish weavers in Spitalfields were torched. The author of the Relief Act, Sir George Savile, was chased from his home in Leicester Fields and made to watch as it was plundered, then razed to the ground. Terrified for their lives, members of Parliament refused to remain in session, thus adding to the sense that law and order had broken down. One by one the centres of London's authority were seized and sacked. The home of the Chief Justice, Lord Mansfield, became the site of a mini-massacre when a platoon of Foot Guards was ordered to open fire on rioters. While troops managed successfully to defend the Bank of England and the Royal Exchange from a full-frontal assault, the offices of the Bow Street Runners were less fortunate.

Attention then turned to the city's prisons, sparking a wave of unrest that earned 7 June 1780 the nickname 'Black Wednesday'. Though the Fleet and the King's Bench prisons, along with the string of smaller compters and roundhouses that littered London, were systematically ravaged, by far the rioters' greatest trophy was Dance's lavish monument to civic control – the second most expensive structure in the city after St Paul's – the newly refurbished Newgate Prison. Though history has blurred the composition of the mob into an anonymous mass of destructive opportunists, critical scholarship has managed to distinguish at least one face on the front flank of the offensive – a 23-year-old art student enrolled at the Royal Academy by the name of William Blake. The aspiring poet and engraver, who would in later life compose the great English anthem 'Jersusalem', was a rebellious and disaffected youth when he happened upon the army of agitators marching down Great Queen Street. Overwhelmed by the infectious frenzy, William abandoned his errand, grabbed a truncheon from a fellow rioter, and set off in the direction of The Gaol.

Londoners were appalled by the wave of violence consuming the city, and the sacking of Newgate was seen by many as constituting the climax of the devastating drama. Among those to witness the mob's descent on the prison at first hand was the 26-year-old poet George Crabbe. 'You have no conception,' Crabbe wrote, 'of the frenzy of the multitude.'

> Akerman's house now a mere shell of brickwork, they kept a store of flame there for other purposes. It became red-hot, and the doors and windows appeared like the entrance to so many volcanoes. With some difficulty they then fired the debtors' prison, broke the doors, and they, too, all made their escape . . . But I must not omit what struck me most: about ten or twelve of the mob getting to the top of the debtors' prison, whilst it was burning, to halloo, they appeared rolled in black smoke mixed with sudden bursts of fire – like Milton's infernals, who were as familiar with flame as with each other . . .
>
> I went home, and returned again at eleven o'clock at night. I met large bodies of horse and foot soldiers, coming to guard the Bank, and some houses of Roman Catholics near it. Newgate was at this time open to all; any one might get in, and, what was never the case before, any one might get out. I did both, for the people were now chiefly lookers-on. The mischief was done, and the doers of it gone to another part of the town.

Once a place of awesome impenetrability, Newgate had been reduced by the riots into a flimsy fabric. Were he not mesmerised by the silhouetted shapes shifting into and out of the inferno raging before his eyes, Crabbe might have noticed in the crowd beside him the portly figure of Dr Johnson, no less hypnotised by the carnage. 'One might see,' Johnson later wrote, 'the glare of conflagration fill the sky from many parts. The sight was dreadful. Some people were threatened . . . Such a time of terrour you have been happy in not seeing.'

With the destruction of the city's prisons, the Gordon Riots had reached a crescendo of municipal unrest. By Friday, 9 June, the city had begun more efficiently to organise and deploy troops; Foot Guards now found themselves charged with taking whatever action was necessary to quell the violence. When it was all over, nearly three hundred rioters had been killed. Of the four hundred or more agitators who were arrested, sixty-two were eventually sentenced to death. The executions were conducted throughout the city, with gibbets being erected as near as possible to the many sites where the condemned had been seen contributing to the mayhem.

Many felt that the incendiary events of early June 1780 would leave a permanent scar not only on the city's infrastructure, but on its soul. 'A metropolis in flames,' William Cowper wrote to the Reverend John Newton, 'and a Nation in Ruins.' A sufficient clamour was raised demanding that someone be held responsible for instigating the uprising that Lord George Gordon was eventually seized and charged with high treason. Held for eight months in the sooty husk of a crudely restored Newgate, in February 1781 Gordon was tried at the Old Bailey, where he was robustly defended by a clever young attorney and future Lord Chancellor, Thomas Erskine. Erskine endeavoured to convince the court that Gordon had committed no crime in rallying support for his measure to repeal the Catholic Relief Act and that he should not be held responsible for the hijacking of the occasion by violent rioters beyond his control. The jury deliberated for a mere thirty minutes before agreeing to acquit him.

Over the course of its long history, Newgate had suffered a seemingly endless series of convulsions both from within and from without. Repeatedly damaged by fire – from the Peasants' Revolt to the Great Fire – the structure had always managed to re-emerge from the ashes a more menacing institution than before. But the Gordon Riots were different. To many, the atmosphere in which the events of 1780 unfolded was apocalyptic in its intensity. Whereas earlier catastrophes had led to a rebirth of the prison, after the Gordon Riots it was utterly irredeemable. Dance had already exhausted the budget on what could be afforded for penal refurbishment. Newgate would have to hobble on in its damnified, ramshackle state – gutted, caked in soot – in every way living up to Henry Fielding's description of the place as den of depravity, 'a prototype of hell itself'.

15

Crinkums

'**CRINKUMS**, *the foul Disease.*'

In April 1790, adrift in choppy waters off the coast of False Bay in the Cape of Good Hope, a band of convicted felons bound for New South Wales was overheard whispering ways to take the vessel by force. With nearly every detail of their plot in place, the mutineers were suddenly overtaken, one by one, by the ship's officials, whipped with sea-soaked rope, and shackled to the soggy deck.

The ruse had been rumbled by a fresh-faced young lad called Samuel Burt, whose mild manners and dandyish dress might have tipped off the others that he wasn't really one of them. Once word of the near-insurrection en route to Botany Bay reached England, the heart-rending circumstances that had resulted in Burt's unlikely appearance aboard a transportation ship would be reported in the London newspapers. 'Being rejected by a woman he wished to marry,' an article in *The Times* would recount,

[Burt] committed forgery, and immediately afterwards surrendered himself at Bow-street, declaring to his friends he had done it for the purpose of getting hanged. Being considered as an object of compassion, he was offered his Majesty's most gracious pardon, which he twice or thrice refused. The lady at length consented to marry him; he then became as solicitous to live as he had before been anxious for death; but during her repeated visits to him in Newgate, she caught the gaol fever and died.

Gaol fever had been a pernicious hazard of prison life since at least the beginning of the fifteenth century, when Stow first records that 'in the yeare 1414, the Gaylors of *Newgate* and *Ludgate* dyed, and prisoners in *Newgate* to the number of 64'. Epidemic typhus is caused by a rod-shaped bacterium, *Rickettsia prowazekii*, and is spawned in the gut of lice that thrive on human skin. The louse provokes its human host to scratch, whereby blood vessels are exposed to the vermin's bacteria-rich excrement, causing infection. Symptoms are said to set in quickly and mercilessly, causing excruciating headaches, fevers, coughing, muscle pain, chills, plummeting blood pressure, sensitivity to light, and a swimming stupor. A hallmark of the fever is the livid rash that appears on the chest five days after symptoms have appeared, spreading to the victim's torso and extremities – stopping just short of the palms and soles.

Relatively light punishments were often cruelly converted into death sentences by the disease, generating tragic stories that only fuelled The Gaol's murky mystique. In 1723, one of the great beauties of the eighteenth century, Sarah Pridden, was sent to Newgate for a year after driving a bread knife through the forearm of her lover, the Honourable John Finch, third son of the second Earl of Nottingham, during an argument in a Covent Garden tavern. Initially, Sarah had counted herself lucky, having dodged a charge of murder for which she would have been executed. The eldest daughter of a bricklayer, Pridden had worked her way up from the scruffy brothels of Mother Needham, 'a noted Bawd', and Mother Wyburn around Drury Lane to become one of the most sought-after courtesans in English society. Having forged the name Sally Salisbury for herself after being told that she bore a resemblance to Lady Salisbury, it wasn't long before Sarah's clients included such formidable figures as Lord Bolingbroke, the Duke of Buckingham and the Prince of Wales. But the Christmas Eve scuffle in the Three Tuns tavern in Chandos Street, Covent Garden, where John Finch sustained his knife-wound, triggered a chain of events that left Sarah dead from the fever a mere six weeks before she was scheduled to be released.

Perhaps the most colourful figure to succumb to the disease was the one whose actions were thought by many to be responsible for exacerbating the dilapidated state of the prison. Though acquitted of having intentionally incited the riots that left The Gaol gutted, Lord George Gordon found himself falling foul of the law a few years later. A provocative pamphlet in which he flaunted his victory over the prosecution, entitled *Innocence vindicated, and the intrigues of popery and its abettors displayed*, was deemed seditious for its assault on the judicial process. To this were added bizarre charges of libel against the French Queen Marie Antoinette, for which Gordon was arrested in 1787 on his return from a brief exile in the Netherlands.

But the man who was convicted on both counts, and sentenced to five years in Newgate, had changed greatly since the riots that engulfed London in the summer of 1780. Since 1783, Gordon had become obsessed with Judaism and the prospect of the imminent millennium that might bring about the return of the Jews to Israel. Shortly before his arrest, at the age of 36, Gordon converted to Judaism – undergoing circumcision, growing a beard and changing his name to Israel Abraham George Gordon. Like many fresh converts to a new faith, Gordon was especially earnest in observing the dogmas of his adopted religion. Once in Newgate, the gaolers humoured Gordon's efforts to transform his cell into a cramped synagogue. Kosher meats and wine were allowed in and the smell of freshly baked challah wafted through the Press Yard. Jewish robes, fringed with tzitzit, and leather-strapped tefillin gave the place an authentically Hebrew feel. But not even the mezuzah, with its tight scroll of scripture, bolted to the doorpost of his cell, could prevent the encroachment of indiscriminate fever. On 1 November 1793 a delirious rendition of the French Revolutionary song 'Ça ira' could be heard issuing from Gordon's cell just before he died.

Occasionally, the fever grabbed hold of a whole corridor and refused to let go. Flare-ups of the foul disease could wipe out an entire ward of The Gaol. In 1750 an outbreak that spread from the prison to the adjoining Sessions House left forty-three people dead, including a pair of judges and the Lord Mayor of London, Sir Thomas Abney. The tragedy inspired a local parson, Dr Stephen Hales, to perfect a ventilation system that he had been toying with for some time, which made use of a windmill and a complex system of extraction pipes. The apparatus was affixed to the roof of the prison in 1752 and, initially at least, seemed to improve the circulation of air through the building. But the pipes were easily clogged and the regular unblocking that they required presented real dangers. While working on the apparatus, Clayton Hand, a journeyman engineer, accidentally opened 'one of the tubes of the old ventilator, which had stood there for three or four years'; 'such an offensive smell issued from it', a contemporary recorded, that Hand was 'immediately seized with a nausea and sickness'. It says something of the constitution of these individuals, and the times they lived in, that after eight days Hand would stoically insist that 'besides frequent retching to vomit, a trembling of his hands, and a constant head-ach', he otherwise felt fine. Of the dozen men it took to install Dr Hales's device, eight died of the fever.

It wasn't long before the contraption, which had been devised to alleviate the horrors of gaol fever, became itself the most feared apparatus in the city. One pamphlet from the period describes the fate of a 15-year-old boy whom 'some of the journeymen working in Newgate had forced . . . to go down into the great trunk of the ventilator, in order to bring up a wig, which one [of] them had thrown into it . . . As the machine was then working, he had almost been suffocated with the stench, before they could get him up.' Not only did the boy suffer horribly, 'the two men who helped him out, by receiving the foul steam from the trunk, were both set a vom-

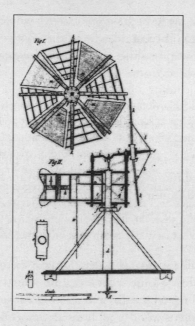

*32. Dr Stephen Hales's ventilation machine designed to
alleviate the threat of gaol fever*

iting so violently as to bring up blood.' Some years later, in a
bid to modernise the system, the celebrated chemist and
inventor of the coal miner's safety lamp, Humphry Davy, was
summoned to Newgate to inspect the cogs and tubes, whereupon he too contracted the illness, though he eventually
recovered.

Newgate's reputation as a distillery of disease, or 'tomb for
the living' as it was called, only added to its repulsive allure.
Though physicians refused to visit, amateur herbalists relished
the challenge of concocting a repellent salve for the prison and
Sessions House, which could be rubbed deep into the stone
fabric of the building. 'To keep out the foul air while in court',
according to Daniel Peter Layard — copies of whose 1772
manual *Directions to prevent the contagion of the jail-distemper,*

commonly called the jail-fever were carried by gaolers and Old Bailey officials in the last decades of the eighteenth century – one must follow a miasmic recipe of complicated and 'hastily thrown together' ablutions:

> candided orange or lemon peel, preserved ginger, and garlic if not disagreeable, cardamom, caraway, or other comfits, may be very useful; and should the mouth be clammed, dry raisins, currants, or lemon drops, will cool, and quench thirst, which, should it increase, may be assuaged by small draughts of old hock and water, or small punch. Smelling to good wine vinegar during the trials, will not only refresh, but revive, more agreeably and coolly, than the use of spirituous waters distilled from lavender or rosemary, and more than any other scents.

According to Layard, in order to make the prison and the adjacent Sessions House proof against infection, a fragrant fumigation of 'tobacco stalks and dried aromatic herbs', 'mint, rosemary, southern wood' and 'bruised juniper berries' were to be burned 'by means of large braziers, pans, or coppers' before the court came into session. Fumes of the bizarre mixture would mingle with the acrid stench of 'wet gunpowder and frankincense' heaped on 'hot iron shovels', while 'the steams of boiling hot vinegar' were 'conveyed to all parts of the building'. 'While the court is sitting,' Layard suggested finally, 'great relief, and refreshment, might be procured, by burning tar in the yard, now and then, which would exhale . . . an agreeable smell.' It is difficult to believe that Layard's complex fumigation of the prison and court was ever followed to the letter and even harder to imagine what the inmates must have smelt like if it was. As already mentioned, efforts to keep the courtroom well-ventilated by removing an entire wall of the lower floor, along the lines of an al fresco Italianate design, did less to combat disease than to strengthen comparisons between English justice and open-air entertainment. 'If crime and detection rely upon disguise,' Peter Ackroyd has noted, 'so London punishment had

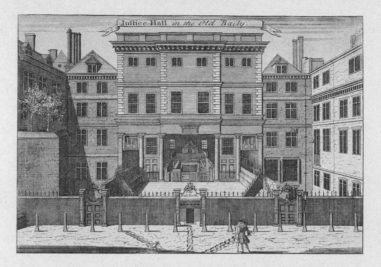

33. View of the Sessions House when proceedings were conducted al fresco

its own theatre of judgement and pain. The Old Bailey itself was designed as a dramatic spectacle, and was indeed compared with "a giant Punch and Judy show" where judges sat within the open portico of a Sessions House which resembled a theatrical backdrop.'

By the time the prison was finally abandoned at the end of the nineteenth century, this particularly virulent strain of typhus, which spread like wildfire through Newgate's fetid cells, had claimed more lives than all of the relentlessly innovative forms of execution dreamed up there put together. For every felon that the prison hung out to dry, it has often been estimated that four died of gaol fever. Incubated by incompetence, gaol fever amounted to little less than passive poisoning. Not to be confused, of course, with the more active kind . . .

16

Twist

'**TWIST**, *half Tea, half Coffee: Likewise Brandy and Eggs mixed. Hot-Pot. Also to Eat; as,* To Twist lustily; *To feed like a Farmer.*'

It all started with a batch of burnt dumplings.

A maidservant and cook, a petite and by all accounts beautiful girl by the name of Elizabeth Fenning (everyone called her 'Eliza'), had been anxious to try her hand at making dumplings for her employer's family, the Turners, for weeks. Eliza finally got round to doing so for tea on the afternoon of Tuesday, 15 March 1815. Dumplings, as everyone knows, are meant to puff to a fine fluffiness and getting the consistency right requires a finesse that one would be lucky to achieve on a first attempt. Whatever words one might want to attach to Eliza Fenning – and before the week was out she would be described as many things, from murderous to maligned – 'lucky' would not be one of them.

Trying to put a brave face on a botched job, the 22-year-old slid the would-be dumplings one by one on to the plates of Orlibar Turner, his son Robert and his daughter-in-law Charlotte, before setting some aside for the Turners' apprentice, Robert Gadsden. Eliza even crunched courageously into one herself, blushing inwardly as she wondered how many more bungled suppers she could risk before being given the sack. But before the evening was out, Eliza's charred dumplings were doing more than merely causing embarrassment. Robert Gadsden was the first to fall ill, clutching his gut and vomiting violently. 'I felt considerable heat across my stomach,' he would later testify in the Old Bailey, 'and chest and pain.' Eliza was next and then, in turn, the Turners. Each was as ill as the other, delirious with fever and desperate to know what was wrong. 'I felt myself very faint', Charlotte would recall in court, 'and an excruciating pain; an extreme violent pain which increased every minute.'

The search for the cause of the illness that gripped No. 68 Chancery Lane in the same week that Napoleon escaped from exile in Elba and prepared to enter Paris, would leave one person suspended from the gallows, another propelled to fame, and Newgate reasserted, yet again, as the curious epicentre of English consciousness.

At 9 p.m., another of the Turners' apprentices, Thomas King, fetched a couple of surgeons from around the corner. As Henry Ogilvy ministered to those in agony upstairs, rubbing the victims' abdomens with warm flannel and dosing them with drops of laudanum, John Marshall poked about in the pantry, running his fingers over the dishes and spoons scattered across the kitchen, sniffing the contents of dirty ramekins and sticky bowls. He had begun to wonder whether curdled cream, perhaps, or rancid eggs could be to blame when his eye fell on the burnt pan in which the dumplings had failed to rise. In the blackened residue of caked flour he noticed, so he later said, a scattering of crystals, which piqued his interest. Fumbling for his pocket scalpel, Marshall scraped loose a sample of the suspicious substance, which, he said, instantly corroded the metal an ominous black. Then, employing a method that would make modern-day crime-scene investigators cringe, he 'dissolv[ed] the dough in warm water' in order to see whether the crystals would sink. Sinking crystals, so Marshall later explained, are a sure sign of arsenic. The crystals sank.

Still suffering from nausea, Eliza was taken into custody and marched the short distance to Hatton Gardens police office where she was charged with attempting to poison the members of her employer's residence before being transferred to Newgate. Handling the case for the Crown was the notorious womaniser, Recorder Sir John Silvester, or 'Black Jack' as he was known to those familiar with his methods of eliciting co-operation from female defendants in exchange for leniency. Silvester was infamous for his opposition to any efforts by more progressive judges to mop up the 'Bloody Code' by reducing the number of capital offences it had absorbed along the way. His cantankerousness became the object of merciless caricaturing by Cruikshank and other illustrators whose acerbic sketches made much of Black Jack's grotesque girth and legendary lechery.

Silvester liked the look of Eliza Fenning from the first and would later be accused of having turned spiteful when she refused to play his brand of penal poker. Certainly his exclusion of any exonerating evidence that might be put before the jury and his ferocious summing-up seemed to suggest that personal animus was fuelling his performance as much as any allegiance to justice. Aware that his case rested on nothing more than scant circumstantial evidence, Silvester slyly spun it to the credulous court that insinuation was often sounder than proof. 'Although we have nothing before us but circumstantial evidence, yet it often happens that circumstances are more conclusive than the most positive testimony.' Swallowing it whole, the jury succumbed to Black Jack's bullying and retired for only a few minutes before returning a verdict of guilty.

Lodged in the condemned ward of The Gaol while her lawyers exhausted a string of unpromising appeals, Eliza became the object of obsessive interest across the capital as tabloids competed to publish anecdotes that pointed to her innocence on the one hand and rumours confirming her guilt on the other. Particularly tantalising was the hypothesis that Eliza was taking revenge on her employer for having been punished a few evenings earlier for entering the servants' bedroom naked from the waist up. Though there was no truth in it, the story stuck and helped to fuel the public's fascination with Fenning.

After three months of inept efforts to have the Fenning case reopened, Eliza's counsel conceded defeat. She would be executed by means of the portable contraption known austerely as 'the new drop', the clamorous erection of which outside the Debtors' Door in Old Bailey could be heard reverberating through the prison at crack of dawn on hanging days. Gone was the era of trundling convicts two-and-a-half miles to Tyburn. The famous procession had come to an end in the autumn of 1783 when the highwayman John Austin was hanged there for the fatal stabbing of John Spicer on Bethnal Green. Having recovered from the trauma of watching his masterwork gutted in the Gordon Riots, George Dance was summoned yet again to the prison in 1787. He was commissioned to devise a scaffold that could more efficiently be dismantled and reassembled after it was discovered that the initial prototype required the recruitment of 'twenty men from ten o'clock on Tuesday night to seven the next morning' at a liquid cost to The Gaol of 'twenty pints of porter' to keep the carpenters' elbows well greased.

By moving the site of execution to Newgate, it was hoped that the gathering of enormous crowds, which had begun to clog the arteries of Edgware Road and Oxford Street, would be discouraged. This was not the case, however. The thousands, sometimes tens of thousands, who would devote part of their day to witnessing the last gasps of a condemned felon, managed to squeeze themselves into the narrow wedge of space outside the prison. 'The age is running mad after innovation,' an irate Dr Johnson had whinged to Boswell on hearing of the relocation, and 'Tyburn is not safe from the fury of innovation.' 'No, Sir, it is not an improvement,' Boswell replied. 'They object that the old method drew together a number of spectators. Sir, executions are intended to draw spectators. If they don't draw spectators, they don't answer their purpose.'

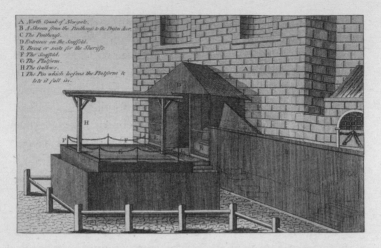

A *North Road of Newgate.*
B *A Screen from the Penthouse to the Prison door.*
C *The Penthouse.*
D *Entrance on the Scaffold.*
E *Beam or seats for the Sheriffs.*
F *The Scaffold.*
G *The Platform.*
H *The Gallows.*
I *The Pin which loosens the Platform & lets it fall in.*

34. The so-called 'new drop', erected outside The Gaol on execution days. It was on such a contraption that Eliza Fenning was hanged in June 1815 as the journalist and radical publisher William Hone looked on

Occasionally the overcrowding outside the prison on execution days proved as lethal as the cramped conditions within. A few years before the Fenning affair, in February 1807, over forty thousand Londoners had elbowed their way into the slim space between The Gaol and St Sepulchre's to witness the simultaneous execution of Owen Haggerty, John Holloway and Elizabeth Godfrey, a 34-year-old woman who had been convicted of 'petty treason' after fatally stabbing Richard Prince through his left eye on Christmas Day. As the platform floor swung open, snapping taut the three lengths of slipknot rope, a four-legged stool that stood beside the Debtors' Door, from which a pair of bakers had been selling pies to the gathering crowd, collapsed. The sudden crack startled the anxious audience, triggering a stampede that left more than a hundred people dead.

Witnesses to the carnage watched in horror as a girl, who carried her infant child on her hip, was pushed over and as she fell 'forced the baby into the arms of the man nearest her, requesting him, for God's sake, to save its life'. In the wave of violence that followed, the man in turn 'threw the infant from him, but it was fortunately caught at a distance by another man, who finding it difficult to ensure its safety or his own, got rid of it in a similar way.' Tossed from stranger to stranger, the child was eventually grabbed by a man 'who contrived to struggle with it to a cart, under which he deposited it until the danger was over, and the mob had dispersed.'

When the day of her execution arrived, Eliza, who had been the only child of eight to survive infancy, put on the dress that had been saved by her parents for her wedding. The unlikely link between a marriage ceremony and the London hanging fairs stretched like a trampled bridal train back through the eighteenth century. There are bizarre references to Tyburn as the 'Wedding Gallows' and a tradition of condemned highwaymen adopting as their last costume the attire of a groom. 'I believe I am come,' announced John Weskett, who was sentenced to hang for stealing from his master, the Earl of Harrington, a handful of shiny knick-knacks, including a diamond button, a repeating watch, a silver candlestick and three gold snuff-boxes, 'to an untimely end, in order that my Soul might be saved; and I look upon this as my Wedding-Day.'

The link ignited a curious chemistry between the convict and the audience, who had come to watch a body jerk orgasmically, then collapse. 'The combination of nuptial clothing of the hanged felon,' according to the historian Peter Linebaugh, 'with the undercurrents of sexuality among the crowd at Tyburn opens Swift's ballad "Clever Tom Clinch Going to be Hanged"':

> As clever Tom Clinch, while the Rabble was bawling,
> Rode stately through Holbourn, to die in his Calling;
> He stopt at the George for a Bottle of Sack,
> And promis'd to pay for it when he'd come back.
> His Waistcoat and Stockings, and Breeches were white,
> His Cap had a new Cherry Ribbon to ty't.

The Maids to the Doors and the Balconies ran,
And said, lack-a-day! he's a proper young Man.
But, as from the Windows the Ladies he spy'd,
Like a Beau in the Box, he bow'd low on each Side . . .'

Sexual chemistry had invigorated the Fenning story from the outset and would continue to influence the way that her reputation would be both defended and damned for decades. 'Her white muslin gown tied with a satin riband and pale-lilac laced boots,' Ben Wilson has commented, 'symbolised not only the death of innocence, but a concept of unobtainable maidenhood, and the transition from virtue to burgeoning sexuality. The image of a young bride swinging on the gallows is a powerful one, but also deeply disturbing.'

On 26 June 1815, fifty thousand people pressed their way into the narrowing thoroughfare that stretched between The Gaol and the adjoining Sessions House. Witnesses to the event that warm summer morning said that Eliza moved gracefully across the platform, the first of three who were booked in to die that morning. As a final affront to the astonishing composure Eliza had maintained throughout the ordeal, the hangman attempted ineptly to stretch a cotton nightcap over her head, which must have been knitted for a child as it was too small even for Eliza's petite skull. The performance approached grim pantomime when the hangman produced two more hoods, each as ill-fitting as the first. Abandoning this, he then pulled a stained and crumpled handkerchief from his pocket and started to drape it over Eliza's face when her composure finally cracked. 'Pray do not put that on, pray do not. Pray do not let them put it on.'

The scene was excruciating to behold. Among those to be drawn into the theatre of inhumanity that late June morning was a 35-year-old struggling journalist and radical bookseller called William Hone. Hone's antennae were acutely attuned to injustice and a year earlier he had been responsible for exposing the unconscionable conditions suffered by the insane in the

35. *A highly eroticised likeness of Eliza Fenning.*
Such depictions of female defendants titillated readers of
contemporary broadsheets and pamphlets, boosting sympathy
and sales

city's lunatic asylums. Hone's wrenching accounts of what he saw festering inside these asylums were vividly enlivened by the illustrator Cruikshank and the reports they put before Parliament make gruelling reading to this day. Among the litany of abuses Hone helped to uncover was the sustained torture of an American called James Norris in New Bethlem Hospital – that warehouse of human wretchedness to which the archetypal label 'Bedlam' was attached. When Hone and his co-investigator, Edward Wakefield, revealed that Norris had been chained to a wall for twelve years, as he slowly wasted into a living ghost, the hospital administration was forced to explain itself, triggering a campaign of reform.

As Hone jostled for position among the impatient crowd, staring up at the makeshift scaffold, he was overwhelmed by an intuition that great injustice was once again dangling before his very eyes. 'Before the just and almighty God, and by the faith of the holy sacrament I have taken,' Eliza stated calmly, as invisible workmen greased the hinge beneath her feet, 'I am innocent of the offence with which I am charged.' The trapdoor slipped and before Eliza's body had stopped twitching, a court clerk began drawing up the fourteen-shilling invoice for recovery of her body, which would be presented to her father. Hone lacked the stomach for the second and third hangings and as he slid from the throng to his shop around the corner from the prison in Fleet Street, something inside him hardened. By the afternoon, and the appearance of government-friendly broadsheets insisting that Eliza had died 'with a lie upon the lips', Hone had already begun plotting what would become a seminal work in the history of British journalism and investigative reporting: a 240-page exposé of the judicial capriciousness that left an innocent girl twisting in the wind, entitled *The important results of an elaborate investigation into the mysterious case of Eliza Fenning* (1815).

Over the next four and a half months, and at great personal cost to his family in both emotional and financial terms, Hone set about dismantling the prosecution's paper-thin case. The first half of his report was devoted to unpicking the over-zealous Recorder's harangues to the jury, to reveal how Silvester had wilfully misinterpreted evidence, concealed facts that proved Eliza's innocence, and dissuaded witnesses from telling the truth. Insinuations that Fenning had been the only member of the household to have had access to the dumpling mixture were exposed as maliciously manufactured by the Turner family, as were suggestions that Fenning had been given notice of her dismissal days before the incident. Most damning of all was the fresh testimony that Hone provided, in part two of the volume, of key witnesses who had come forward during the course of the trial, only to be sent away by Silvester as irrelevant. As to why the Turner family would quietly collude in implicating the hapless cook, Hone uncovered a compelling scenario, which the sinister Silvester had swept under the carpet. Throughout the proceedings there were whispers that her employer's son, Robert, suffered bouts of violent depression. Hone traced these rumours back to a chemist called Mr Gibson of Corbyn & Co. in Holborn. Gibson revealed to Hone that Robert had paid him a visit shortly before the events of the ides of March that year 'in a wild and deranged state'. Giving vent to what Gibson described as 'violent and incoherent expressions', Robert confessed to being seized with a frenzy of destructive impulses. 'Get me secured or confined,' Robert is alleged to have said, 'for if I am at liberty . . . I shall destroy myself and my wife. I must and shall do it, unless all means of destruction are removed out of my way . . . something from above tells me I must do it.'

With each outrageous revelation of the ways in which Fenning had systematically been framed, Hone's resolve to avenge execution deepened. 'I took lodgings away from my family,' he later remembered, describing how his obsession with the investigation brought even his adoring and patient wife to breaking point, 'and for three weeks I was wholly engrossed on the case of Eliza Fenning . . . On the fourth Saturday evening my wife came to ask me for money – but I had none. I told my wife to go home, and that I would bring her the money, but I had no idea where to get it; I had not sixpence.' Hone had holed up in a shabby room opposite Newgate in Old Bailey, a few yards from where the legendary thief-taker Jonathan Wild had masterminded the capital's criminal underworld a century earlier. Hone's scribbling into the small hours, in the shadow of Fenning's final residence, was interrupted only by the occasional shouts of criminals being hauled into the prison's lodge.

When *The important results* was finally published in November 1815, it caused a stir, propelling its author into instant notoriety as an indefatigable defender of the underdog. In reconstructing the heroine of his damning indictment, Hone capitalised on the sexual allure that had been concocted by the popular press from the moment of Eliza's arraignment in Hatton Gardens. 'She seems,' according to Hone's recent biographer Ben Wilson, 'too good to be true. And so she was; the maid of Hone's book was carefully crafted to rouse public opinion and engrave the memory of the victim on the popular mind.' With her innocence ravaged by the gallows before it could be lost to a lover, Eliza Fenning became an icon of suspended virginity against a backdrop of male cruelty and incompetence. Fenning's refusal to confess on the scaffold had helped swing popular sentiment further behind her. Over ten thousand people followed her body to the grave, exceeding the numbers who turned out to receive the bodies of soldiers who fell that week in the Battle of Waterloo. 'The crowds,' according to *The Times*, 'were immense':

> The funeral began to move from the house of her father in Eagle-street, Red Lion Square, about half past three o'clock. It was preceded by about a dozen peace officers, and these were followed by nearly 30 more; next came the undertaker, immediately followed by the body of the deceased. The pall was supported by six young females, attired in white: then followed eight persons, male and female, as chief mourners, led by the parents. These were succeeded by several hundred of persons, two and two, and the whole was closed by a posse of peace officers. Many thousands accompanied the procession, and the windows, and even tops of the houses, as it passed, were thronged with spectators. The whole proceeded in a regular manner, until it reached the burying ground of St George the Martyr.

The embarrassment that Hone's report caused to the grandees who stood impassive as Fenning was needlessly sacrificed, particularly Lord Chief Justice Ellenborough and the Home Secretary Lord Sidmouth, was considerable and left the fearless publisher marked out as a target for future prosecution. Hone would get his comeuppance two years later when he was brought to book on a string of trumped-up libel charges. His championing of Eliza Fenning stood him in good stead when he was called upon to defend himself during a series of court appearances in the Guildhall, which remain among the great triumphs for the underdog in British legal history.

17

Dag

'DAG, *a gun.*'

By the beginning of the nineteenth century and the final era of The Gaol's existence, the status of Newgate as the pre-eminent theatre in which the capital's dramas unfolded was indisputable. A century earlier, the distance between stage and cell began to blur as the profiles of real and invented figures, from the legendary Claude Duval to the iconic Macheath of *The Beggar's Opera*, drifted into one another: the influence of footpads on fiction and vice versa was one of the strangest and most alluring social pirouettes in British cultural history. In May 1812, a play scheduled to open at the Theatre Royal by Theodore Hook (a talented young prankster famous for the 'Great Berners Street Hoax') which had been widely advertised under the intriguingly permissive title *Killing No Murder*, was forced by the Lord Chamberlain to change at the last minute to the bland *Buskin and Belvi*, out of respect for the real-life saga that was then unravelling across town in a heavily guarded cell in Newgate.

This is where John Bellingham, a 42-year-old commercial agent, had been brought on the evening of 11 May by a cir-cuitous route from the Houses of Parliament. Here, at 5.15 p.m. and at point-blank range, he had drawn a pistol from a secret pocket recently stitched into his coat and sent a ball of lead through the unsuspecting heart of the young Prime Minister,

36. *One of the many depictions of the assassination of Prime Minister Spencer Perceval to appear in newspapers and magazines in May 1812*

Spencer Perceval. Within minutes, news of the assassination had spread like wildfire through the alehouses and coffee-shops scattered across the capital. By 6 p.m., the carriage route from Westminster to Newgate had begun to fill with incredulous onlookers anxious to catch a glimpse of either the monster or the hero – depending on who was doing the looking – of the latest figure to take centre-stage in London's long-running opera of fire.

Among the first to congregate outside Westminster were members of London's ultra-radical groups, sympathisers of the underground agrarian reformer Thomas Spence, who were desperate to ascertain whether it was one of their men who had taken matters into his own hands. Since the beginning of that year, a scheme had begun to take shape, sponsored by a political agitator called Arthur Thistlewood, whereby an emissary would be dispatched to Paris charged with persuading Napoleon to invade Britain and re-establish 'Saxon' control. Resentful at what they felt was the continued disenfranchisement of the working classes and a spiteful resistance on the part of Spencer Perceval's government to parliamentary reform, for many, news of the murder sparked hope that the implausible plan to import revolution from France may have got off to an auspicious start.

But the truth that would emerge in the frantic days that followed, as prosecution lawyers jostled with reporters for information from anyone connected to the assassin's past, was at once more chilling and more poignant than anyone could have imagined. Bellingham, so the papers would report, was not party to any fringe political movement or underground nest conspiring to ignite radical reform. His was less a political grievance than a personal grudge – a gripe that had begun eight years earlier, thousands of miles away from London in an icy, rat-infested prison cell near the White Sea in the far north of Russia.

Born in 1770 in St Neots, Huntingdonshire, the son of a painter of miniatures, Bellingham suffered an emotionally choppy childhood. His father died from mental illness when Bellingham was nine and when he was 14 he ran away from home after an abortive apprenticeship with a jeweller in Whitechapel. By the age of 17, he found himself briefly employed as a midshipman on the East Indian boat *Hartwell*, though the vessel sank on 23 May 1787 after ramming a reef off the coast of Bonavista. Lurching from crisis to disappointment, Bellingham next tried his hand at working in a tinplate shop in Oxford Street, but by the early 1790s he was forced to declare himself bankrupt. Bellingham's subsequent incarnation – his last before reinventing himself as the only man in history to assassinate a British prime minister – was as a merchant broker, negotiating imports and exports from Russia, shuttling back and forth between Liverpool and Archangel.

In the summer of 1804, Bellingham set out, together with his new young wife and their infant son, on what would prove to be his final journey to Russia. When his family embarked, Bellingham had no way of knowing that they were sailing into a convoluted trap that would change the course not only of his life, but of British political history. The previous autumn, a Russian-owned commercial ship called the *Sojus* sank in the White Sea. When its owner, a prominent member of a Russian merchant family and Mayor of Archangel, Vasily Popov, attempted to collect on an insurance policy, which was held by Lloyd's Coffee House, the claim was refused. Lloyd's had begun to suspect that the *Sojus* had been destroyed intentionally and that the claim amounted to fraud. For reasons that remain a mystery to this day, Popov was led to believe that the person responsible for tipping off Lloyd's was Bellingham.

Infuriated by his loss, Popov had the Bellinghams' travel passes confiscated on the eve of their return to England, thus preventing them from leaving Archangel even to conduct business in St Petersburg or to seek advice at the Embassy there. Meanwhile, a lengthy investigation was undertaken into what were almost certainly trumped-up charges of debt against them. Eventually thrown into prison, Bellingham watched as his alleged liability swelled farcically from a few roubles to over 38,000 without the Russian officials ever providing proof of the debt. To make matters worse, Bellingham's portmanteau of business documentation, which contained any paperwork he might have that could assist him in demonstrating his innocence, was spitefully seized. Desperate, Bellingham made appeals to the Governor-General for diplomatic intercession on his behalf. At first these appeared to work and the British Consul initiated a dialogue with the Russian officials who were prosecuting the hapless merchant. But as months turned into years and the Russian position hardened, Bellingham found it increasingly difficult to disguise his frustration. 'Indecorous' outbursts from his cell slowly soured the Consul's sympathy. Bellingham was soon in receipt of correspondence from the British Ambassador that was as deliberately obtuse in its reluctance to offer assistance as the charges against him had been maliciously invented: 'I am sorry,' Lord Granville Leveson Gower wrote to Bellingham,

> to find that you are involved in so unpleasant a dispute at Archangel, but however desirous I may be of assisting you, it is not in my power to forward any Application for permission for you to come to St Petersburgh on your sole representation of the Circumstances of the Transaction in question, particularly as I find this Statement contradicted by the Letter of the Governor General of Archangel to Mr Shairp.
>
> At the same time, however, that I say this, I wish you to understand, that provided you can furnish me with such Evidence of your having been unjustly used, as will authorize my Interference on this subject, I shall very readily take such steps in your behalf as the occasion may appear to me to require.

For five years John Bellingham was 'bandied from prison to prison, and from dungeon to dungeon', as debt after dubious debt was alleged and abandoned. A contemporary witness to the appalling conditions in Russian gaols during this period reeled at what he called these 'abodes of wretchedness and misery' where 'great filthiness prevail[ed]'. 'Various kinds of vermin are numerous,' the French Quaker missionary and prison reformer Stephen Grellet recalled, 'the bed-bugs are seen in clusters on the walls, like swarms of bees on the sides of their hives. The air is noxious.' Having exhausted every means by which they could harass their helpless subject, short of banishing him to Siberia, the Russian authorities finally released Bellingham without having squeezed a single rouble out of his emaciated hands: 'At length the Senate, quite tired out by these severities, in 1809 I received, at midnight, a discharge from my confinement, with a pass, and an order to quit the Russian dominions.' And as he headed home, bankrupt and embittered, to be reunited with his estranged wife and son, something began to ossify inside Bellingham. His indignant displays of impassioned umbrage had slowly hardened into silent rage. His life had been ruined. Someone was going to pay.

Indeed, that was literally what he wanted: payment. Some kind of compensation for the years of lost life and wages. Once back in England, even before making contact with his family, on 27 December 1809 he wrote to the Foreign Secretary, the Marquis of Wellesley, laying out the particulars of his case and explaining why he had felt abandoned by his government. A polite reply a month later, in which Bellingham was told that the 'government [was] precluded from interfering', was followed by a barrage of brush-offs, which, one by one, would bring Bellingham to the brink. A letter petitioning the Right Honourable Lords and Commissioners of His Majesty's Treasury met with almost immediate rebuff. The Privy Council followed suit. Bellingham's hopes were briefly raised in May 1810, when he took the notion that a rising star in government, Spencer Perceval, who was known for his judicial fairness and was then serving as Attorney-General, must surely be in a position to redress such prima facie injustice as he had suffered. But to Perceval himself, all access was denied. 'The time for presenting private petitions,' Bellingham was informed by the minister's secretary, 'has long since passed . . . Mr Perceval cannot encourage you,' the letter went on tauntingly to explain, 'to expect his sanction in introducing into the House a petition, which Mr Perceval thinks is not of a nature for the consideration of Parliament.'

Spurned at every turn, for the next eighteen months Bellingham retreated into himself. His wife and business contacts were disturbed by his introversion, which occasionally erupted into cryptic outbursts asserting a victim's right to revenge. By the beginning of 1812, Bellingham was basing himself in London, with one hand on the tiller of his lagging mercantile business, as his wife loyally looked after the family back in Liverpool. By March, he had whipped up a final flurry of petitions, which he subtly laced with hints of vengeance, should he continue to be ignored. Too subtly, it seems. A letter to the Magistrates of the Public Office, in Bow Street, which insisted that 'should this reasonable request be finally denied, I shall then feel justified in executing justice myself', was met with the same cold shoulder.

On 20 April, Bellingham made the short stroll from his lodgings near Coldbath Fields, up Gray's Inn Road and across Holborn Bridge, to Snow Hill, just short of Newgate. At No. 58 Skinner Street, he paid the gunsmith W. Beckwith four guineas for a brace of seven-inch steel pistols, which he carried to Primrose Hill to practise firing in broad daylight at tree trunks and the skittish demons of his soul who ducked behind them.

On his walk back to his rented rooms in No. 9 New Millman Street, he met a local clothier, James Taylor, along Guilford Street, and invited him back for a drink. Taylor had recently fitted Bellingham with a new waistcoat and trousers and was pleased to be asked whether he might consider another trifling commission. Disappearing for several minutes, Bellingham returned and handed him a heavy charcoal-grey coat. Puzzled by what appeared to be a coat in fine condition, and which seemed already to be Bellingham's size, Taylor asked his host what work he could possibly wish him to undertake. 'He accordingly gave me a bit of paper', Taylor would later testify in the Old Bailey, a pattern 'about the length of nine inches' and 'gave me directions to make him a pocket on the left side, so as he could get at it conveniently'. 'Did you execute that order?' Taylor was eventually asked by the prosecution. 'I did, he was very particular to have it home that evening.'

On the morning of 11 May 1812, Bellingham breakfasted and spent an hour putting his affairs in order. He wrote letters to his wife and to a handful of business associates and tried to forget about an altercation he had had with a laundrywoman the night before, whom he felt had slightly overcharged him to wash his dressing gown. He laid a prayer book, which he had purchased a few days earlier, on his bedstand and agreed to accompany his landlady, Rebecca Roberts, and her son on a visit to the European Museum in King Street, St James's Square (which would later become the home of Christies auction house). As the three strolled around the exhibition, amicably discussing the pictures on display, nothing in Bellingham's outward demeanour betrayed to his companions the truth of what he had tucked deep into a slender pocket inside his coat. After leaving the museum, the three meandered back towards Leicester Square where Bellingham announced that there was something he had to do in Westminster, an errand.

It had been a bizarrely quiet day in the Houses of Parliament. Fewer than one in ten of the 658 members of the House had been present to consider a motion designed to strengthen a shipping blockade against Napoleon. Debate on the issue had been scheduled to resume at 4.30 p.m. and a messenger had been sent by Henry Brougham, the member responsible for the legislation, to inform the new Prime Minister, Spencer Perceval, an erratic timekeeper, that he was forty minutes late. At 5.15, Perceval burst through the large folding doors that led to the lobby of the House, hustling his way towards the debating chamber. But after eight years, Bellingham was tired of waiting. Expressionless, he rose from the marble bench on which he'd been sitting, as if in some kind of trance, reached behind his lapel and, with the clench of his forefinger, for the first time presented a case to the government that could not be brushed off.

Bellingham was instantly seized by William Jerdan, a reporter for the newspaper *The British Press* who happened to be passing through the lobby at the time, while bystanders tended to Perceval who was heard murmuring, 'Murder,' as blood trickled from both corners of his sagging mouth. According to witnesses, Bellingham was a curious paradox of cool-headedness and uncontrollable emotion. 'His chest,' Jerdan would later recall, 'rose and fell a spasmodic action, as if a body as large as the hand were choking him at every breath. Never on earth, I believe, was seen a more terrible example of over-wrought suffering: yet, in language, he was perfectly cool and collected. Someone come from the Speaker's room, and said, "Mr. Perceval is dead!"'

The officials who descended on Bellingham, ripping his clothes open and turning out his pockets, were taken aback by the assailant's resigned compliance. 'I wish I were in Perceval's place,' he confessed. 'I submit myself to justice.' What followed was surreal in its orderliness. Bellingham was escorted to the Bar of the House where the Speaker politely confirmed his name. He was then taken without resistance to the prison room of the Serjeant-at-Arms where he calmly discussed his motives with a group of stunned House members while bystanders were interviewed. Word that all efforts to revive the young head of government had failed trickled through the chambers as ministers scurried hither and yon, debating to whom the miserable task of informing Perceval's wife should fall. There was also the tricky matter of how to transfer the gunman from Parliament to prison without inciting mayhem. By seven o'clock, rumours had begun to spread that anti-government radicals were gathering along the obvious routes between Westminster and Newgate, rehearsing ways of hijacking the carriage that would soon be carrying what each disgruntled group presumed must be a sympathiser.

At eight o'clock, a hackney coach standing outside the gates to Lower Palace Yard was nearly commandeered and its driver roughed up when 'a most ruffianly mob' mistakenly suspected that the prisoner of whom the city was waiting to catch a glimpse might be inside. 'By main force, only,' according to a bystander, Sir George Jackson, 'could they be prevented from mounting the coach-box, clinging to the wheels, and even entering the coach to shake hands with and congratulate the murderer on his deed. They were whipped off; beaten off – there was no other course left – amidst the execrations of the mob on the police and the vociferated applause and hurrahs . . . Not a few captures were made of the most active and daring.' By nine o'clock the crowd outside the Houses of Parliament rivalled those that once gathered around the Triple Tree at Tyburn. A column of Life Guards struggled to keep order as cutpurses and prostitutes circulated, practising their skills, and bewildered ministers paced around contemplating their next move. By all accounts, the calmest man in Parliament that evening was Bellingham, who sat talking with his captor in the House jail, the magistrate Michael Angelo Taylor. It wasn't until midnight when the throng began to thin that those guarding Bellingham saw their chance and, under heavy protection by a column of Dragoon Guards, dared to march the prisoner through the Speaker's Court, foist him into a carriage, and set him off on a circuitous route to Newgate.

If the dust had begun to settle a little around Westminster, at Newgate things were just warming up. Crowds fresh from the alehouses in Fleet Street collided along Old Bailey with a legion of equally inebriated revellers heading west from Cheapside in the hope of cheering on the man whose name, let alone motives, had yet to circulate. Horse Guards kept the peace as the carriage carrying Bellingham clattered to a halt and the prisoner was lifted by his armpits by burly Bow Street Runners awaiting his arrival and briskly bundled inside. He was led by the Keeper, John Addison Newman, through a labyrinth of dark, dank halls – the shuffle of his feet against the filthy stone slabs masking the grunts and expletives that wafted towards him from the adjacent rooms. Eventually they reached his cell, situated beside the chapel. Bellingham seemed to take little notice of the formidable appointments of his new accommodation: the double-barring on the door, the bricks that had been cemented into the small recess where once yawned a tiny window, and the hooped iron ring, rooted in the middle of the stone floor, to which he was immediately tethered. All these precautions were understandable given the nature of the appalling crime that had just been committed. But Bellingham was no Jack Sheppard. He wasn't going anywhere.

As Bellingham slept, officers of the court were furiously investigating whether his confessions of a personal grudge were the whole story and not merely a pathetic cover for a more sinister and far-reaching radical conspiracy. His rooms in New Millman Street had been ransacked for clues and his incredulous landlady, Mrs Roberts, interrogated. Taylor, the tailor, came forward with his long slip of paper. When Bellingham's wife was tracked down in Liverpool, she corroborated every detail of his anguished statement. By morning, London was a heaving contradiction of grief for its heinously slain leader and fascination with the mind of a man who believed his murder was not merely justified, but virtuous. When Bellingham awoke, he resumed his daily habits irrespective of his new surroundings, and spent the hour before breakfast writing letters. Planning ahead, he wrote to Mrs Roberts:

Tuesday morning, Old Bailey

Dear Madam,

Yesterday midnight I was escorted to this neighbourhood by a noble troop of light horse, and delivered into the care of Mr Newman (by Mr Taylor, the magistrate and M.P.) as a State Prisoner of the first class. For eight years I have never found my mind so tranquil as since this melancholy, but necessary catastrophe: as the merits or demerits of my peculiar case must be regularly unfolded in a Criminal Court of Justice to ascertain the guilty party, by a jury of my country, I have to request the favour of you to send me three or four shirts, some cravats, handkerchiefs, nightcaps, stockings, &c. out of my drawers, together with comb, soap, toothbrush, with any other trifle that presents itself which you think I may have occasion for, and inclose them in my leather trunk, and the key please to send sealed, per bearer; also my great coat, flannel gown, and black waistcoat, which will most oblige, Dear Madam, your very obedient Servant,

JOHN BELLINGHAM

To the above please to add the prayer book.

Bellingham was clearly preparing for a lengthy stay in Newgate, certain that he would not be tried until the next sessions. But events were moving more quickly than he could have imagined and, as it would happen, there would be little need for so many shirts or cravats.

Soon satisfied that Bellingham had indeed acted alone, and that he was in no apparent way connected to any anti-government groups or agrarian agitators for reform who were known to have entertained schemes for destabilising government, prosecutors for the Crown, led by the notoriously sour Attorney-General, Sir Vicary 'Vinegar' Gibbs, turned their attention to the potential defences that were open to the accused. The most obvious of these, of course, was a plea of insanity or derangement. But neither Bellingham's outward demeanour since his incarceration nor his pride would countenance such a defence. His counsel would try, but Bellingham took umbrage at the very suggestion. Indeed, to anyone who came into contact with the assassin in those days between capture and trial, Bellingham appeared utterly in control of his senses and entirely without remorse for what he believed was a mandated deed.

By and large, Bellingham was an easy guest in Newgate, if bemused by all the fuss that was being made over him and the preposterous whisperings of possible conspiracy and links with radical reformers. He seemed neither to take comfort from those who supported him, nor offence at those who condemned his actions. So concerned were the turnkeys and Keepers about the possibility of vigilantism preventing justice from taking its due course that they refused to provide Bellingham with food or drink prepared by anyone but themselves. As information was brought to light about Bellingham's grudge against the government, and his shadowy years spent in Russian detention, sympathetic stories concerning the family life of the slain Prime Minister were splashed across the newspapers. News of his fatherless daughters' confirmation by the

Bishop of London at St Martin-in-the-Fields tugged as hard at the heartstrings of the capital as some wished to see the noose drawn tightly round the assassin's neck. By the time Bellingham was led into the Old Bailey on Friday morning, 15 May, barely three days after the 'necessary catastrophe', no one in London remained indifferent to his fate.

Dressed neatly in striped waistcoat and nankeen trousers, Bellingham had been led down the warren of fusty hallways from his cell to the Sessions House next door. That morning, he had managed to hold down only an orange at breakfast, and for a brief moment, hit by the full horror of how his actions would affect the future of his family, he broke down. By the time he reached court, he was once again fully composed. The proceedings began with a lengthy tussle over whether the defence could be granted a postponement and therefore more time to produce evidence and witnesses, which Mr Peter Alley, Bellingham's chief counsel, claimed could demonstrate that the accused was in fact insane when he committed the crime. But Vinegar Gibbs would have none of what he perceived as playing for time by the defence, and implored the judge, Sir James Mansfield, to refuse any such delay and immediately empanel a jury.

Instructing the twelve men who had been summoned to decide Bellingham's fate to consider nothing other than 'whether the Prisoner at the Bar was, or was not, capable of distinguishing between right and wrong, at the time when the crime which he was now called on to answer, was perpetrated', Mansfield motioned to Gibbs to proceed with the prosecution's case. The first called to testify was William Smith, a member of Parliament who happened to be engaged in a conversation in the lobby of the House when Bellingham stepped forward and shot Perceval through the chest. 'I stopped to speak to a gentleman whom I met with there; while in conversation with that gentleman I heard the report of a pistol, which appeared to have been fired close by the entrance of the door of the lobby.' Smith explained how he had helped move Perceval's body on to a nearby table. 'Had you afterwards,' Gibbs asked, helping Smith reconstruct the tragic scene, 'any opportunity of seeing where Mr Perceval was wounded?' 'The wound was very near the nipple of the left breast,' Smith explained, 'a little above it and within it; the orifice appeared to me to be large for a pistol ball, and when Mr Lynn probed it, it seemed clearly that the ball had slaunted downwards, but it appeared clearly that the ball had penetrated the cavity of the breast, for the probe did not touch it.'

One by one, witnesses were called forward to help establish what no one in attendance doubted for a second – Bellingham's sole responsibility for planning and committing the audacious crime. Henry Burgess, a respected solicitor who was on business in Westminster when the shot was fired, testified to the condition of the firearm, which he seized from Bellingham's hand after hearing the blast. 'It was warm, it had the appearance of having been recently discharged.' Much attention was paid to Bellingham's coat. James Taylor told the court about the unusual pistol-shaped pocket that Bellingham wanted sewn inside it and held up 'a bit of paper about nine inches in length', with which the defendant had provided him as a pattern. Newman, Keeper of Newgate, was asked to verify whether the coat in question was in fact the one that the prisoner had been wearing upon arrival at the prison. John Vickery, a Bow Street Runner, who had been despatched on the evening of the murder to search Bellingham's rooms in New Millman Street, described the evidence of lethal obsession he had discovered among the defendant's belongings – 'the small powder flask' and 'gunpowder in a paper box', 'small flints', 'a pistol key, and a mould for casting bullets'. The jury did its best to remain focused as the testimony droned on, and to put aside the well-known fact that Bellingham had surrendered himself immediately after firing the fatal shot and had never for a moment denied the extent of his premeditation.

What they longed to hear was the defendant's version of events and to have the opportunity to measure just how far down the flickering corridors of madness he had strayed.

After four hours of tedious testimony and a brief recess, the court was finally ready for Bellingham to explain himself. 'Now is the time,' Mansfield instructed the accused, 'for you to make any defence you have to offer or to produce any witnesses that you wish to be examined.' The judge's overture inviting witnesses for the defence to be brought forward was, as everyone in attendance knew, cynically disingenuous. Having hastened the proceedings so that fewer than seventy-two hours had elapsed since the crime had been committed, Mansfield made certain that the defendant was in no position to produce either family members or business associates from Liverpool who might be able to attest to his state of mind or corroborate his story. British due process, Bellingham discovered, could be as capricious as Russian. Whatever the defendant wanted the jury to hear, it would have to come from his lips. For years Bellingham had felt that the government deserved to stand trial for its cavalier disregard of his rights and failure to protect his freedom. And as he rose to address the court, it struck him that, ironically, this was the stage he had constructed for those long-overdue proceedings. One man had already been killed for the attention he was now receiving. And he knew that, no matter what he said, the death toll would be likely to double.

Never before in his life had Bellingham been called upon to speak in public. And it showed. Sweat beaded his brow and his hands began to rattle the wad of papers in his hands. He tried to steady himself by sounding a note of gratitude to the prosecution for refusing to countenance his counsel's efforts to have his actions excused as the product of derangement. 'I feel great personal obligations,' he insisted, 'to the learned Attorney-General for the objections that he made to the defence set up by my counsel on account of insanity':

37. *A portrait of John Bellingham who stood accused
of assassinating the Prime Minister Spencer Perceval in
1812*

it is far more fortunate for me that such a plea as that should be
unfounded, and at the same time I am under the same obligation to my learned counsels for their zeal in my defence in
setting up the plea that I am insane by the desire of my friends,
or that I have been insane. I am not apprised of a single instance
in Russia where my insanity was made public except in one
single instance, when the pressure of my sufferings had exposed
me to that imputation . . .

Once he had started, there was no going back. For nearly
two hours, in an impassioned speech, which was interrupted
only by his own tears, Bellingham addressed the jury in whose
hands his fate now rested. Appealing to its sense of compassion,
he painstakingly reconstructed his years of suffering in Russia
and his own government's refusal to offer him assistance:

Reflect now, gentlemen, if you can imagine yourselves in a
state of such accumulated misery; what must have been your
feelings? and from thence judge of mine. I had been but
recently married to a wife, then only twenty years of age, with

an infant at her breast, and pregnant with a second child; yet
was I doomed to continue immured in a dungeon in Russia for
six months longer . . . I had no friend beside: I was surrounded
by enemies . . . (*The Beauties of England and Wales, Or, Delineations,
Topographical, Historical, and Descriptive*, London, 1815, p. 60)

His voice shaking, squeezing syllables through clenched
teeth, Bellingham described his steadfast resistance to Russian
efforts to extort money from him and how he had been
'dragged about the streets with offenders who had been guilty
of the most atrocious crimes'. As a leitmotif to his testimony,
he read extracts from the mountain of letters he had received
from government officials, each explaining why his grievance
was unworthy of action. In attributing individual blame,
Bellingham singled out Lord Leveson Gower and Sir Stephen
Shairp, whom he felt had abandoned him to his fate. When it
came to the question of why, therefore, he ultimately set his
sights on Spencer Perceval – the only point on which the jury
would be able to convict or acquit him – his logic was muddled
and one could sense the sympathy that he had masterfully mus-
tered, only moments before, slowly seeping away. 'Gentlemen,
a refusal of justice,' Bellingham maintained, 'was the sole cause
of this fatal catastrophe:

His Majesty's ministers have now to reflect upon their conduct
for what has happened. Lord Gower is now in court, I call on
him to contradict, if he can, the statement I have made, and,
gentlemen, if he does not, I hope you will then take my statement to be correct. Mr Perceval has unfortunately fallen the
victim of my desperate resolution. No man, I am sure, laments
the calamitous event more than I do. If I had met Lord Gower
he would have received the ball, and not Mr Perceval. As to
death, if it were to be suffered five hundred times, I should
prefer it to the injuries and indignities which I have experi-
enced in Russia, I should consider it as the wearied traveller
does the inn which affords him an asylum for repose, but government, in the injustice they have done me, were infinitely

more criminal than the wretch, who, for depriving the traveller of a few shillings on the highway, forfeits his life to the law. What is the comparison of this man's offence to government? or, gentlemen, what is my crime to the crime of government itself? It is no more than a mite to a mountain, unless it was proved that I had malice propense towards the unfortunate gentleman for whose death I am now upon my trial. I disclaim all personal or intentional malice against Mr Perceval.

Unable to accept that the assassination of the Prime Minister was an unavoidable consequence of the defendant's chronic misfortune, and prohibited by Judge Mansfield from dismissing the act as in any way a manifestation of insanity, the jury was left in little doubt as to their obligation to the Crown. Whatever else he was, Bellingham was not a stupid man. He had understood the law perfectly well, yet made no effort to offer a legal defence for his actions. At some point, probably on an unremembered day in an icy cell in Archangel, Bellingham ceased fully to inhabit in the real world. For him, the murder of Spencer Perceval was merely an audition for a performance he had rehearsed in his mind for years without an audience. Desperate for a platform from which he might finally be heard, and after deliberation by the jury of only fifteen minutes, Bellingham was finally given what he had long wanted – only this platform was fitted with a trapdoor.

Once he was in possession of the verdict, the judge did not have to search for words. 'Prisoner at the bar!' thundered Mansfield, 'you have been convicted by a most attentive and a most merciful jury, of one of the most malicious and atrocious of crimes it is in the power of human nature to perpetrate . . . You have shed the blood of a man admired for every virtue which can adorn public or private life.' There is little chance that Bellingham, who had collapsed in a violent fit of emotion, heard the judge's enjoinder that he should 'solicit pardon from the Almighty' before passing a sentence that was as little in doubt before the proceedings began as the defendant's guilt:

'That you be taken on Monday next, to a place of execution, there to be hung by the neck till you are dead, and your body delivered over to be anatomised.'

When Bellingham was escorted back through the corridors connecting the Sessions House with Newgate, he was led to a different wing of the prison from the one he had left that morning. As he entered the cell in the Condemned Hold, past the two guards stationed there who would stand sentry beside the iron-studded door until the hour of his execution, he remarked to himself that the space was strangely cheerful by comparison with his former cell. It seemed odd to him, for instance, that his waiting-room to oblivion should be fitted with a small window, through which the dusky half-light of spring was filtering, where before no access to sun or air was permitted. In his new accommodation, his arms and legs would remain fettered, but there was no ring in the floor to which his shackles were clamped. That the tea and oranges on which he had subsisted previously would be austerely swapped for water and bread, didn't seem to bother Bellingham. Within minutes of returning to Newgate, he was once more fully composed.

The following day – Saturday, 16 May – the plume-bearers and stately carriages, the black-robed mourners of the funeral procession for Spencer Perceval paused on Westminster Bridge to commemorate the murdered man. Ten years earlier, the poet William Wordsworth had stood on that same spot describing 'a calm so deep', composing lines for a sonnet of uncanny prescience:

> Dull would he be of soul who could pass by
> A sight so touching in its majesty:
> This City now doth like a garment wear
> The beauty of the morning: silent, bare . . .

Alas, Wordsworth's anachronistic, unintended elegy was the nearest thing to a decent memorial that Perceval would receive. In an age of literary luminaries, the assassination of the Prime

Minister made virtually no lasting cultural impression. One searches in vain for moving masterpieces such as Walt Whitman's 'When lilacs last in the dooryard bloom'd' or 'O Captain, My Captain!', which were written after the violent death of Abraham Lincoln half a century later. The insipid verses that Perceval's demise inspired seem forever to add insult to injury. The understandably forgotten poet H. Hughes opened a dismal effort with the apology that 'abler Pens will probably do greater justice to the Memory of so great and good a man as Mr Perceval'. Unfortunately, none did:

> No succour I from fancy'd Muse require,
> Lamented Perceval! Thy praise to tell:
> No! let the voice of Truth alone inspire
> The mournful tribute you deserve so well:
> True sorrow speaks with no fictitious views,
> Claims no assistance from Apollo's beams,
> Asks no refreshment from Castalian dews,
> Nor seeks repose by Heliconian streams . . .

Back in Newgate, Bellingham's reaction to the guilty verdict had begun to curdle from grief into disbelief – from disbelief into anger. 'One can imagine with horror,' reflected the historian Mollie Gillen, author of the humane and impeccable investigation *Assassination of the Prime Minister*, 'the anguish of such a mind forced to recognize that his idea of justice was regarded as insanity, that his peace could be nothing more than a treadmill of inescapable memories.' 'Government think to intimidate me,' he was heard muttering, 'but they are mistaken, I have been guilty of no offence, I have only done an act of public justice.'

While many in London chose to follow the casket of the slain parliamentarian, another procession was forming across town of those who wished to catch a glimpse of the lone assassin from Archangel. But Newman, the Keeper, had been informed by the sheriffs that Bellingham was not to become a zoo exhibit, and forbade the parade of spectators, including such dignitaries as the Lord Chamberlain, from purchasing the chance to observe the man in his final hours.

Access was limited to the likes of Dr Brownlow Forde, the Ordinary, and Reverend Daniel Wilson, the minister of St John's Chapel in Bedford Row, who professed an interest in ministering to the condition of the condemned man's soul. Wilson would later record in a pamphlet entitled *The substance of a conversation with John Bellingham . . . the day previous to his execution*, his frustrated attempts to persuade the convict to confess his sins and seek spiritual redemption. The last visitor Bellingham received was Joseph Butterworth, a Fleet Street bookseller who claimed he was already acquainted with him. Butterworth's reason for visiting Bellingham was to put to rest, if he could, the rumours that continued to persist in some of the more dimly lit corners of society, that Bellingham was part of a wider conspiracy to knock the British government off kilter. Bellingham assured his guest that he had acted entirely of his own initiative. As Butterworth left the cell, Bellingham turned to one of the guards and requested pencil and paper. He wanted to wish his wife goodbye. 'As we shall not meet any more in this world,' he wrote, 'I sincerely hope we shall do so in the world to come.' A postscript to his final missive brought the matter back to the few incidentals he clung to: 'Dr Ford[e] will forward you my watch and prayer book . . . I have been called upon to play an anxious card in life.'

The morning of Monday, 18 May 1812, was 'hazy, thick and wet'. Two thousand umbrellas jostled for position along Old Bailey. From inside the prison, the clanging of St Sepulchre's bell and the clatter of hammers erecting the scaffold could be heard as Bellingham prepared for his final performance. Unshaved – indeed, not allowed to shave – and wearing a cravat that would soon be superfluous, together with a pair of Hessian boots, Bellingham looked prepared to embark on an expedition to undiscovered territory. Having been introduced to the veteran executioner, William Brunskill, who had spent three decades honing his skills, Bellingham stood impassively as his fetters were replaced by a simple cord binding his arms behind him.

Among those who witnessed the event were the poet Lord Byron and the radical journalist William Cobbett, though from very different vantage points. The 24-year-old poet, who only two months earlier 'awoke to find [him]self famous' with the sensationally popular publication of *Childe Harold's Pilgrimage*, had managed to rent a window in a house opposite the prison. Cobbett, on the other hand, was at that moment serving a two-year sentence for treasonous libel and was among the scrum of Newgate prisoners who rushed to the window to see the event unfold. 'I saw the anxious looks,' Cobbett remembered, 'I saw the half-horrified countenances; I saw the mournful tears run down; and I heard the unanimous blessings.' Reporters noted too the curiously 'cheerful countenance' Bellingham projected as he was escorted to the scaffold. Amid many shouts of 'God bless you!', he implored Brunskill to forgo the ritual of slipping a white hood over the convict's head. But to no avail. Through the coarse hempen fabric, Dr Forde monitored Bellingham's mood and later recorded that his final words were ones of thanks to God for the gifts of 'fortitude' and 'resignation' with which he embraced his fate. 'The clock struck eight,' the various broadsheets and versions of *The Newgate Calendar* would presently report,

> and while it was striking the seventh time, the clergyman and Bellingham both fervently praying, the supports of the internal part of the scaffold were struck away, and Bellingham dropped out of sight down as far as the knees, his body being in full view, and the clergyman was left standing on the outer frame of the scaffold. When Bellingham sunk, the most perfect and awful silence prevailed, not even the slightest attempt at a huzza or noise of any kind was made.

18

Knot

'KNOT, a Crew or Gang of Villains.'

Motives for silence at an execution varied. A stifled gasp of shock or disbelief choked many, particularly first-time viewers. For others, the twitching bodies proved hypnotising, as if making spectators aware of something hidden and twisting inside themselves. On May Day 1820, an inscrutable silence enveloped a dishevelled member of the enormous audience that had assembled outside Newgate to witness the synchronised 'turning off' of five men convicted of high treason. Dressed in a pigment-smeared apron, the 29-year-old stranger stood transfixed as he stared into the stony, traumatised eyes of one of the conspirators numbly awaiting the executioner's mask. Gripping a pencil in one hand, a sketchpad in the other, it wasn't the first time that the gaunt and stubbled figure had stood face to face with a pedestal of death.

A year earlier, the artist had filled his shabby Parisian studio with a gruesome collection of rotting remains – severed arms and hacked torsos, split thighs and dripping heads – purloined from a nearby hospital. His aim had been to recreate as vividly as possible a model for what he was convinced would be remembered as his masterpiece, *The Raft of the Medusa*. Theodore Géricault's iconic work helped to expose the French government's culpability in a seafaring débâcle that had left over one hundred and thirty people dead and another fifteen clinging

*38. Theodore Géricault's first-hand account of the hanging
of the Cato Street Conspirators in May 1820*

hopelessly to a makeshift vessel for two weeks off the coast of
western Africa. The emotional intensity of the project, which
forced the struggling artist to confront the depths of depravity
the survivors had been forced to plumb, brought Géricault's
brittle psyche to the brink of collapse. Having failed to sell the
painting when it was first exhibited in Paris, Géricault resolved
to take his scrolled up canvas to London, where he hoped it
would meet with greater acclaim. His mission coincided with
the execution outside The Gaol of some of the most audacious
plotters ever to grip the British imagination, the band known as
the Cato Street Conspirators. 'There was something in his darkness and despondency that,' according to the artist's recent biographer Jonathan Miles, 'attracted him to the macabre spectacle
of the hanging.'

In order to understand the conspirators' outlandish scheme,
from its shadowy inception to the dramatic dénouement that

Géricault captured in his unflinching sketch, one must first acquaint oneself with a serial backstabber called George Edwards. After an early apprenticeship on London's streets as a small-time thief, Edwards divided his time between sculpting busts in a model shop in Fleet Street and ingratiating himself with a company of unsuspecting reformists. Model-maker by day, agent provocateur by night, Edwards was soon winning the confidence of followers of the aggressive reformer and editor of the influential radical magazine, *Pig's Meat*, Thomas Spence. By 1817, he had amassed a healthy purse from helping to secure the release of French prisoners of war, only to divulge their whereabouts to officials later in exchange for a generous bounty. Edwards would be remembered later by Charles Knight, in his *Passages of a working life* (1865), as 'a rogue by nature', a 'diminutive animal with downcast look and stealthy face' who 'did not calculate badly when he approached one who . . . had a solid foundation of honesty which made him unsuspicious'.

By 1818, George and his brother William, a former Bow Street police officer, had managed to weasel their way into the affections of the Spencean Philanthropists – those robust radicals who had earlier hoped to claim the inscrutable assassin John Bellingham as one of their number. Visitors to Edwards's home would have had every reason to believe that the reformist zeal of a former occupant, the progressive publisher and defender of Eliza Fenning, William Hone, lived on there. That was certainly the impression Edwards hoped to give by displaying a life-size model of Thomas Paine,which he'd been working on, commissioned by his neighbour, the radical publisher Richard Carlile. But the real sculpting that took place during these secret soirées was of Edwards's unsuspecting guests. Among the most prominent members of society to come under his sway was Arthur Thistlewood, a 46-year-old former estate agent and army officer who had hatched a scheme to overthrow Spencer Perceval before Bellingham had saved him the trouble. By

1816, Thistlewood had emerged as the leader of a splinter group, whose members believed that the principles of Spencean radicalism had been compromised by the organisers of a gathering in Spa Fields, Clerkenwell, in December that year, who had sought to make the movement more popularly appealing.

Stoking Thistlewood's ambition to ignite an uprising in London to rival the earlier convulsions of revolutionary Paris, Edwards indulged him in dizzying brainstorming sessions. Visions of succeeding where Guy Fawkes had failed two centuries earlier in blowing up the Houses of Parliament were conjured up by Edwards in a fog of cigar smoke before being brushed aside as fanciful and risky. Talk of whether Newgate itself might be destroyed as a radical allusion to the iconic Bastille was dismissed as impractical: the Gordon rioters had already tried with the help of thousands, and in any case The Gaol had since become too rich and complex a symbol to stand unambiguously for authority. Then someone mentioned assassination. The Prime Minister, perhaps, or the Attorney-General? Why choose? When George III died on 29 January 1820, the perfect climate of political confusion had been created, Edwards argued, and the group must surely seize it. By whose lips the ensuing plan to murder en masse the entire British Cabinet was uttered will be likely forever to remain a mystery. What is clear is that by the end of January 1820, the clandestine designs of Arthur Thistlewood and two dozen of his Spencean recruits to assassinate the government of Tory Prime Minister Robert Jenkinson, the second Earl of Liverpool, were taking shape as quickly as they were being relayed back to the Home Office by the diminutive double-crosser Edwards.

Anxious that Thistlewood might find the logistics of planning a series of far-flung assassinations daunting, Edwards and his Home Office cronies resolved to keep the plot simmering by making things easier for the gang. A phoney advertisement ran in several newspapers announcing that a lavish Cabinet dinner was to be hosted by Lord Harrowby in Grosvenor

Square on 23 February. Thistlewood could hardly believe his luck. Huddling with a nucleus of trusted agitators, including the butcher James Ings, shoemakers Richard Tidd, Thomas Preston and Robert Adams, an unsuccessful tradesman called John Thomas Brunt, and a black unemployed cabinetmaker by the name of William Davidson, Thistlewood began refining the scheme. Who would stand watch and who would fire the shots? Where would the decapitated heads of Lord Sidmouth and Lord Castlereagh be displayed? Should the assaults on the Bank, the Tower, and the Artillery Ground follow or coincide with the bloodbath at Lord Harrowby's? The conspirators needed a base to operate from, near enough to No. 44 Grosvenor Square in Mayfair, and the baker John Harrison knew just the right spot.

Cato Street is a five-hundred-foot stretch that runs parallel to Edgware Road, approximately five minutes' stroll north of present-day Marble Arch. Along with Homer Street and Virgil Mews, it was one of a handful of classically named streets laid out at the beginning of the nineteenth century on the Portman Estate, which abutted Old Marylebone Road. Number 6, the place Harrison had in mind (today renumbered 1A), was an abandoned stable, the disused hayloft above which was unlikely to meet with disturbance or eavesdropping. From there, access to Grosvenor Square, just south of Oxford Street, was easy.

By two-thirty in the afternoon of 23 February, Thistlewood's men began arriving in Cato Street, unaware that their movements were being monitored from a nearby tavern, the Horse and Groom, by the magistrate Richard Birnie, who had been placed in charge of the case. No sooner had the credulous conspirators settled to a final briefing at around 7.30 p.m., sipping brandy to calm their nerves, than the shutters of the derelict loft were kicked in by a squad of Bow Street Runners, while a column of Coldstream Guards climbed the inner ladder. The ensuing seconds were a frenzy of swords and

39. George Cruikshank's depiction of the storming of a loft in Cato Street where a group of conspirators were plotting to assassinate the British cabinet in February 1820. One of the ringleaders, Arthur Thistlewood, is shown stabbing a Bow Street Runner, Richard Smithers, through the chest. Smithers died from his injury

broken bottles as someone was heard to shout, 'Lay down your arms, we are officers of the peace!' The brave attempt by one Runner, Richard Smithers, to overcome Thistlewood met with a lethal lunge through the chest, before Thistlewood escaped the premises with ten others. Edwards was nowhere to be seen.

The scheme was up. Hasty editions of the morning papers set the extraordinary stakes for the leader's capture: 'Whereas Arthur Thistlewood,' advertised the *The London Gazette*,

stands charged with High Treason, and also with the Wilful Murder of Richard Smithers, a reward of ONE THOUSAND POUNDS is hereby offered to any person or persons who shall discover and apprehend, or cause to be discovered and apprehended the said Arthur Thistlewood, to be paid by the Lords Commissioners of His Majesty's Treasury, upon his being apprehended and lodged in any of His Majesty's Gaols. And all persons are hereby cautioned not to receive or harbour the said Arthur Thistlewood, as any person offending herein will thereby be guilty of High Treason.

The above-named Arthur Thistlewood is about forty-eight years of age, five feet ten inches high, has a sallow complexion, long visage, dark hair (a little grey), dark hazel eyes and arched eyebrows, a wide mouth and good set of teeth, has a scar under his right jaw, is slender made, and has the appearance of a military man, was born in Lincolnshire, and apprenticed to an Apothecary at Newark, usually wears a long blue coat and blue pantaloons, and has been a Lieutenant in the Militia.

It wasn't long before Thistlewood and several of the other principal plotters were apprehended, as the astonished nation came to terms with news of the government's 'narrow escape', as Lord Althorp described it. In the following weeks a predictable rush of judicial bargaining resulted in some of the conspirators turning witness for the prosecution in exchange for immunity, some receiving reduced sentences of transportation to New South Wales, and five – including Thistlewood, Tidd, Ings, Davidson and Brunt – left to pose gruesomely in front of Newgate prison. After being cut down, the heads of the five men were one by one severed from their bodies with a skiver as the crowd's reaction thawed from frozen silence to violent disapproval. A diligent roughing-up awaited the hangman on his descent from the platform, and he barely managed to escape with his life.

Among those caught up in the mêlée, somewhere in the crowd with the mesmerised Géricault, was the poet laureate Robert Southey, silently sketching his own portrait of the 'atrocious traitor, Thistlewood'. 'On the scaffold, his deameanor,' Southey would later recall, 'was that of a man who was boldly resolved to meet the fate he had deserved.' For him, Southey reflected, 'the grand question whether or not the soul was immortal would soon be solved'. Transfixed by the actions of the hangman as he went about his butchery, Southey was suddenly in a state of profound reverie, envisioning the convict's final hours inside Newgate, seeing in his mind's eye Thistlewood 'rise upon his knees . . . repeatedly calling upon Christ his Saviour to have mercy upon him'.

That Newgate should prove so compelling to Southey is perhaps not that surprising, given the strange power that the prison had had over his own life and reputation. In 1794, when he was 20, Southey had entered The Gaol in the hope of arranging with James Ridgway — a reformist publisher then being held on charges of sedition — the publication of a work he had recently completed entitled *Wat Tyler*. Southey was convinced that the fourteenth-century rebel leader and destroyer of Newgate, after whom his verse-drama was named, was in fact a distant relative of his, and he hoped that sales of the book might help defray the cost of an idealistic plan to build a utopian community with the poet Samuel Taylor Coleridge along the banks of the Susquehanna River in Pennsylvania. To Southey's delight, Ridgway consented to take the project on, but for reasons that remain unclear to this day, *Wat Tyler* was not published until pirated editions of the play flooded London's streets more than two decades later. By then — 1817 — Southey's political outlook had dramatically changed, curdling into conservatism, and his dreams of establishing a 'pantisocratic' utopia in the New World had evaporated. The humiliating appearance of radical protestations from his youth — emerging from the shadows of The Gaol like a ghost — would continue to haunt Southey's soul for years to come.

From converging perspectives in the swelling throng, Géricault and Southey stared at the bloodied scaffold. In due course, the jumbled remains of the executed were dragged back inside The Gaol and through the labyrinth of corridors down to the narrow subterranean passageway that stretched behind the prison, linking it with the Sessions House next door, known popularly among the inmates and staff as 'Deadman's

Walk'. While the morbid performance had been playing out in front of Newgate before one of the largest crowds ever to squeeze itself into Old Bailey, the gaolers had been busy prising up the heavy paving stones and digging a shallow grave, smeared with calcium oxide, or quicklime, to mask the stench of the decomposing bodies with which it would soon be loaded. For centuries, this narrow margin of no man's land, which separated the prison's property and the Surgeons' Hospital behind it, had served as a makeshift cemetery for the unclaimed bodies of those who had died inside. On the bleak stone walls that enclosed the slender passage, only a constellation of etched initials hinted at what was buried there.

Tremors from the Cato Street Conspiracy continued to be felt for months. Sixteen weeks after the executions, a gang of vigilantes wielding torches gathered at the home of the physician and future founder of the medical journal *The Lancet*, Thomas Wakely, in Argyll Street. Though Wakely had not even been present at Newgate that day, rumours had rippled through London in the hours after the hangings that it was he who had been behind the decapitations. He was brutally beaten and stabbed, and his practice destroyed by the ensuing blaze.

By relying on the testimony of Thistlewood's co-conspirators, the Home Office had sought to shield Edwards's role in fomenting the plot. But not everyone was willing to let the matter rest and by the end of May 1820, an indictment had been issued against him. 'HIGH TREASON' read a notice in *The Times* on 25 May:

ONE HUNDRED GUINEAS REWARD. A True Bill of Indictment having been found by the Middlesex Grand Jury against GEORGE EDWARDS for HIGH TREASON, whoever will apprehend and lodge the said George Edwards in any of his Majesty's Gaols, shall, on application to Mr James Harmer, of Hatton-garden, London, receive the above reward. The said George Edwards is by trade a modeller, he is about 5 feet 3 inches high, thin and pale faced, with an aquiline nose, gray eyes, and light brown hair: he has lately gone by the name of Wards, and is supposed to be about to leave this country for New Brunswick under that assumed name.

It was too late. By the time the papers had begun advertising for his arrest, Edwards was already forging new identities for himself from Germany to Guernsey, supporting himself on the meagre honoraria that his contacts at the Home Office continued to send him. Edwards's scheme to ensnare Thistlewood and his radical cohorts had worked, but the cost was his own disappearance as well. He was never heard from again.

19

Rum-mort

'RUM-MORT, a Queen, or great Lady.'

By the middle of the nineteenth century, The Gaol had served for over seven hundred years as a cauldron of curious acquaintances. Artists and writers such as William Hogarth and John Gay had been frequent visitors – each keen to witness at first-hand the notorious inmates who were featuring in their paintings and plays. This is where such literary figures as Horace Walpole and Samuel Johnson rubbed elbows with unkempt Newgate canters, where the Flowerpot plotters conspired at the end of the seventeenth century and the shadowy Christopher Marlowe is said to have hooked up 'with one Poole . . . who hath great skill in the mixture of metals' and, 'having learned some things of him', may have dabbled in the coining of 'French crownes, pistolets, and English shillings'.

On 31 January 1842, at approximately three o'clock in the afternoon, one of the most peculiar alignments in The Gaol's history occurred. The occasion for the encounter was the first state visit to London of the handsome new King of Prussia, Frederick William IV, who had succeeded his father to the throne two years earlier. Unlike his long-serving predecessor, who had helped negotiate favourably for Prussia the terms of the Congress of Vienna in 1815, by temperament Frederick William was more of a genteel intellectual than a clever strategist – an amateur draughtsman more interested in recording the subtle shapes of medieval turrets and flying buttresses than shaping territorial boundaries. The 47-year-old King was a loyal patron and friend of fellow Prussian artists and a keen student of architecture and gardening.

As the itinerary for his tour of England in early 1842 was taking shape, few in his entourage were surprised by the King's insistence on spending as much time tracing the buildings of Christopher Wren across the English capital, as shaking hands with the royal counterparts and diplomats with whom he would be dealing in the coming years. But however agile Frederick William's social sensibility may have been, few could have anticipated his determination that an audience be arranged not with any of the great engineers or artists of the day – Isambard Brunel, say, or J. M. W. Turner – but with a Quaker woman whose unusual behaviour had made her a constant presence in the noisome soot-caked walls of Newgate Prison for nearly thirty years.

Remarkable as it may seem to us today, by the early 1840s, in a city that could boast such sensational cultural attractions as Robert Barker's rotating panorama in Leicester Square and the lush delights of Vauxhall Gardens, among the most eagerly sought-out spectacles was the philanthropist Elizabeth Fry ministering to the hundreds of wretched women who were marooned inside the infamous Female Quadrangle of Newgate Prison.

For Elizabeth, it had all begun in 1813 when a friend, Stephen Grellet – a French Quaker missionary who, twenty years earlier, had narrowly escaped the turbulence of revolutionary Paris – told her of the horrors he had witnessed on a brief visit to The Gaol. Moved by Grellet's emotional response to what he had seen, Elizabeth, who several months earlier had confided to her diary that 'I feel my life slipping away to little purpose' – even though she had nine children to care for – resolved to visit the women's side of the prison, to which

Grellet had been refused entry on grounds of safety. Upon declaring her interest in entering the women's wards, Fry met with considerable discouragement from the prison's Governor who confessed that he was himself 'reluctant to go amongst them'.

Agreeing merely to leave her watch behind in the Governor's office, which he had promised her would otherwise be wrenched from her wrist, Elizabeth Fry went through with her intention to observe for herself the conditions in which some members of society had been condemned to live. The misery and discord, filth and disease that Fry encountered – over three hundred women crammed into a space designed for no more than fifty, piles of human faeces lying within inches of newborn babies gasping for what little air there was amid the thick fug of tobacco smoke, the stench of urine, and the howling of the insane – reduced her to tears but also led to a lifelong commitment to prison reform. 'In short,' she would later relate to Grellet, 'all I tell thee is a faint picture of the reality: the filth, the closeness of the room, the ferocious manners, and the abandoned wickedness which everything bespoke are quite indescribable.'

Over the next three years, as Elizabeth wrestled with the domestic burdens that such a large family had placed on her shoulders and those of her husband, the merchant banker Joseph Fry, her determination to return and help those she had encountered inside Newgate was unwavering. Having helped to establish a successful school for girls in her own neighbourhood of East Ham, she was convinced that education was the crucial resource that the women prisoners were denied access to inside The Gaol. In late 1816, Elizabeth raised the matter with a clutch of bemused prison officials and eventually succeeded in enlisting their support for the creation of a girls' curriculum inside the prison walls.

Humouring her, a small space was cordoned off amid the hubbub, from which Elizabeth was permitted to conduct what the prison administration regarded as an 'almost hopeless experiment'. Among Elizabeth's first objectives was the acquisition of decent provisions for the hungry and half-clothed cohort she had adopted – and, of course, Bibles. Lots of Bibles. Using her Quaker connections, she mobilised an efficient team of charity workers and her cramped corner became a base of operations. She began her assault on the depravity that had raged inside the Female Quadrangle by a clever campaign of divide-and-conquer. The inmates were put into groups of no more than a dozen, depending on the nature of the alleged crime or the sentence being served – each group supervised by a matron.

The transformation in prisoner morale and discipline was miraculous. Crass conversation and bawdy behaviour was replaced with spiritual tutorials, hair-pulling with knitting, and caterwauls with quiet prayer. Before long, Elizabeth had managed to convince the stunned gaolers to accept a raft of reforms, which included the prohibition of liquor from the Female Quadrangle, the adoption of uniform dress and the daily patrolling of the wards by a gentle army of Quaker ladies who patiently read to the inmates from the Bible. Within a year, De Haan says, Elizabeth Fry had founded the influential Ladies' Association for the Reformation of the Female Prisoners in Newgate, whose widely publicised good works subsequently gave birth to the British Ladies' Society for Promoting the Reformation of Female Prisoners – the first nationwide women's association.

News of Elizabeth's success in improving the quality of life inside the female wings of Newgate spread across Europe. By 1821, her compassionate methods for cultivating learning and esteem among the prison population were being emulated in gaols from Holland to Russia. To many, she was a living saint who had brought salvation to the women of Newgate and her achievement became the object of quasi-religious pilgrimages to the prison. 'I went and requested permission to see Mrs Fry,' a visitor later reported, offering an account of a place so different from the one Grellet had been prohibited from entering that it was hard to believe it was enclosed within the same walls, 'which was shortly obtained, and I was conducted by a turnkey to the entrance of the women's wards':

> On my approach, no loud or discordant sounds or angry voices indicated that I was about to enter a place which, I was credibly assured, had long had for one of its titles that of 'Hell above ground.' The courtyard into which I was admitted, instead of being peopled with beings scarcely human, blaspheming, fighting, tearing each other's hair, or gaming with a filthy pack of cards for the very clothes they wore, which often did not suffice even for decency, presented a scene where stillness and propriety reigned. I was conducted by a decently dressed person, the newly appointed yards-woman, to the door of the ward, where, at the head of a long table, sat a lady belonging to the Society of Friends. She was reading aloud to about sixteen women prisoners, who were engaged in needlework around it. Each wore a clean-looking blue apron and bib, with a ticket, having a number on it, suspended from her neck by a red tape. They all rose on my entrance, curtsied respectfully, and then, at a signal given, resumed their seats and employments.

'The Royal carriage,' according to a reporter for *The Times*, 'stopped in front of the Governor's House [of the prison], and its presence soon collected a mob in that crowded and thickly populated locality.' Amid the kind of cheering that Londoners had come to associate more with an agitated exit from Newgate than with an elegant entrance to it, the King of Prussia was escorted into the Governor's house trailing an entourage of anxious minders whose expressions suggested that they much preferred Frederick William's visits to palaces and cathedrals than to prisons. Awaiting his arrival, 'already assembled', were the City's Sheriffs and Aldermen, the Lady Mayoress of London, the prison's Ordinary and Surgeon, together with an assortment of silk-suited dukes and lords, eager to catch sight of the illustrious visitor.

40. Elizabeth Fry first visited The Gaol in 1813

Standing behind the group of redundant dignitaries, 'a large body of ladies forming the committee of the Benevolent Society formed for the purpose of reforming criminals' beamed serenely. But before any of the prison's receiving party could step forward and offer their well-rehearsed pleasantries, the King focused his attention on the gentlewoman whose communion he had so eagerly awaited, bowed briefly, and offered her his arm. As Elizabeth led Frederick William through the dank warren of corridors to the women's wards at the south end of the prison, the two conversed as old friends. They had, after all, met before — two years earlier, in the spring of 1840, a month before Frederick William acceded to the throne.

The occasion of their first meeting was one of Elizabeth's by then celebrated tours of European countries, during which she lobbied for the kind of penal reform she had initiated in

London as well as the alleviation of religious discrimination wherever it existed. Prussian persecution of Lutherans was among the many issues that vexed Elizabeth and she seized upon the opportunity of an invitation from the King's sister – a great admirer of Fry's philanthropy – to meet with her in the lavish Hotel de Russie in Berlin.

When the Crown Prince himself suddenly appeared at the meeting, eager to make the acquaintance of the fêted 'Angel of the Prisons', Elizabeth courageously challenged protocol by presenting him with a petition in which she forcefully appealed to his father's humanity for the immediate cessation of Lutheran oppression. Knowing that the risk of offending her royal hosts was considerable, the anxiety with which Elizabeth awaited the Crown's reply was made tolerable only by the quiet confidence that she had in the moral soundness of her actions. When the reaction came the next morning, decency had begot decency: 'the Spirit of God', the King is said to have written, 'must have helped them to express themselves as they have done'. Fry's righteous rebuke had been royally registered.

This was not, of course, Elizabeth's first encounter with the powers-that-be. In 1818, Thomas Fowell Buxton, Elizabeth's brother-in-law, was elected to Parliament and among his chief concerns was the appalling state of British prisons. Inspired by the selfless dedication of his brother's wife, Buxton had done his homework and was determined to enlist parliamentary support in accelerating the momentum of Elizabeth's initiative. In the past, government inquiries had managed to expose much and change little. John Howard's investigation of penal abuse in the 1780s and '90s, during which he brought to light, among much else, the disgraceful neglect that had left over a hundred and fifty women crammed into the space of three uninhabitable cells in Newgate, ultimately resulted in resolutions that were at best half-heartedly enforced and more often utterly ignored. Investigations in 1811 and again in 1814 further exposed the endemic over-crowding that had made life inside Newgate unbearable.

The opulent prison that George Dance the Younger had designed to hold, at most, five hundred inmates, was regularly forced to accommodate over eight hundred and fifty. In terms of floor space, for those unable to afford rent or a mattress in either the Press Yard or on the Masters' side, this equated to a sleeping space of eighteen inches of lice-strewn stone per debtor or felon. Members of the 1814 investigative committee registered their disgust at the enduring custom of Keepers charging prisoners fees – which nearly every task force for half a millennium had censured – as well as the informal ritual, enforced by the inmates themselves, of extracting garnish from other prisoners. But the growing adulation surrounding Elizabeth Fry convinced Buxton that the climate was changing and that real reform was not only necessary but possible.

Feeding the zeitgeist for reform were intellectual arguments asserting that the philosophical premises behind Newgate were as brittle as The Gaol's crumbling cells. As Buxton conducted his 1818 inquiry – inviting, among others, his famous sister-in-law to appear before Parliament – a formidable metaphor for his efforts was simultaneously being erected in Millbank, Pimlico, on the site of the present-day Tate Britain gallery. This is where construction had begun in 1812 of a massive human machine, which promised to render obsolete the failed experiments of antiquated incarceration of which Newgate was the most egregious example. The Millbank prison was designed by a series of eminent architects – William Williams, who was succeeded by Thomas Hardwick, who in turn handed the baton to Sir Robert Smirke, who was fresh from having created the British Museum to house the national collection of antiquities, prints and drawing. But the real brain behind the Millbank machine was the political philosopher Jeremy Bentham, who, for over twenty years, had had the extinction of dinosaurs like Newgate squarely in his sights.

Since 1790, Bentham had been perfecting the rationale and proposed layout of a curious penal system that he called 'The

Panopticon'. He believed that incarceration should focus on the rehabilitation of prisoners and that the physical structure of a gaol was fundamental to achieving that end. Criminals committed crimes, according to Bentham, because they lacked a conscience, and a conscience, he believed, functioned not unlike a prison guard who patrols one's actions and thoughts. If the experience of prison could be used to reconnect inmates with their missing conscience, or 'inner gaze', offenders could potentially be returned to society as useful members. But as they stood, Bentham was convinced, prisons in Britain and elsewhere in Europe at the beginning of the nineteenth century merely reinforced the psychological deficiencies to be found in prisoners. Left to moulder in the shadowy corridors of Newgate, the atrophied psyches of convicted criminals were encouraged to rot even further. The old prison plans, which featured quadrangles of communal cells loosely connected by a labyrinth of passageways, only made matters worse.

In an age in which all manner of visual gadgets were being invented or were undergoing dramatic reinvention, Bentham wanted to focus attention on the prisoner's psyche by constructing an apparatus that could hold the convict's consciousness steady like a specimen under a microscope. 'The Panopticon', according to Bentham's plan, would comprise a ring of individual cells (the isolation of each prisoner was crucial), radiating around a central watchtower like the segments of a sliced orange. The interior of each cell would be visible to the warden in the watchtower at all times of the day and night, but the warden himself would be hidden from the prisoners by means of an ingeniously devised system of blinds. Never certain when the warden might be exerting his gaze, the prisoner would, over time, internalise this sense of ceaseless surveillance, thus nurturing the conscience he had previously lacked. It was, Bentham would confess in an unpublished letter, 'a way of obtaining power, power of mind over mind, in a quantity hitherto without example.'

Not everyone was convinced, however, and Bentham would spend nearly twenty years lobbying for his private obsession. There were concerns about the cost and feasibility of constructing such a complex prison layout. To many, the expense of lavishing individual accommodation on every criminal was a luxury that London could neither countenance nor afford. Others simply doubted that such a plan would work and feared that, on the contrary, it might have the opposite effect to what its creator had in mind, unleashing monsters beyond social control. 'The jailer (the most unhappy wretch of all),' according to one critic of Bentham's hobbyhorse,

> sits in the centre of his transparent dominion, and sees to the utmost recesses of its crimes and its filthiness, all the proceedings of his aggregation of slaves. The poets give us a terrible idea of *solitude*; but eternal solitude is paradise to society under such everlasting inspection. The panopticon would soon become Bedlam, the keeper going mad first.

But Bentham was a determined man and in 1812 permission for the first prison based on the philosopher's design, to be constructed near Vauxhall Bridge along the Thames, was finally granted. Dogged by setbacks, including the partial collapse of the structure's freshly laid foundation, which rested on marshy ground, the penitentiary cost the then exorbitant sum of £1 million to complete. And though it was nearly a decade before the first inmate was led into one of the thousand isolated cells that comprised the prison, Millbank Penitentiary is more significant for what it stood for than for how long or how successfully it stood (it would be declared defunct only forty years later). It is, in a sense, the lost monument for the momentum of penal reform in the first half of the nineteenth century that Elizabeth Fry helped to accelerate.

Though often regarded as a separate tributary of social progress and enlightenment, the sensibility behind prison reform in the first quarter of the nineteenth century contributed to, and profited from, the growing pressure that was being exerted to condemn other evils, particularly slavery. To Thomas Buxton, the two issues were inextricable: social tolerance of the abuse of prisoners in Newgate – in the very heart of the British Empire – merely fostered a climate in which the continued enslavement of Africans could more easily be countenanced on its colonial fringes. The publication of the findings of Buxton's investigation into penal abuses, *An inquiry whether crime and misery are produced or prevented by our present system of prison discipline* (1818), was a runaway bestseller, not only in England, where it ran to several editions, but across Europe and the subcontinent, triggering a rash of international inquiries into local abuses. Joining forces with the indefatigable abolitionist, William Wilberforce, Buxton parlayed his reputation as a defender of human dignity into potent political clout on the issue of ending slavery in the colonies. A crusade for heightened respect for humanity that had begun inside Newgate Prison under the influence of Elizabeth Fry culminated fifteen years later – after years of setbacks and frustrations – in a bill championed by Buxton emancipating colonial slaves. It was passed on 23 August 1833 and enacted the following year.

As Frederick William IV of Prussia strolled through the quiet passageways of the Female Quadrangle of The Gaol in 1842, he was fully aware that the person whose company he had eagerly sought, with whom he now linked arms and chatted amiably, was not merely a kind and well-intentioned woman of pensionable age, but a formidable humanitarian force, a national treasure.

By the time of her death in the autumn of 1845, Elizabeth Fry had managed to transform the image of Newgate from a place of intractable despair into a harbour of hope. Within a few short years, the prison would begin showing palpable signs of winding down. By 1850, its population would dramatically start to decline. From then on, only inmates yet to be tried or those condemned to execution would continue to haunt its corridors. In the last decade of her miraculous ministry, as Elizabeth continued to stoke change from within, a shift in The Gaol's meaning was simultaneously being orchestrated beyond its walls at the hands of a very different, though no less culturally colossal, individual. Rumours would later abound that the two figures had, for the briefest moment, aligned like significant planets and exchanged glances across Newgate's fusty firmament, before slipping back into their respective orbits. It was November 1835, Guy Fawkes Day, and the English imagination would never be the same again.

20

Quit

'**QUIT**, to set free, to discharge. *The Autem-Bawler will soon quit the Hums*; The Parson will soon discharge the Congregation.'

The cab came to a halt as rain slipped from the brim of the driver's silk topper and the three huddled passengers – one more than the law permitted – clambered from the carriage on to the slushy gravel in front of The Gaol and ducked into the dank lodge of the Governor's house. The party consisted of a young publisher called John Macrone, 29-year-old Nathaniel Parker Willis (an American journalist and poet), and 'a young paragraphist for the *Morning Chronicle* who wished to write a description' of the prison – a 23-year-old by the name of Charles Dickens.

Charles's reputation as a gifted scribbler had begun to grow over the course of the previous two years as his stories had started to appear in newspapers and literary reviews under the eye-catching *nom de plume* 'Boz'. Having persuaded Macrone to publish a collection of these sketches, Dickens was eager to round off the volume – 'to make weight,' he said – by adding a piece that would alone justify the whole. It would have to explore a topic about which all Londoners cared deeply, but reinvented through his own imagination and language so as to be presented to the public as if for the very first time. 'With this view', he wrote to Macrone a fortnight earlier, he had 'begged' his editor at the *Morning Chronicle*, John Black, to arrange a meeting with one of London's Aldermen, Matthew Wood, to take him inside The Gaol – not just through the familiar corridors to which the public already had access, but to its hidden heart.

Macrone had told the driver to head for Furnival's Inn, Holborn, beside the popular Bull and Mouth tavern where coaches were allowed to loiter. Slushing down the Strand, dodging umbrella'd pedestrians taking umbrage at the splashing cabs, Macrone spotted Willis, whose spirited American travelogue, *Pencillings by the Way*, he had agreed to publish later that year, idly window-shopping. Macrone persuaded the rather jaunty and self-possessed Willis to accompany him as he collected Dickens on the way to Newgate. Willis's subsequent description of his first encounter with Dickens captures the young writer on the threshold of unprecedented popularity – his ego still in check, deferential to his publisher, Macrone, and only moments before setting foot inside that structure around which his literary consciousness would revolve in scene after scene, novel after novel, for the rest of his life. 'In the most crowded part of Holborn', Willis recalled, 'we pulled up at the entrance of a large building used for lawyers' chambers':

Not to leave me sitting in the rain, Macrone asked me to dismount with him. I followed up long flights of stairs to an upper storey, and was ushered into an uncarpeted and bleak-looking room, with a deal table and two or three chairs and a few books, a small boy [Charles's fourteen-year-old brother, Frederick] and Mr Dickens for the contents. I was only struck at first with one thing (and I made a memorandum of it that evening, as the strongest instance I had seen of English obsequiousness to employers) – the degree which the poor author was overpowered with the honour of his publisher's visit! I remember saying to myself, as I sat down on a rickety chair, 'My good fellow, if you were in America, with that fine face and ready quill, you would have no need to be condescended to by a publisher!'

Dickens was dressed very much as he has since described 'Dick Swiveller' [in *The Old Curiosity Shop*] – minus the 'swell look'. His hair was cropped close to his head, his clothes scant, though jauntily cut, and after changing a ragged office-coat for a shabby-blue, he stood by the door, collarless and buttoned up, the very personification, I thought, of a close sailor to the wind.

Charles was desperate for a chance to penetrate The Gaol's imposing façade and anxiously awaited Alderman Wood's approval of Black's application for a visit. Though initially distracted by Dickens's peculiar magnetism, Willis soon found himself mesmerised by the hulking reality of being inside Newgate – its mystique, conveyed through the pages of the popular *Newgate Calendar*, having likewise enthralled American readers. 'Though interested in Dickens's face, I forgot him naturally enough after we entered the prison, and I do not think I heard him speak during the two hours.'

Intriguing as the interlude may have proved, for Nat Willis and John Macrone the excursion to Newgate amounted to little more than cultural tourism. But for Charles, The Gaol was a symbol of something existentially deeper. The opportunity to penetrate Newgate dislodged something inside himself – like a rock falling from a precipice, the force of which would continue to drag against his consciousness for years to come. It had not, of course, been the young author's first visit to a place of detention. His father had been committed to the Marshalsea for debt in 1824, when Charles was 12 – a shame that scarred his soul. Prison had wrecked Charles's childhood, crushed his father's spirit, and hobbled his family's happiness. As the great archetype for all such places, Newgate loomed in his consciousness like a realm of trapped spirits. He wrote in horror of his fellow city-dwellers who, 'day by day, and hour by hour, pass and repass this gloomy depository of the guilt and misery of London in one perpetual stream of life and bustle, utterly unmindful of the throng of wretched creatures pent up within it':

nay, not even knowing, or if they do, not heeding, the fact, that as they pass one particular angle of the massive wall with a light laugh or a merry whistle, they stand within one yard of a fellow-creature, bound and helpless, whose hours are numbered, from whom the last feeble ray of hope has fled for ever, and whose miserable career will shortly terminate in a violent and shameful death. Contact with death even in its least terrible shape, is solemn and appalling. How much more awful is it to reflect on this near vicinity to the dying – to men in full health and vigour, in the flower of youth or the prime of life, with all their faculties and perceptions as acute and perfect as your own; but dying, nevertheless – dying as surely – with the hand of death imprinted upon them as indelibly – as if mortal disease had wasted their frames to shadows, and corruption had already begun.

Having presented their credentials, Macrone, Willis and Dickens were ushered into one of a series of little rooms adjacent to the Governor's house where they waited for their guide amid the displayed fetters of Jack Sheppard and the lidless stares of 'casts of the heads and faces' of 'notorious murderers'. The moulding of plaster-of-Paris death masks from the faces of the executed was intended to preserve for future physiognomic examination the countenances of the condemned. According to the increasingly popular principles of the late-eighteenth-century theorist Johann Kaspar Lavater, the Swiss poet and pastor, the paths of vice could be traced in the lineaments of the face and skull. After the prison's demolition, the ghastly gallery displayed inside Newgate would be moved to Scotland Yard to join the secret holdings of penal relics in what has become known as the 'Black Museum'.

From the Governor's wing, the three men were led through what Dickens would later describe as a 'maze of confusion' where 'narrow and dismal stone passages' fed like terrifying tributaries into 'tortuous and intricate windings, guarded in their turn by huge gates and gratings, whose appearance is

41. *Dickens's visit to The Gaol in 1836 transformed
his imagination*

sufficient to dispel at once the slightest hope of escape'. 'If we
noticed,' he wrote in his 'Visit to Newgate', 'every gate that
was unlocked for us to pass through, and locked again as soon
as we had passed, we should require a gate at every comma.' As
they wound their way from ward to ward, Dickens's heart
twisted with each anguishing encounter he witnessed between
prisoners and visitors – meetings, he later reflected, where
'neither hope, condolence, regret, nor affection was expressed
on either side'. In the women's ward, the party were able to
observe at first hand the edgy discipline with which Elizabeth
Fry was investing the place. 'The women rose hastily, on our
entrance,' Dickens recalled, 'and retired in a hurried manner to
either side of the fireplace. They were all cleanly – many of
them decently – attired, and there was nothing peculiar, either
in their appearance or demeanour.'

The situation could hardly have been more different around
the corner in that part of the building known cynically as the

'school' – a portion of the prison reserved for under-teen boys. When Macrone, Willis and Dickens entered the cell, the children, all awaiting trial for pick-pocketing, 'were drawn up in a line' for the visitors' inspection. 'There were fourteen of them in all,' Dickens recorded, 'some with shoes, some without; some in pinafores without jackets, others in jackets without pinafores, and one in scarce any thing at all . . . Fourteen such terrible little faces we never beheld . . . there was not one redeeming feature among them.' Leaving behind these 'hopeless creatures of neglect', the three continued through dismal passages, visiting in turn 'the yard for men', where 'idle and listless' the unemployed inmates (on whom no such angel as Elizabeth Fry had ever descended) 'sauntered moodily about', before examining the prison chapel and Press Yard.

In the Press Room below, which had long-since ceased to function as such, three men averted their humiliated eyes upon hearing the approaching footsteps and 'seemed to be unconsciously intent on counting the chinks in the opposite wall'. The trio had been condemned to die a week earlier in the Old Bailey. One, a 32-year-old private soldier in the Scotch Fusilier Guards, called Robert Swan, had been convicted of robbery but was said to have reason to hope that he might soon be in receipt of a reprieve and paced 'up and down the court with a firm military step'. The other two, John Pratt and John Smith, had been found guilty of committing an 'unnatural offence' and were under no illusion about the certainty of their fate. 'No plea could be urged,' Dickens wrote, 'in extenuation of their crime, and they well knew that for them there was no hope in this world.' 'The two short ones,' the turnkey is said to have whispered to Dickens as he stared into their wretched half-turned faces 'motionless as statues', 'were dead men.'

Hypnotised by what he had seen, Dickens was anxious to commit his observations to writing, a desperation made all the more frustrating by the sequence of reporting deadlines that prevented him from focusing on the Newgate sketch for nearly two weeks. Determined to 'get on in good earnest', he resolved to cancel a meeting he had looked forward to with his fiancée, Catherine Hogarth, lest he begin suffering, he said, 'difficulty in remembering the place, and arranging his materials'. When *Sketches by Boz* was published by Macrone a year later, 'A Visit to Newgate' was widely heralded as the finest piece in the collection. It is, one reviewer wrote, 'the most remarkable paper in the book . . . written throughout in a tone of high moral feeling, and with great eloquence, and must leave a deep and lasting impression on the mind of every reader.' For Dickens, the sketch was a watershed of psycho-geographical orientation. For the ensuing three decades, in book after book – from *The Adventures of Oliver Twist* (first published in serial form between February 1837 and April 1839) to *Great Expectations* (December 1860 to August 1861), from *The Life and Adventures of Nicholas Nickleby* (April 1838 to October 1839) to *Barnaby Rudge* (February to November 1841) – The Gaol looms as the ancient hinge on which the soul of London opened and closed. 'There, at the very core of London,' he would write in *Nicholas Nickleby*, 'in the heart of its business and animation, in the midst of a whirl of noise and motion: stemming as it were the giant currents of life that flow ceaselessly on from different quarters, and meet beneath its walls: stands Newgate.'

The accelerating popularity of *The Newgate Calendar* and other true-crime 'penny-blood' broadsheets had created an appetite for penal prose, which Charles Dickens was by no means the first to cater to. Dating back at least to Defoe's *Moll Flanders*, the 'Newgate Novel', as the genre came disparagingly to be known by critics who bristled at its glamorisation of crime and criminals, had been invested with some literary respectability in the mid-1790s by William Godwin, author of the influential utilitarian treatise *Political Justice* (1793) and future husband of the pioneering feminist Mary Wollstonecraft. Godwin's *Caleb Williams: or things as they are* (1794) was a rollicking page-turner, the narrative of which relied on readers' familiarity with the format and morbid morality plays embodied by *The Newgate Calendar*. The genre was further refined during the first two decades of the nineteenth century by a circle of successful writers that included Harrison Ainsworth, Edward Bulwer-Lytton and William Makepeace Thackeray. Adopting in turn some of the most sensational cases from the pages of the *Calendar* – from the prison-breaker Jack Sheppard (Ainsworth) to the philologist and murderer Eugene Aram (Bulwer-Lytton) and the spousicide Catherine Hayes (Thackeray) – the Newgate novelists capitalised on the astonishing fame that these mythic malefactors continued to enjoy in popular culture, all the while denying that their work in any way celebrated criminality. Some measure of their phenomenal success may be gauged by a report of the 1840s, published by the Children's Employment Commission, which recorded with horror that underprivileged youths ignorant of figures from the Bible or members of the royal family, nevertheless possessed detailed knowledge of the lives and adventures of Dick Turpin and Jack Sheppard.

But Dickens's imagination was too restless for the recycling of familiar sagas, and over the course of his many works he reinvigorated Newgate's opera of fire by introducing a fresh mythology all his own. Such unforgettable figures as the frisky fence, Fagin, inhabited The Gaol's stage as compellingly as any of the actual inmates ever could, and helped trigger an imaginative apotheosis of the prison. By the time the heroic young Oliver visits his malign mentor Fagin, who had callously endeavoured to enlist the lad in a life of crime, the Condemned Hold had achieved a kind of mythic literary status, like a circle in Dante's *Inferno*, or a sphere in the classical underworld. The character of Fagin had himself been based on a real-life receiver of stolen goods, a career criminal and procurer of child pickpockets called Isaac ('Ikey') Solomons (a name that Thackeray would mischievously adopt as a pseudonym), who had languished in Newgate on more than one occasion and was transported to New South Wales in 1831 for violating the statutes that Jonathan Wild once inspired. But Dickens was eager to forge human archetypes, not historical caricatures, and Fagin's resemblance to Ikey Solomons remains merely generic.

Dickens's preoccupation with prisons in general and with Newgate in particular was not only, or even primarily, literary. He frequently gravitated to The Gaol, whether alone, late at night, for the purpose of simply 'touching its rough stones', as if it were an enormous talisman, or as part of a surging tide of onlookers eager to catch a glimpse of an execution against its rugged frontage. Two years after first penetrating its walls with Macrone and Willis, Dickens was back inside in May 1837 acting as tour guide to a larger party consisting of his friend and future biographer, John Forster, the actor William Charles Macready, and two illustrators, George Cattermole and Hablot Knight Browne, better-remembered by posterity as 'Phiz'. The visit would leave a lasting impression on Phiz, who, decades later, would be called upon by Dickens to illustrate Barnaby Rudge's imprisonment in Newgate for his role in the Gordon Riots; this image was among the most powerful and disturbing of the artist's oeuvre and helped permanently to imprint the icon of The Gaol on to the minds of Londoners. As the group wove their labyrinthine way through the echoing building, Macready suddenly startled the others with a deep gasp at the shadow-entombed sight of Thomas Wainewright, the cele-brated artist and poisoner who was then awaiting trial for forgery.

In early June 1840, Dickens, along with much of London, stayed up all night in anticipation of the hanging of François Benjamin Courvoisier, a French coachman convicted of slitting the throat of his employer, Lord William Russell, a month earlier – an act, Courvoisier allegedly admitted on the scaffold, that had been inspired by one of Ainsworth's novels. Thackeray was also present in the crowd and the spectacle filled both him and Dickens with almost unutterable revulsion for the brutal ritual. Six years later, a piece that Dickens wrote for the *Daily*

News would reveal just how vivid and unremitting an impression the execution made: 'I was, purposely, on the spot,' he explained, 'from midnight of the night before':

> and was a near witness of the whole process of the building of the scaffold, the gathering of the crowd, the gradual swelling of the concourse with the coming-on of day, the hanging of the man, the cutting of the body down, and the removal of it into the prison. From the moment of my arrival, when there were but a few score boys in the street, and those all young thieves, and all clustered together behind the barrier nearest to the drop – down to the time when I saw the body with its dangling head, being carried on a wooden bier into the gaol – I did not see one token in all the immense crowd; at the windows, in the streets, on the house-tops, anywhere; of any one emotion suitable to the occasion. No sorrow, no salutary terror, no abhorrence, no seriousness; nothing but ribaldry, debauchery, levity, drunkenness, and flaunting vice in fifty other shapes. I should have deemed it impossible that I could have ever felt any large assemblage of my fellow-creatures to be so odious. I hoped, for an instant, that there was some sense of Death and Eternity in the cry of 'Hats off!' when the miserable wretch appeared; but I found, next moment, that they only raised it as they would at a Play – to see the Stage the better, in the final scene.

And yet Dickens returned for encore after encore. Despite having confessed to a friend that he had 'no excuse for going', he was one of over thirty thousand to gather outside Horsemonger Lane Gaol in November 1849 for the first husband-and-wife execution for nearly a century and a half. The condemned were George and Maria Manning, who had crammed the lifeless body of their lodger, Patrick O'Connor, under the floorboards of their kitchen in Bermondsey. The couple had excited the interest of the public when it was revealed that Maria had taken the lead in the killing by shooting O'Connor in the chest before George gratuitously defaced the corpse's head 'with a ripping chisel'. 'I give in, about the

Mannings,' Dickens wrote to the caricaturist John Leech, a few days before the scheduled double execution, adamant that he would not attend so as to 'avoid another such horrible and odious impression'. But still he went.

The Mannings' execution provoked Dickens to shift his earlier objection to capital punishment to a position that he thought was more likely to win favour with legislators. Writing to *The Times*, he began advocating not the outright abolition of executions, but a removal of the theatrical dimension from public hangings – that they might be conducted instead behind prison walls and away from the opera-glasses and cries of 'Down in front!' which had come to define them. Though change was slow in coming, Dickens would live to see the adoption of the Capital Punishment Within Prison Bill, which was passed in May 1868, two years before the novelist's death. On 26 May 1868, Michael Barrett, an Irish Nationalist convicted of igniting a bomb in Clerkenwell, which killed four people, would become the last person to be publicly executed in Britain.

The removal of the hanging spectacle from the public eye to within the walls of The Gaol and a makeshift 'Execution Shack' erected near 'Deadman's Walk' signalled a slow implosion of Newgate's iconic status. No longer providing a stage for public drama, Newgate's obsolescence was assured. Over the following two decades, committee after committee concluded that the historic prison was incapable of conversion to the principles of modern penal reform, not only architecturally but spiritually. Such judgements coincided with an acknowledgement by the City Corporation that an expanded Sessions House was urgently needed. In 1898, the site of Newgate Prison was sold to the City Corporation of London for £40,000 to make way for a new Criminal Court, and plans to transfer The Gaol's inmates to Pentonville and Holloway penitentiaries began taking shape.

On 6 May 1902, George Woolfe, who had been convicted of murdering his girlfriend, became the last of some 1,169 individuals to be executed at Newgate since the gallows had been moved there from Tyburn in 1783. Three months later, on 15 August, demolition of The Gaol began. 'A little crowd soon gathered,' according to one account, 'to watch the operations. The old pigeons, rough and grimy as the prison itself compared with other flocks in London, fluttered about . . . evidently talking over the event with much excitement. The doom of the gaol was being carried out at last.'

Early the next year, an announcement of the 'Historic Sale of Relics' from the prison attracted a crush of amateur and professional collectors, eager to walk away with grim mementoes. When the Bastille was pulled down in July 1789, Parisians conducted bizarre baptisms of the prison's stones, purging them in elaborate ceremonies of fire. It somehow seems appropriate, however, given the gawdy theatre that had surrounded Newgate almost from its inception, that rather than undergoing rituals of spiritual atonement, some of its celebrated cells, including the one in which Lord George Gordon had been confined, should be carted away, stone by stone, by buyers for Madame Tussaud's wax museum where they could be reassembled and live on as a macabre diorama.

Acknowledgements

For the opportunity to conjure the ghosts of Newgate, I should like to extend warm thanks to Roland Phillips at John Murray. I am also grateful to my editors, Gordon Wise and Rowan Yapp, for their advice and encouragement, and to my copyeditor, Jane Birkett, from whom I have learned a great deal. The manuscript for *The Gaol* could not have been completed without a generous award from the Arts and Humanities Research Council, which I received in 2006–7. I first became interested in Newgate's role in shaping the British imagination while working for the *Dictionary of National Biography* as a graduate student at Oxford University. My task was to excavate obscure sources that contributors might have missed, and I would like to thank my mentors on the project, Michael Thornhill and Philip Carter, for the many research skills they taught me. Though the actual site of Newgate Prison has been erased and reinscribed by the Central Criminal Court of the Old Bailey, the spirit of the The Gaol continues to haunt London and I am grateful to the Court's senior clerk Robin Shrimpton and to Tarnjit Carter for allowing me access to the premises and for helping me unlock its subterranean secrets. Acknowledgement is also due to the staff of several archival institutions, without whose guidance and kindnesses many of the resources here would not have been tapped: the Ashmolean Museum, the Bodleian Library, the British Library, the Guildhall Library, the John Rylands University Library of Manchester, the National Maritime Museum, the National Library of Wales, and the Public Record Office. I would like also to extend my deepest thanks to John Saddler, the best agent anyone could have, and to the many colleagues and friends who encouraged me as the book took shape, particularly Matthew Bevis, Lindsay Duguid, Matthew Francis,

ACKNOWLEDGEMENTS

Robert McCrum, Kevin Mills, Anthony Mosawi, Jem Poster, Sinéad Sturgeon, Kathryn Sutherland, Richard Marggraf Turley, and Damian Walford Davies.

Thanks are due to the following institutions for permission to reproduce the various copyright illustrations:

British Library: xvii (Title-page, *A new canting dictionary*, 1725), 10 (*Peine forte et dure*), 22 (Thomas Nashe in leg irons), 49 (Mary Frith), 111 (Title-page, *The Arraignment, trial, and condemnation of Captain William Kidd, for Murther and Piracy, upon six several indictments*, 1701), 159 (Claude Duval), 186 (Title-page, *The New & Complete Newgate Calendar*, 1795).

Bridgeman Art Gallery: 42 (Woodcut of the burning of Anne Askew at Smithfield in 1546), 259 (Théodore Géricault's 'Execution in London', 1820).

Guildhall Library, London: 12 (View of prisoners exercising at Newgate Prison), 28 (Newgate in 1679), 41 (Burning of John Rogers in 1555), 54 ('The Cock Lane ghost, or the invisible humm bug'), 70 ('The London rairey shows or who'll step into Ketch's Theatre'), 80 (Scene at Tyburn showing crowds gathered to watch a hanging, 1696), 92 ('Wenceslas Hollar's map of the City of London and surrounding area showing the extent of the damage caused by the Great Fire of London in 1666'), 115 ('A pirate hanged at Execution Dock'), 136 ('Eleven views with descriptions charting how Jack Sheppard escaped from Newgate Prison, Old Bailey in 1724'), 152 ('View of Daniel Defoe in the pillory at Temple Bar surrounded by a crowd'), 203 (Henry Fauntleroy on trial in the Old Bailey), 209 (A crowd sets fire to Newgate during the Gordon Riots), 212 (George Dance the Younger's design for Newgate), 223 (The 'Italianate' Sessions House before it was enclosed), 228 (The 'new drop'), 263 (The storming of the Cato Street loft, by George Cruikshank).

Henry E. Huntington Library and Art Gallery, San Marino, California: 66 (Title-page, *The Blacke Dogge of Newgate*, 1596), 90 ('Hieroglyphic' from William Lilly's *Monarchy, or no monarchy*, 1651).

National Maritime Museum: 5 (Richard Whittington).

Mary Evans Picture Library: 16 (Newgate in the 16th Century),

ACKNOWLEDGEMENTS

65 (Ben Jonson), 130 (Invitation to the execution of Jonathan Wild), 140 (engraving of James Thornhill's portrait of Jack Sheppard), 167 (James Hind), 175 (James Maclaine), 200 (William Dodd), 237 (John Bellingham shoots prime minister Spencer Perceval), 251 (John Bellingham giving evidence in the Old Bailey), 273 (Elizabeth Fry, after Charles Robert Leslie), 286 (Charles Dickens).

Sources

The astonishing story of Newgate has attracted the attention of many scholars since the end of the nineteenth century, and I am particularly indebted to Arthur Griffiths's comprehensive history *The Chronicles of Newgate* (1883), to Donald Rumbelow's rich and investigative *The Triple Tree: Newgate, Tyburn and Old Bailey* (1982), to Arthur Babington's humane and judicious *The English Bastille: A History of Newgate Gaol and Prison Conditions in Britain, 1188–1902* (1971), and to Stephen Halliday's splendid recent study *Newgate: London's Protoype of Hell* (2006). I have learned a great deal from the varied perspectives and expertise of each of these works and an attempt to coalesce and reconcile their emphases, chronologies and sources can be felt throughout *The Gaol*.

No writer on London can proceed without constant consultation of Ben Weinreb and Christopher Hibbert's magisterial *The London Encyclopedia* (1983), which has proved especially helpful in unravelling the histories of streets and neighbourhoods which together comprise the larger story at the centre of which The Gaol looms. From the beginning of the eighteenth century, an organic biography of Newgate and Tyburn began to take shape on London's streets under the generic title 'Calendar', and while these volumes were as unreliable as they were irresistible, they nevertheless formed the basis of every subsequent history of the prison and have likewise helped shape the present story. An important dimension of Newgate's saga is the dramatic development of English law and, in particular, the theatrical courtroom antics that played out only feet away from Newgate in the Sessions House of the Old Bailey. Tim Hitchcock and Robert Shoemaker's pioneering archival database, *Old Bailey Proceedings Online*, which electronically chronicles the minutes of the

Criminal Court from April 1674 to October 1834, has proved an invaluable resource.

My understanding of the history of London – political, sociological, economic and psychological – and of the criminal underworld that underpins it, has been shaped by the works of several modern historians and I would especially recommend as further reading, for anyone interested in pursuing these threads, works by Peter Ackroyd, V. A. C. Gatrell, Christopher Hibbert, Stephen Inwood, Peter Linebaugh, Frank McLynn, Lucy Moore, Roy Porter, E. P. Thompson, Iain Sinclair and Jerry White.

In addition to Griffiths, Rumbelow and Halliday, the sources to which I am gratefully indebted for each of the individual chapters are as follows:

Chapter 1: Whit

Bernardi, J., *A short history of the life of Major John Bernardi* (1729)

Bloomfield, R., 'The Architect of Newgate', in *Studies in Architecture*, ed. R. Bloomfield (1905)

Fitz Stephen, William, *Description of the city of London, newly translated from the Latin original; with a necessary commentary* (1772)

Hobley, B., *Roman and Saxon London: a reappraisal* (1985)

Holdsworth, Sir W. S., *History of English Law* (1923–31)

Hooper, W. E., *The history of Newgate and the Old Bailey* (1935)

Maitland, W., *History and survey of London from its foundation to the present time* (1775)

Norman, P., 'Roman and later Remains found during the Excavations on the Site of Newgate Prison, 1903–1904', in *Archaeologia: miscellaneous tracts relating to antiquity*, vol. IX (1904), pp. 125–42

Notes and Queries, 'Obituary: Philip Norman', vol. clx (3 May 1931), p. 396

Pollock, Sir F., *The history of English law before the time of Edward I* (1895)

Richardson, J., *London and its people: a social history from medieval times to the present day* (1995)

—— *The annals of London: a year-by-year record of a thousand years of history* (2000)

Stow, J., *A suruay of London contayning the originall, antiquity, increase, moderne estate, and description of that citie, written in the yeare 1598* (1598)

Vincent, N., *Peter des Roches: an alien in English politics, 1205–38*, in *Cambridge Studies in Medieval Life and Thought*, 4th ser., 31 (1996)

Chapter 2: Bone

Anon., *The complaint of Mrs Celiers and the Jesuits in Newgate, to the E of D and the lords in the Tower, concerning the discovery of their new sham-plot* (1680)

Anon., *The tryal and sentence of Elizabeth Cellier for writing, printing and publishing a scandalous libel called Malice defeated, &c.* (1680)

Barron, C. M., *London in the Later Middle Ages: government and people 1200–1500* (2005)

Bassett, M., 'Newgate Prison in the Middle Ages', in *Speculum*, 18 (1943), pp. 233–46 [my chief source for the Keepers]

Beattie, J. M., *Policing and punishment in London, 1660–1750: urban crime and the limits of terror* (2001)

Carpenter, J., *Liber Albus*, Riley, H.T. edn (1861)

Cellier, E., *Malice defeated, or, A brief relation of the accusation and deliverance of Elizabeth Cellier, together with an abstract of her arraignment and tryal, written by herself* (1680)

Chapman, P., 'George Flint', *Oxford Dictionary of National Biography* (2004)

Chew, H. M., and Kellaway, W., *London assize of nuisance, 1301–1431: a calendar* (1973)

Defoe, D. [probable], *The history of the Press Yard* (1717)

Foxe, J., *Acts and Monuments* [called 'Book of Martyrs'], 3 vols., (1641)

Holmes, R., *Dr Johnson and Mr Savage* (1993)

Johnson, S., *An account of the life of Mr Richard Savage*, ed. C. Tracy, (1971)

Loades, D. ed., *John Foxe and the English Reformation* (1997)

—— ed., *John Foxe: an historical perspective* (1999)

Margaret, T. B., *Letters of Queen Margaret of Anjou and Bishop Beckington and others* (1863)

Mozley, J. F., *John Foxe and his book* (1940)

Oldys, W., *The Harleian Miscellany; or, A Collection of scarce, curious, and entertaining pamphlets and tracts, as well in manuscripts as in print, found in the late Earl of Oxford's library; interspersed with historical, political, and critical notes* (1808–11)

Pugh, R. B., 'Newgate between two fires', in *Guildhall Studies in London History*, 3 (1979), pp. 137–63

Radcliffe, A., *The works of Alexander Radcliffe* (1696)

Roll A 9: *Calendar of the plea and memoranda rolls of the city of London*, vol. 1, 1323–1364 (1926)

Sharpe, R. R., *London and the kingdom: a history derived mainly from the archives at Guildhall in the custody of the corporation of the city of London* (1894)

Shoemaker, R. B., *Prosecution and punishment: petty crime and the law in London and rural Middlesex, c.1660–1725* (1991)

Thomas, H., *The ancient remains, antiquities, and recent improvements of the city of London* (1830)

Tyacke, N., *England's Long Reformation, 1500–1800* (1998)

Wales, T., 'Bodenham Rewse', *Oxford Dictionary of National Biography* (2004)

—— 'Thief-takers and their clients in later Stuart London', *Londinopolis: essays in the social and cultural history of early modern London*, ed. P. Griffiths and M. S. R. Jenner (2000), pp. 67–84

Chapter 3: Glimmer

Barron, C., *Revolt in London: 11th–13th June 1381* (1981)

Beilin, E. V., *The examinations of Anne Askew* (1996)

Brigden, B., *London and the Reformation* (1989)

Brooks, N., 'The organisation and achievements of the peasants of Kent and Essex in 1381', in *Studies in medieval history presented to R. H. C. Davies*, ed. H. Mayr-Harting and R. Moore (1985), pp. 247–70

Camm, B., ed., *Lives of the English martyrs declared blessed by Pope Leo XIII in 1886 and 1895*, 1 (1904)

—— *The martyrs of the London Charterhouse* (1893)

Chauncy, M., *History of the sufferings of eighteen Carthusians in England* (1890)

SOURCES

Chester, J. L., *John Rogers* (1861)

Clebsch, W. A., *England's earliest Protestants, 1520–1535* (1964)

Daniell, D., 'John Frith' and 'John Rogers', *Oxford Dictionary of National Biography* (2004)

—— *William Tyndale: a biography* (1994)

Dobson, R. B., ed., *The Peasants' Revolt of 1381*, 2nd edn (1983)

Flaherty, W. E., 'The great rebellion in Kent of 1381 illustrated from the public records', in *Archaeologia Cantiana*, 3 (1860), pp. 65–96

Fox, L., ed., *The whole workes of W. Tyndall, John Frith, and Doct. Barnes* (1572–3)

Froude, J. A., *History of England*, new edn, 12 vols. (1870–75), vol. 2, pp. 363–82

Hendriks, L., *The London Charterhouse: its monks and its martyrs* (1889)

Hogg, J., 'John Houghton', *Oxford Dictionary of National Biography* (2004)

Huggarde, M., *The displaying of the protestantes* (1556)

Knott, J. R., 'Heroic suffering', in *Discourses of martyrdom in English literature, 1563–1694* (1993), pp. 33–83

Loades, D., *Mary Tudor: a life* (1989)

MacCullough, D., *Thomas Cranmer* (1996)

Marshall, P., 'John Forest', *Oxford Dictionary of National Biography* (2004)

—— 'Papist as heretic: the burning of John Forest, 1538', in *Historical Journal*, 41 (1998), pp. 351–74

Pratt, J., ed., *The acts and monuments of John Foxe*, 8 vols. (1877)

Prescott, A., 'Wat Tyler', *Oxford Dictionary of National Biography* (2004)

Starkey, D., *Elizabeth: apprenticeship* (2000)

—— *The reign of Henry VIII: personalities and politics* (1991)

The Parliamentary Register; or, History of the proceedings and debates of the House of Commons, vol. VI (1802), Sir William Meredith's speech, 13 May 1777, pp. 175–82

Tittler, R., *The reign of Mary I*, 2nd edn (1991)

Watt, D., 'Anne Askew', *Oxford Dictionary of National Biography* (2004)

Wriothesley, C., *A chronicle of England during the reigns of the Tudors*

from AD 1485 to 1559, ed. W. D. Hamilton, I, CS, new ser., II
(1875)

Chapter 4: Crank

Annual Register (1762)

Anon., *A letter from Kent of the rising at Rochester* (1648)

Anon., *A true account of the tryal of Mrs Mary Carlton, at the sessions in
the Old Bayly, Thursday the 4th of June, 1633, she being indicted by the
name of Mary Mauders alias Stedman, sometime supposed by Mr Carlton
and others, to be a princess of Germany* (1663)

Bernbaum, E., *The Mary Carleton narratives 1663–1673: a missing chapter
in the history of the English novel* (1914)

Burnet, G., *The history of the Reformation of the Church of England*, rev.
N. Pocock, new edn, vol. 2 (1865)

Capp, B., *Cromwell's navy: the fleet and the English revolution, 1648–1660*
(1989)

Carleton, J., *Ultimum vale of John Carleton, of the Middle Temple London,
gent. being a true description of the passages of that grand imposter, late a
pretended Germane-lady* (1663)

Carleton, M., *An historical narrative of the German princess, containing all
material passages, from her first arrivall at Graves-End, the 30th of March
last past, untill she was discharged from her imprisonment, June the 6th
instant . . . written by her self* (1663)

—— *The memoires of Mary Carleton, commonly stiled the German princess.
Setting forth the whole series of her actions, with all their intrigues, and
subtile contrivances from her cradle to the fatal period of her raign at
Tiburn, being an account of her penitent behaviour, in her absteining from
food and rest, in the prison of Newgate* (1673)

—— *The case of Madam Mary Carleton, lately stiled the German princess,
truely stated, with an historical relation of her birth, education, and fortunes; in an appeal to his illustrious highness Prince Rupert* (1663)

Carter, M., *A most true and exact relation of that as honourable as unfortunate expedition of Kent, Essex, and Colchester by M.C., a loyall actor
in that engagement, Anno Dom. 1648* (1650)

Court of Common Council, *A declaration from the City of London with
instructions from the Court of Common Councell . . . also a message*

concerning Prince Charles, read in the House of Lords, from Sir Thomas Dishington (1648)

Gentleman's Magazine, 1st ser., 32 (1762), pp. 43–4, 81–4

Goldsmith, O., *The mystery revealed, containing a series of transactions and authentic memorials respecting the supposed Cock Lane ghost* (1762)

Grant, D., *The Cock Lane ghost* (1965)

Hahn, D., 'Elizabeth Crofts', *Oxford Dictionary of National Biography* (2004)

Kingdomes Weekly Intelligencer, 262 (23–30 May 1648)

Kirkman, F., *The counterfeit lady unveiled, being a full account of the birth, life, most remarkable actions, and untimely death of Mary Carleton, known by the name of the German princess* (1673)

Lang, A., *Cock Lane and common-sense* (1894)

Seccombe, T., and Shore, H., 'Elizabeth Parsons', *Oxford Dictionary of National Biography* (2004)

Stow, J., *Chronicles of England* (1592)

Thornbury, G. W., and Walford, E., *Old and new London: a narrative of its history, its people, and its places*, 6 vols. (1873–8)

Timbs, J., *Romance of London: strange stories, scenes, and remarkable persons of the great town*, 3 vols. (1865)

Todd, J., and Spearing, E., eds., *Counterfeit ladies* (1994)

Todd, J., 'Mary Moders', *Oxford Dictionary of National Biography* (2004)

Wright, S., 'Cornelius Evans', *Oxford Dictionary of National Biography* (2004)

Chapter 5: Pink'd

Bakeless, J., *The tragicall history of Christopher Marlowe*, 2 vols. (1942)

Donaldson, I., 'Benjamin Jonson', *Oxford Dictionary of National Biography* (2004)

Eccles, M., 'Jonson and the spies', *Review of English Studies*, 13 (1937), pp. 385–91

—— 'Marlowe in Newgate', *Times Literary Supplement*, 6 Sept. 1934, p. 604

Field, P. J. C., 'Sir Thomas Malory', *Oxford Dictionary of National Biography* (2004)

SOURCES

—— *The life and times of Sir Thomas Malory* (1993)

Holt, J. C., 'Robin Hood', *Oxford Dictionary of National Biography* (2004)

—— *Robin Hood*, 2nd edn (1989)

Hutton, L., *Luke Huttons lamentation* (1598)

—— *The black dogge of Newgate* (*c.*1596)

—— *The discovery of a London monster* (1638)

Judges, A. V., *The Elizabethan underworld* (1930)

Kay, W. D., *Ben Jonson: a literary life* (1995)

Keen, M., *The outlaws of medieval legend* (1961)

Knight, S., ed., *Robin Hood: an anthology of scholarship and criticism* (1999)

Lee, S., 'Sir Thomas Malory', DNB archive

Nicholl, C., 'Christopher Marlowe', *Oxford Dictionary of National Biography* (2004)

—— *The reckoning: the murder of Christopher Marlowe* (1992)

Riggs, D., *Ben Jonson: a life* (1989)

Shrank, C., 'Luke Hutton', *Oxford Dictionary of National Biography* (2004)

Wraight, A. D., and Stern, V., *In search of Christopher Marlowe* (1965)

Chapter 6: Gape

Anon., *The Tyburn ghost: or, The strange downfal of the gallows* (1678)

Anon., *The plotters ballad, being Jack Ketch's incomparable receipt for the cure of trayterous recusants* (1678)

Anon., *The Man of destiny's hard fortune, or, Squire Ketch's declaration concerning his late confinement in the Kings-Bench and Marshalsea, whereby his hopeful harvest was like to have been blasted* (1679)

Anon., *The man of destiny's hard fortune, or, Squire Ketch's declaration* (1679)

Anon., *The Romanists best doctor* (1680)

Anon., *A dialogue between Jack Ketch and his journey-man* (1683)

Anon., *Jack Catch his Bridewel oration, or a word or two of advice to his friends* (1686)

Anon., *Pleasant discourse by way of dialogue between the old and new Jack Catch* (1686)

Anon., *An account of the late Lawrence, Earl Ferrers* (1760)

SOURCES

Anon., *The trial of Lawrence, Earl Ferrers for the murder of John Johnson* (1760)

Barrow, G. W. S., 'The bearded revolutionary', in *History Today*, 19 (1969), pp. 679–87

Benson, L., ed., *The book of remarkable trials and notorious characters, from 'Half Hanged Smith', 1700, to Oxford who shot at the queen, 1840* (1871)

Bethel, S., *A bill and answer betwixt Jack Catch plaintiff, and Slingsby Bethel, & al., defendants of the year 1681* (1686)

Bland, J., *The common hangman* (1984)

Bleackley, H. W., *The hangmen of England* (1929)

Davenport-Hines, R., 'Laurence Shirley', *Oxford Dictionary of National Biography* (2004)

Dixon, W. H., *The London prisons, with an account of the more distinguished persons who have been confined in them: to which is added a description of the chief provincial prisons* (1850)

Dunning, R., *The Monmouth episode: a guide to the rebellion and bloody assizes* (1984)

Ellwood, T., *The history of the life of Thomas Ellwood* (1714)

Gatrell, V. A. C., *The hanging tree: execution and the English people, 1770–1868* (1994)

Gent, B. E., *A new dictionary of the . . . canting crew* (1699)

Harris, T., 'James Scott, duke of Monmouth', *Oxford Dictionary of National Biography* (2004)

—— *London crowds in the reign of Charles II* (1987)

Howlett, R., ed., *Chronicles of the reigns of Stephen, Henry II, and Richard I* (1885)

Ketch, J. [pseud.], *The apologie of John Ketch, esq.; the executioner of London, in vindication of himself as to the execution of the late Lord Russel* (1683)

Leach, R., *The Punch and Judy: history, tradition and meaning* (1985)

Marks, A., *Tyburn Tree: its history and annals* (1908)

Ollard, R., *Pepys, a biography* (1974)

Pottle, F. A., *James Boswell: the earlier years, 1740–1769* (1966)

The Antiquary, vol. 3–4 (1873), p. 205

Thornbury, W., and Walford, E., *Old and new London: a narrative of its history, its people, and its places* (1892)

Tomalin, C., *Samuel Pepys: the unequalled self* (2002)

SOURCES

Wales, T., 'John Catch', *Oxford Dictionary of National Biography* (2004) [an excellent collation of disparate sources and myths]

Watson, J. N. P., *Captain-general and rebel chief: the life of James, duke of Monmouth* (1979)

White, B., 'Hannah Dagoe', *Oxford Dictionary of National Biography* (2004)

Wright, L. M., *The literary life of the early Friends, 1658–1725* (1932)

Chapter 7: Smoke

Anon., *The German princess revived, or, The London jilt: being a true account of the life and death of Jenney Voss, who after she had been transported for being concerned with Sadler about eight years past in stealing my lord chancellors mace, and several times since convicted of repeated fellonies was executed on Friday the 19th of December, 1684, at Tyburn. Published from her own confession* (1684)

Ashmole, E., *Autobiographical and historical notes*, ed. C. H. Josten, 5 vols. (1966)

Baxter, R., *Richard Baxter's dying thoughts upon Phil. I. 23.* (1683)

Capp, B. S., 'Sir George Wharton', *Oxford Dictionary of National Biography* (2004)

—— *Astrology and the popular press: English almanacs, 1500–1800* (1979)

Curry, P., 'William Lilly', *Oxford Dictionary of National Biography* (2004)

—— *Prophecy and power: astrology in early modern England* (1989)

Evans, Arise, *An eccho to the voice from heaven, or, A narration of the life, and manner of the special calling, and visions of Arise Evans by him published, in discharge of his duty to God, and for the satisfaction of all those that doubt* (1652)

Evelyn, J., *The diary of John Evelyn*, ed. E. S. De Beer (1959)

Geneva, A., *Astrology and the seventeenth-century mind: William Lilly and the language of the stars* (1995)

Gonzales, M., *London in 1731* (1888)

Langley, B., *An accurate description of Newgate. With the rights, privileges, allowances, fees, dues, and customs thereof, which alone offers a detailed tour of the famous premises* (1724)

Lilly, W., *Anglicus, peace, or no peace, 1645 a probable conjecture of the state*

304

of England, and the present differences betwixt His Majestie and the Parliament of England now sitting at Westminster, for this present yeer, 1645, an exact ephemeris of the daily motions of the planets: with an easie introduction to the use thereof, monethly-observations, a table of houses, and explanations thereof : to which is added, a modest reply to M. Wharton, and the prognostication of his present almanak printed at Oxford, for 1645 (1645)

—— Merlinus Anglicus: or, England's Merlin. Prophetically fore-telling, the admirable events, and wonderful effects, that shall befall the king of Scots, the states of Holland, and the Parliament of England, in all their consultations, warlike actions, and naval designes, both by sea and land, for the year of our Lord, 1653 (1653)

—— Monarchy or no monarchy in England (1651)

—— Mr William Lilly's history of his life and times: from the year 1602, to 1681, 2nd edn (1715)

Noorthouck, J., A new history of London: including Westminster and Southwark (1773)

Parker, D., Familiar to all: William Lilly and astrology in the seventeenth century (1975)

Pepys, S., The diary of Samuel Pepys, 11 vols., ed. R. Latham et al. (2000)

Smith, A., The history of the lives of the most noted highway-men (1714)

Tinniswood, A., By permission of heaven: the story of the Great Fire of London (2003)

Vincent, T., God's terrible voice in the city (1667)

Waterhouse, E., A short narrative of the late dreadful fire in London (1667)

White, B., 'Jane Voss', Oxford Dictionary of National Biography (2004)

Chapter 8: Whip

A person of quality, A full account of the actions of the late famous pyrate, Capt. Kidd. With the proceedings against him and a vindication of the right honourable Richard earl of Bellamont . . . (1701)

Anon., The arraignment, tryal, and condemnation of Captain William Kidd, for murther and piracy, upon six several indictments (1701)

Bonner, W. H., Pirate Laureate: the life and legends of Captain Kidd (1947)

Brooks, G., ed., *The trial of Captain Kidd* (1930)

Giovanopolous, A. C., 'Captain Kidd and the King: piracy and politics in Restoration England', in *In the grip of the law: trials, prisons and the space between*, ed. M. Fludernik et al. (2004), pp. 3–22

Hinrichs, D. M., *The fateful voyage of Captain Kidd* (1955)

Lorrain, P., *The ordinary of Newgate: his account of the behaviour, confessions, and dying-words of Captain William Kidd* (1701)

Milligan, C., *Captain William Kidd, gentleman or buccaneer* (1932)

Ritchie, R. C., 'William Kidd', *Oxford Dictionary of National Biography* (2004)

—— *Captain Kidd and the war against the pirates* (1986)

Chapters 9 and 10: Chive & Stag

Anon., *A narrative of all the robberies, escapes, &c of John Sheppard, written by himself and printed by John Applebee of Blackfriars: giving an exact description of the manner of his wonderful escape from the castle in Newgate* (1724)

Anon., *The history of the lives and actions of Jonathan Wild, thief-taker. Joseph Blake alias Blueskin, foot-pad. And John Sheppard, housebreaker* (1725)

Anon., *The lives of the most remarkable criminals*, 3 vols. (1735)

Applebee's Original Weekly Journal, July–November 1724

Backscheider, P. R., *Daniel Defoe: his life* (1989)

Bleackley, H., and Ellis, S. M., *Jack Sheppard* (1933)

Daily Journal, July–November 1724

Daily Post [London], July–November 1724

Defoe, D. [as D. H. Clerk of Justice], *The life of Jonathan Wild, from his birth to his death* (1725)

—— *The history of the remarkable life of John Sheppard* (1724) [the seminal account of Sheppard's remarkable story, from which all subsequent lives stem]

—— *The true and genuine account of the life and actions of Jonathan Wild* (1726)

E. G. [Gentleman in town], *Authentic memoirs of the life and surprising adventures of John Sheppard, who was executed at Tyburn, November the*

16th, 1724. By way of familiar letters from a gentleman in town, to his friend and correspondent in the country (1724)

Gay, J., *The Beggar's Opera* (1728)

Hibbert, C., *The road to Tyburn: the story of Jack Sheppard and the eighteenth-century underworld* (1957)

Hollingsworth, K., *The Newgate novel, 1830–1847* (1963)

Howson, G., *Thief-taker general: the rise and fall of Jonathan Wild* (1970)

Lyons, F. J., *Jonathan Wild, prince of robbers* (1936)

McKenzie, A., 'Joseph Blake' and 'Jonathan Wild', *Oxford Dictionary of National Biography* (2004)

Moore, L., *The thieves' opera: the remarkable lives and deaths of Jonathan Wild, thief-taker, and Jack Sheppard, house-breaker* (1998) [a brilliantly engaging reconstruction and my chief authority]

Nokes, D., *John Gay: a profession of friendship* (1995)

Purney, T., *The ordinary of Newgate: his account, of the behaviour, confession, and last dying words of the malefactors, that were executed at Tyburn, on Friday the 8th of February, 1722–3* (1723)

Rawlings, P., *Drunks, whores and idle apprentices: criminal biographies of the eighteenth century* (1992)

Smith, A., *Memoirs of the life and times, of the famous Jonathan Wild, together with the history and lives, of modern rogues, several of 'em his acquaintance, that have been executed before and since his death* (1726)

Sugden, P., 'John Sheppard', *Oxford Dictionary of National Biography* (2004)

Sutherland, J., *Defoe* (1937)

Swift, J. [disputed], *Newgate's garland: being a new ballad, shewing how Mr Jonathan Wild's throat was cut, from ear to ear, with a penknife by Mr Blake, alias Blueskin, the bold highwayman, as he stood at his trial at the Old-Bailey* (1724?)

—— *The correspondence of Jonathan Swift*, ed. H. Williams, 5 vols. (1963–5)

Chapter 11: Snaffle

Allen, F., *An account of the behaviour of Mr James Maclaine* (1750)

Anon., *The declaration of Captain James Hind (close prisoner in New-gate)* (1651)

Anon., *The true and perfect relation of the taking of Captain James Hind* (1651)

Anon., *Another victory in Lancashire obtained against the Scots by Major General Harrison, and Collonel Lilburn* (1651)

Anon., *The life of Deval: Shewing how he came to be a highway-man; and how he committed several robberies afterwards. Together with his arraignment and condemnation. As also his speech and confession, at the place of execution* (1669)

Anon., *Devol's last farewel: containing an account of many frolicksom intreigues [sic] and notorius robbers which he committed: concluding with his mournful lamentation, on the day of his death* (1670)

Anon., *No jest like a true iest being a compendious record of the merry life and mad exploits of Captain James Hind the great robber of England* (1670)

Anon., *A full and true account of the apprehending James Whitney* (1693?)

Anon., *The life of Captain James Whitney* (1693)

Anon., *A compleat and true account of all the robberies committed by James Carrick, John Malhoni, and their accomplices* (1722)

Anon., *A complete history of James Maclean, the gentleman highwayman* [1750]

Anon., *A genuine account of the life and actions of James Maclean, highwayman* [1750]

Anon., *An account of John Rann, commonly called Sixteen String Jack* (1774)

Boswell, J., *London Journal, 1762–63*, ed. F. A. Pottle (1950), vol. 1

Butler, S., *To the memory of the most renowned Du-Vall: a pindarick ode* (1671)

Carter, P., 'Paul Lewis', *Oxford Dictionary of National Biography* (2004)

Daily Advertiser, November 1749

Evans, H., and Evans, M., *Hero on a stolen horse* (1977)

Faller, L. B., 'James Whitney', *Oxford Dictionary of National Biography* (2004)

—— *Turned to account: the forms and functions of criminal biography in late seventeenth- and early eighteenth-century England* (1987)

Fidge, G., *Hind's ramble, or, The description of his manner and course of life* (1651)

—— *The English Gusman, or, The history of that unparallel'd thief James Hind* (1652)

Harper, C. G., *Half hours with the highwaymen* (1908)

Hesse, J. H., *Memoirs of the court of England during the reign of the Stuarts, including the Protectorate* (1855)

J. S., *An excellent comedy, called, The Prince of Priggs revels: or, The practises of that grand thief Captain James Hind, relating divers of his pranks and exploits, never heretofore published by any* (1651)

Linebaugh, P., 'The Tyburn riot against the surgeons', in *Albion's fatal tree: crime and society in eighteenth-century England*, ed. D. Hay et al. (1985), pp. 65–117

London Evening-Post, September 1750

Mackdonald, Capt., *A general history of the lives and adventures of the most famous highwaymen, murderers, pirates, street-robbers, and thief-takers. Particularly the four last most noted villains, viz. MacDaniel, Salmon, Eagan and Berry* (1758)

McKenzie, A., 'James Carrick'; 'James Maclaine', *Oxford Dictionary of National Biography* (2004)

Meades, O. M., *The adventures of Captain James Hind of Chipping Norton: the Oxfordshire highwayman* (1985)

Penny London Post, July–October 1750

Phillips, G. L., 'Two seventeenth-century flue-fakers, toolers, and rampsmen', in *Folk-lore: transactions of the Folk-lore Society*, vol. LXII, no. 2 (June 1951), pp. 289–95

Pope, W., *The memoires of Monsieur Du Vall: containing the history of his life and death. Whereunto are annexed his last speech and epitaph* (1670)

Smith, J. T., *Nollekens and his times*, ed. W. Whitten, 2 vols. (1920)

Spraggs, G., *Outlaws and highwaymen: the cult of the robber in England from the Middle Ages to the nineteenth century* (2001)

Spurr, J., *England in the 1670s: 'this masquerading age'* (2000)

Sugden, P., 'John Rann', *Oxford Dictionary of National Biography* (2004)

The Gentleman's Magazine, 1st ser., 20 (1750)

Toynbee, P., ed., *Supplement to the Letters of Horace Walpole*, vol. 3 (1918–1925), pp. 132–5

—— ed., *The Letters of Horace Walpole* (1903–5)

Wales, T., 'John Thrift', *Oxford Dictionary of National Biography* (2004)

White, B., 'John Bennet'; 'William Davis'; 'Claude Duval'; and 'John Hind', *Oxford Dictionary of National Biography* (2004) [taken together, Barbara White's contributions to the *ODNB* comprise one of the best biographical resources available on seventeenth- and eighteenth-century highwaymen and -women]

Chapter 12: Clack

Anon., *The Tyburn chronicle: or, villainy display'd in all its branches. Containing an authentic account of the lives, adventures, tryals, executions, and last dying speeches of the most notorious malefactors of all denominations who have suffered for . . . from the year 1700, to the present time* (1768)

Anon., *The malefactor's register; or, the Newgate and Tyburn calendar. Containing the authentic lives, trials, accounts of executions, and dying speeches, of the most notorious violators of the laws of their country; who have suffered death, and other exemplary punishments, in England, Scotland, and Ireland from the year 1700 to Lady-Day 1779*, 5 vols. (1779)

Carter, P., 'Elizabeth Brownrigg' and 'Catherine Hayes', *Oxford Dictionary of National Biography* (2004)

Hammelmann, H., *Book illustrators in eighteenth-century England*, ed. T. S. R. Boase (1975)

Jackson, W., *The new and complete Newgate calendar; or, Villany displayed in all its branches*, 6 vols. (1795)

Johnson, Capt. C., *A complete history of the lives and adventures of the most famous highwaymen, murderers, street-robbers etc.* (1720?)

Knapp, A., and Baldwin, W., *Criminal chronology, or, the new Newgate Calendar*, 4 vols. (1810–11)

—— *The Newgate Calendar; comprising interesting memoirs of the most notorious characters who have been convicted of outrages on the laws of England since the commencement of the eighteenth century*, 6 vols. (1824–6)

Norton, R., *Mother Clap's molly house: the gay subculture in England, 1700–1830* (1992)

SOURCES

Smith, Capt. A., *A complete history of the lives and robberies of the most notorious highwaymen, footpads, shoplifts, & cheats of both sexes* (1714)

Sullivan, M. G., 'Samuel Wale', *Oxford Dictionary of National Biography* (2004)

Wilkinson, G. T., *The Newgate calendar improved; being interesting memoirs of notorious characters who have been convicted of offences against the laws of England, during the 17th century; and continued to the present time*, 5 vols. (1830–6)

Chapter 13: Skrip

Andrew, D. T., and McGowan, R., *The Perreaus and Mrs Rudd: forgery and betrayal in eighteenth-century London* (2001)

—— 'Daniel Perreau', 'Robert Perreau', and 'Margaret Caroline Rudd', *Oxford Dictionary of National Biography* (2004)

Anon., *The trials of Robert and Daniel Perreau's on the King's Commission of the Peace, Oyer and Terminer . . .* (1775)

Anon., *An explicit account of the lives and trials of the twin brothers* (1775)

Anon., *The life, trials and dying words of the two unfortunate twin brothers* (1776)

Bakewell, S., *The smart* (2001) [an excellent resuscitation of the intrigue and pathos surrounding the Perreau/Rudd affair]

Bleackley, H., *Some distinguished victims of the scaffold* (1905)

Boswell, J., *Life of Johnson* (1791)

Catnach, J., *An account of the trial, execution, and dying behaviour of Henry Fauntleroy* (1824)

Clayton, T., 'William Wynne Ryland', *Oxford Dictionary of National Biography* (2004)

Davenport-Hines, R., 'Henry Fauntleroy', *Oxford Dictionary of National Biography* (2004)

Egan, P., *Account of the trial of Mr Fauntleroy for forgery* (1824)

Fitzgerald, P., *A famous forgery, being the story of the unfortunate Dr Dodd* (1865)

Howson, G., *The Macaroni Parson* (1973)

McLynn, F., *Crime and punishment in the eighteenth century* (1991)

Morning Post, 1775–6 [as quoted in S. Bakewell]

SOURCES

Perreau, D., *Mr Daniel Perreau's narrative of his unhappy case; wherein every particular transaction between Mrs Rudd, his brother, and himself, from the commencement of Mr Daniel Perreau's connexion with Mrs Rudd, until the time of his trial, is most truly and candidly laid before the public; together with his defence. Published by himself* (1775)

Rawlings, P., 'William Dodd', *Oxford Dictionary of National Biography* (2004)

Smith, J. H., *Celebrated trials of all countries, and remarkable cases of criminal jurisprudence* (1847)

Theodosia, *Genuine memoirs of the Mess. Perreau* (1775)

Villette, J., *A genuine account of the behaviour and dying words of William Dodd, LL.D.* (1777)

Chapter 14: Twig

Aikin, J., *A view of the character and public services of the late John Howard* (1792)

Brown, J. B., *Memoirs of the public and private life of John Howard, the philanthropist* (1818)

Crabbe, G., *The Poetical Works of the Rev. George Crabbe: with his letters and journals* (1834)

De Castro, J. P., *The Gordon Riots* (1926)

Donovan, R. K., *No popery and radicalism: opposition to Roman Catholic relief in Scotland, 1778–1782* (1987)

Field, J., *The life of John Howard* (1850)

Haydon, C., *Anti-Catholicism in eighteenth-century England, c. 1714–80: a political and social study* (1993)

Howard, J., *The state of the prisons in England and Wales with preliminary observations, and an account of some foreign prisons* (1777)

Kalman, H. D., 'Newgate prison', *Architectural History*, vol. 12 (1969), pp. 50–61

Morgan, R., 'John Howard', *Oxford Dictionary of National Biography* (2004)

Stroud, D., *George Dance, architect, 1741–1825* (1971)

Thornbury, W., *Old and new London*, vol. 2 (1878), chs. LII–LIII

Watson, R., *The life of Lord George Gordon* (1795)

SOURCES

Chapter 15: Crinkums

Adlard, J., *The softer paths of pleasure: a life of Sally Salisbury* (1980)

Allan, D. G. C., and Schofield, R. E., *Stephen Hales: scientist and philanthropist* (1980)

Anon., *Authentick memoirs of the life, intrigues and adventures of the celebrated Sally Salisbury with true characters of her most considerable gallants by Capt Charles Walker* (1723)

Anon., *The genuine history of Mrs Sarah Prydden, usually called Sally Salisbury, and her gallants* (1723)

Clark-Kennedy, A. E., *Stephen Hales, D.D., F.R.S.: an eighteenth-century biography* (1929)

Creighton, C., *A history of epidemics in Britain*, 2 vols. (1891–4)

Gordon, Lord G., *Innocence vindicated, and the intrigues of Popery and its abettors displayed, in an authentic narrative of some transactions, hitherto unknown* (1783)

Layard, D. P., *Directions to prevent the contagion of the jail-distemper, commonly called the jail-fever* (1772)

Porter, R., *Disease, medicine and society in England, 1550–1860* (1987)

Pringle, J., 'An Account of Several Persons Seized with the Goal-Fever, Working in Newgate; And of the Manner, in Which the Infection Was Communicated to One Intire Family', in *Philosophical Transactions (1683–1775)*, vol. 48 (1753–4), pp. 42–55

White, B., 'Sarah Pridden', *Oxford Dictionary of National Biography* (2004)

Chapter 16: Twist

Hackwood, F. W., *William Hone: his life and times* (1912)

Hone, W., *The important results of an elaborate investigation into the mysterious case of Eliza Fenning* (1815)

The Times, 31 March and 12 April 1815

Wilson, B., *The laughter of triumph: William Hone and the fight for the free press* (2005) [an excellent reconstruction of Hone's involvement in the Fenning affair and compendium of relevant sources]

SOURCES

Chapter 17: Dag

Anon., *A full report on the trial of John Bellingham* (1812)

Anon., *An authentic account of the horrid assassination of the Honourable Spencer Perceval* (1812)

Courier, 13 May 1812

Forbes, J., *An account of the trial of John Bellingham* (1812)

Gillen, M., *Assassination of the Prime Minister: 'the shocking death of Spencer Perceval'* (1972) [the most comprehensive and humane of investigations and the one to which I am most indebted]

Gower, Lord G. L., *Private Correspondence: 1781 to 1821*, 2 vols. (1916)

Grellet, S., *Memoirs of the life and gospel labors of Stephen Grellet* (1860)

Jackson, Sir G., *Bath archives: a further selection of the diaries and letters of Sir George Jackson from 1809 to 1816* (1873)

Jerdan, William, *Autobiography*, 4 vols. (1852)

The Times, 12–18 May 1812

Wilson, D., *The substance of a conversation with John Bellingham . . . the day previous to his execution* (1812)

Chapter 18: Knot

Athanassoglou-Kallmyer, N., 'Géricault's Severed Heads and Limbs: The Politics and Aesthetics of the Scaffold', in *The Art Bulletin*, vol. 74, no. 4 (December 1992)

Boime, A., *Art in an age of counterrevolution, 1815–1848* (2004)

Browne, C. T., *Life of Robert Southey* (1854)

Chase, M., 'Arthur Thistlewood' and 'Cato Street conspirators', *Oxford Dictionary of National Biography* (2004)

—— *The people's farm: English radical agrarianism, 1775–1840* (1988)

Healey, R. M., 'George Edwards', *Oxford Dictionary of National Biography* (2004)

Knight, C., *Passages of a working life during half a century: with a prelude of early reminiscences* (1865)

McCalman, I., *Radical underworld: prophets, revolutionaries, and pornographers in London, 1795–1840* (1988)

Miles, Jonathan, *Medusa: the shipwreck, the scandal, the masterpiece* (2007)

Southey, R., *Wat Tyler: a dramatic poem in three acts* (1817)

Stanhope, J., *The Cato Street conspiracy* (1962)

The London Gazette, 1820

The Times, 1820

Wilkinson, G. T., *An authentic history of the Cato Street conspiracy* (1820)

Chapter 19: Rum-mort

Bentham, J., *The Panopticon; or, the inspection-house: containing the idea of a new principle of construction applicable to any sort of establishment, in which persons of any description are to be kept under inspection: and in particular to penitentiary-houses, prisons* (1791)

Blackwood's Edinburgh Magazine, 1865

Blouet, O. M., 'Sir Thomas Fowell Buxton', *Oxford Dictionary of National Biography* (2004)

Buxton, C., *Memoirs of Sir Thomas Fowell Buxton, baronet, with selections from his correspondence* (1848)

Buxton, T. F., *An inquiry whether crime and misery are produced or prevented by our present system of prison discipline* (1818)

Corder, S., *Life of Elizabeth Fry: compiled from her journal* (1855)

De Haan, F., and Van Drenth, A., *The rise of caring power: Elizabeth Fry and Josephine Butler in Britain and the Netherlands* (1999)

De Haan, F., 'Elizabeth [née Gurney] Fry', *Oxford Dictionary of National Biography* (2004)

Fry, E., *Memoir of the life of Elizabeth Fry, with extracts from her letters and journal*, ed. K. Fry, and R. E. Cresswell, 2 vols. (1847)

Gurney, J. J., *Brief memoirs of Thomas Fowell Buxton and Elizabeth Fry* (1845)

Howard, D. L., *The English prisons: their past and their future* (1960)

Semple, J., *Bentham's Prison: a study of the Panopticon penitentiary* (1993)

Whitney, J., *Elizabeth Fry: Quaker heroine* (1937)

SOURCES

Chapter 20: Quit

Ackroyd, P., *Dickens* (1990)

Allen, M., *Charles Dickens's childhood* (1988)

Carlton, W.J., 'The Third Man at Newgate', in *The Review of English Studies*, new ser., vol. 8, no. 32 (Nov. 1957), pp. 402–7 [my source for Nathaniel Parker Willis and his connection with Dickens]

Collins, P., *Dickens and Crime* (1964)

Dickens, C., *Barnaby Rudge* (1841)

—— *Great Expectations* (1861)

—— *Sketches by Boz: illustrative of every-day life and every-day people* (1836)

—— *The Adventures of Oliver Twist* (1838)

—— *The Letters of Charles Dickens 1812–1870*, ed. W. J. Carlton, et al., 12 vols. (1865–2002)

—— *The Life and Adventures of Nicholas Nickleby* (1839)

Duckworth, J., *Fagin's children: criminal children in Victorian England* (2002)

Halliday, S., *Newgate: London's Prototype of Hell* (2006)

Rumbelow, D., *The Triple Tree: Newgate, Tyburn and Old Bailey* (1982)

Index

Index

NOTE: Page numbers in *italic* indicate illustrations and captions

INDEX

Read more ...

Henry Hitchings

DR JOHNSON'S DICTIONARY: THE EXTRAORDINARY STORY OF THE BOOK THAT DEFINED THE WORLD

The story of one of the most heroic feats of lexicography ever undertaken

The decision by the obscure near-hack, Samuel Johnson to accept the commission to produce the first ever complete dictionary of the English language, illustrated by examples of usage, was a moment of matchless audacity – a decision that would be followed by years of toil and ultimate triumph. This entertaining, rigorously researched account of Johnson's adventure reveals all the effort it involved, all the fascination of the process of capturing the meanings of words, and all the rambunctious energy of Johnson's personality.

'So good, so apposite, so chewy and edible . . . buy Hitchings's book' Will Self, *New Statesman*

'Clever, wittily written and amusingly arranged' Andrew Motion, *Guardian*

'A masterful account of one of the greatest literary triumphs of the eighteenth century' Giles Milton

'Highly entertaining . . . Anyone interested in dictionaries, Dr Johnson or the English language will surely spend many happy hours with this book' *Independent*

Order your copy now by calling Bookpoint on 01235 827716 or visit your local bookshop quoting ISBN 978-0-7195-6632-5 www.johnmurray.co.uk